ACROSS THE THREE PAGODAS PASS:
THE STORY OF THE THAI-BURMA RAILWAY

POWs Laying sleepers along the Thai-Burma railway. Drawing by Ewart Escritt from a photograph by Lieut Ketsu Fujii

ACROSS THE THREE PAGODAS PASS

THE STORY OF THE THAI-BURMA RAILWAY

BY

YOSHIHIKO FUTAMATSU

TRANSLATED AND INTRODUCED BY EWART ESCRITT

EDITED WITH A FOREWORD BY PETER N. DAVIES

RENAISSANCE BOOKS

ACROSS THE THREE PAGODAS PASS:
THE STORY OF THE THAI-BURMA RAILWAY

First published 2013 by
RENNAISANCE BOOKS
PO Box 219
Folkestone
Kent CT20 2WP

Renaissance Books is an imprint of Global Books Ltd

© Renaissance Books 2013

ISBN 978-1-898823-07-0

British Library Cataloguing in Publication Data
A CIP catalogue entry for this book is available
from the British Library

 The Great Britain
SASAKAWA
FOUNDATION
グレイトブリテン・ササカワ財団

The publishers wish to acknowledge the kind
support of The Great Britain-Sasakawa Foundation
in the making of this book

Set in Adobe Garamond Pro 11 on 12.5 pt by Dataworks
Printed in England by TJ International, Padstow, Cornwall

*I wish to dedicate this work
to the late Professor Yoshinori Suzuki of Kanagawa University
and his wife Minako.
Both have provided constant support and assistance
over many years for my research on Japanese topics
and I am most grateful for their kindness.*

PETER N. DAVIES

CONTENTS

ACKNOWLEDGEMENTS

My detailed knowledge of wartime events in the Far East came from an invitation to write the biography of Colonel Sir Philip Toosey who was the senior British Officer present during the building of the so-called *Bridge on the River Kwai*.

Sir Philip was a prominent businessman who became the Liverpool Agent for the merchant bank Baring Brothers. As such. his duties included acting as a non-executive director for many of the firms advised by Barings and amongst these was Liner Holdings – the parent company of the Elder Dempster Shipping Line.[1] As the official historian of this enterprise I was already acquainted with Sir Philip and had always enjoyed a good personal relationship with him. I was aware of the fact that he had been taken prisoner-of-war by the Japanese during the Second World War but until he approached me I had little idea of his special role as a POW and of the affection with which he was held by many former prisoners who knew him at that time.

Sir Philip was a very private person who had no desire for publicity. It was only as a result of the film: *The Bridge on the River Kwai*[2] in which he was portrayed by Alex Guinness as a collaborator of the Japanese that he was persuaded to take action so that the real story could be told. Thus, in the years prior to his death in 1975 I was able to assess his records and obtain almost fifty hours of taped interviews.[3] I was also able to visit many of the sites in Thailand and Malaya where Toosey had been a prisoner and there, and elsewhere, met many of the individuals who shared his experiences in various ways.

As my academic interests in Japanese shipping and shipbuilding[4] took me to Japan on several occasions I found it possible to interview a number of Japanese who had been involved in the building of the Bridge and Railway. One of these was Teruo Saitoh who, as the second in command at Tamarkan – the Bridge camp – was well known to Toosey and was an excellent source of valuable information.[5] Two others, Yoshihiko Futamatsu and Renichi Sugano, were contacted as a result of an introduction by Carl Fritsche – an American pilot who I had met to discuss his bombing raids on the Kwai Bridge.[6] This resulted in several meetings during which I learned much about their joint wartime careers in the 4th Special Railway Bridging Unit and the 9th Railway Regiment. Later on, I became extremely interested to discover that Futamatsu had written an account of this wartime exploits. This was given extra emphasis by the knowledge that although there have been numerous accounts of the Thai-Burma Railway showing the Western view of events only two small works have been produced in English which outlined the Japanese attitude to its construction.[7]

It was clear to me, therefore, how desirable it would be for Futamatsu's work to be translated and published in English but at first this seemed to be a very distant possibility. However, a letter in the *Sunday Times* began a train of events which was to transform this situation. The author of the letter was Louis Allen,[8] an eminent expert on Japanese military affairs, and his references to his Japanese sources led me to seek his advice. On one particular point he then suggested that I contact a certain Ewart Escritt who he was sure would be able to assist me.

This certainly proved to be the case and my initial query was quickly answered. Of much greater significance was that this link with Ewart Escritt was to provide me with expert backup on many aspects of the Japanese records as well as giving me the benefit of his personal knowledge of life as a prisoner of war. It seems that he had volunteered for the Territorial Army in 1938 and thus was called up into the RASC when war broke out the following year. As Captain C.E. Escritt he then arrived in Singapore with the 18th Division on 5 February 1942 and was captured when the garrison surrendered ten days later. He was at first interned in Changi but was subsequently moved to Thailand to work on the Railway. He was then to serve in many different camps and became well acquainted with Toosey who he regarded with great respect. Although he had no previous understanding of Japanese, Escritt had a good ear for language and during his captivity he devoted himself to learning the language – eventually becoming adept in both spoken and (very impressively) written Japaneswe. This latter skill was to be of tremendous value in his post-war years when he combined his career as a senior administrator at Oxford University with an ongoing interest in the Japanese archives of the Railway.[9]

My developing relationship with Escritt then proved to be very helpful in assessing the background evidence for my biography of Colonel Toosey. In the course of our correspondence I mentioned Futamatsu's work and the need for its publication in English and this led to a direct link between the two men although they never met. This, then, resulted in Escritt spending a number of years translating the work while at the same time I was able to persuade my publisher at that time – The Athlone Press – that, suitably revised and edited, it would make an ideal companion volume to my own study of Toosey. In this way it was to be anticipated that these two very different, viewpoints would give posterity a better perspective in judging the actual events.

Sadly, although my biography was duly published as planned,[10] the proposed publication of Futamatsu's work did not proceed. This was partly due to the publisher requiring both a substantial revision of the manuscript and a large subsidy. Both of these difficulties might well have been resolved over time but the death of Escritt in 1991 was a critical factor which could not be easily overcome. At that time I was extremely busy with my own research projects and committed to other publications[11] so could not step into the breach and accordingly a long hiatus ensued. However, I did retain permission from both Futamatsu and from Escritt's widow, Mrs Ruth Escritt, to publish the translation and with other studies completed[12] have now been able to give the biography the attention it deserves. A further essential factor has been the support of The Great Britain Sasakawa Foundation for the research, preparation and publication of the completed manuscript. Without this assistance it is almost certain that the entire project would have remained stillborn and I am, therefore, greatly indebted to both Peter Mathias and Stephen McEnally for their continued encouragement and practical help.

In the meantime Yoshihiko Futamatsu died and thus did not see the final outcome of a project close to his heart; however, his former colleague, Renichi Sugano, has been most helpful in clarifying many uncertain points in Futamatsu's text. I am also most grateful to Professor Kunio Katayama,[13] my academic collaborator, who kindly facilitated my final meeting with Sugano in Tokyo in October 2011 and whose skill in translation was a major factor in its success. The culmination of this work thus owes much to the assistance provided by Sugano and Katayama and their ongoing dedication deserves my sincere thanks. This support was considerably aided by that provided by Mrs Atsuko Broadbridge whose Japanese background proved to be most valuable in helping my understanding of many aspects of the original manuscript. I would also wish to acknowledge the huge contribution made to the study by Mrs Gill Wilson. Her skill and enthusiasm in preparing successive drafts for publication clearly demonstrated her great interest and commitment to the project and she clearly deserves the highest possible commendation for all her efforts.

Publisher's Note: Japanese Names

In the title and introductory pages to this book, we have followed the Western custom of presenting the given name before the family name, thus Yoshihiko Futamatsu, whereas Japanese names are normally presented with the family name first followed by the given name – thus Futamatsu Yoshihiko. The Japanese convention, however, has been followed by translator Ewart Escritt.

FOREWORD
Peter N. Davies

The root cause of The Pacific War lay in Japan's invasion of Manchuria and China for eventually this led the United Stated to restrict its exports of oil and scrap metal on which Japan was heavily reliant. This policy was intensified after Japan joined the Tripartite Pack with Germany and Italy and a total ban on all strategic materials was imposed by Britain, Holland and the USA after Japan had occupied parts of French Indo-China in 1940–41.

This development left Japan with only two real choices – to withdraw from China and Indo-China as a condition for the lifting of the sanctions or to make itself self-sufficient by seizing the remaining territories of the South-East Asia.[14] The weakness of the Western powers following the German victories in 1940 then encouraged those who favoured what was thought would be a short war and on 7 December 1941 Japan launched her secret attack on the United States' fleet based at Pearl Harbour in Hawaii. This was largely successful so that although the American aircraft carriers escaped damage as they were out of port the Japanese established temporary superiority at sea. However, what was regarded as an act of treachery had the effect of uniting the American nation and it became grimly determined to defeat Japan and its European allies.[15]

At about the same time Japanese forces began landing in Thailand and were quickly able to advance down the Malayan Peninsula. Japanese tactics were then to prove so decisive that on 15 February 1942 Singapore itself had been captured. These victories were achieved at relatively little cost due to the weakness of the British armed forces which was partly due to most of their intended equipment – especially aircraft and tanks – being diverted to aid Russia.[16] However, this very success created its own problems for the Japanese authorities. In Singapore these were caused by the very large numbers of troops taken prisoner for whom little or no preparation had been made.[17] On the wider front other early victories resulted in Japan gaining control over the Philippines, the Dutch East Indies and Burma. Further attempts to cut communications between the United States and Australia by seizing Samoa, Fiji and New Caledonia and plans to secure the Aleutian Islands and Port Moresby in New Guinea were then to be frustrated by defeats in the Battles of Midway and the Coral Sea. These failures ensured that from May 1942 Japanese expansion in the Pacific was at an end but also meant that a defensive perimeter needed to be created to protect the vast area she had already occupied.[18]

The resulting lines of communication were of enormous length and placed huge burdens on the Japanese merchant marine. This was already finding it difficult to fulfil its prime task of bringing oil and other raw materials from the conquered territories to the homeland for it should be noted that in the last year of peace Japanese vessels had only been able to carry 65% of her imports.[19] Although the production of cargo ships was to be greatly increased during the war their numbers and tonnage were never sufficient to offset those being sunk and this was to remain a major constraint on Japanese strategy.[20] The overall decline in available merchant vessels together with the ever increasing scale of attacks by American submarines and aircraft then obliged the Japanese to examine ways in which economies could be made. As part of this process it was decided that the supply of their forces in Burma should be via Bangkok instead of using the port at Rangoon.

This proposed re-arrangement of routes offered two specific advantages. In the first place it was appreciated that a saving of over 1,200 miles could be made if Rangoon could be replaced by Bangkok as the shipping terminus. Second, was also understood that the attacks from aircraft based in India which were already causing heavy losses to shipping approaching Rangoon were likely to intensify. Thus, a potentially safer and shorter route had much to commend it but the problem with implementing such a scheme was that there was no existing provision for the ongoing movement of cargo landed at Bangkok to be carried into Burma. For this to be resolved required the Thai and Burma rail networks to be connected which was, in fact, a matter which the Japanese had already examined in their pre-war planning. This had resulted in a feasibility study being commissioned in 1939 and 1940 which was completed by a civilian consultant named Kuwabara. His conclusion was that such a project could be finalized in a year if sufficient resources were availablebut given wartime constraints military engineers revised this estimate to five or six years.[21]

Japan had not ratified the Geneva Convention of 1929 but as it had signed The Hague Agreement of 1907 it was still legally committed to the principle that prisoners of war must not undertake work that would be helpful to their captors. In spite of this a decision was made to utilize the massive pool of labour which had become available after the fall of Singapore. It was, indeed, only the existence of this resource that convinced those in power that the construction of a rail link with Burma was a viable proposition. Thus, as early as March 1942 preliminary preparations were begun and British prisoners started to move to Thailand at the end of June 1942. At about the same time a large unit of Australian prisoners which had previously been employed to help repair the former British airfields in Burma was re-deployed to begin building the track towards the Thai frontier at the Three Pagodas Pass. Eventually, more than 60,000 British, Dutch, Australian and a few Americans were to be engaged in Thailand and Burma in constructing the rail link. It should be emphasized that all of this vast workforce were employed purely as unskilled labourers as all of the technical and skilled tasks were the responsibility of the estimated 12000 to 15000 Japanese who were allocated to the project.[22] A further substantial number of labourers, perhaps over 150,000, were recruited locally and from the occupied territories but their high mortality due to tropical disease and the poor organization provided by their Japanese masters seems to have greatly limited their contribution to the work.

The net result of the activities of this diverse workforce was that in spite of appalling conditions including heavy rainfall, little medical provision and a complete lack of capital equipment the track was completed over a distance of 415 kilometres (262 miles) in just over eighteen months. This tremendous achievement owed much to Japanese ingenuity – many existing lines were cannibalized to obtain rails and machinery – and even more to a ruthless determination to ignore the human cost. Thus, it has been calculated that 20% of allied personnel died during the construction of the Railway. Over the same period only 4% of the Japanese engaged in the enterprise were lost – on the other hand at least 26% of the indigenous labourers failed to survive a single year[23] and it is estimated that over 90,000 were eventually to die working on the project.

The extent to which this massive cost in lives can be justified by the military situation should now be considered. The original plan was for the Railway to be able to carry 3,000 tons per day but by the time it was completed this had already been reduced to a target of 1,000 tons. This revised figure was due to a recognition of the poor quality of the track and rolling stock which was accepted as being the best that could be expected in the circumstances of the time. In practice, even this lower throughput was seldom possible on account of the rising severity of allied air raids which led to much disruption and thus by 1944 the daily average was seldom above 300 tons.[24] However, it should be appreciated that the Railway also transported large numbers of troops into Burma who would otherwise have had to march long distances with all their equipment. It is thought that these amounted to as many as seven divisions together with many Corps and Headquarters personnel. In addition, at least 10,000 casualties were evacuated via this route which later, after the abortive attack on India, was used by many units to withdraw into Thailand. The fact that these troops were able to retire in good order meant that they were soon able to set up a strong defensive position at the Three Pagodas Pass and had the war not been ended by events elsewhere they would undoubtedly have caused the British forces many problems.[25]

The delivery of men and supplies to Burma on the Japanese side was paralleled by comparable events on the British side. Following their retreat from Burma British army formations established new defensive positions along the Indian frontier. The need to supply and reinforce these troops presented a major logistical problem given the fact that there was no through road from the nearest port at Calcutta some 600 miles away. At first, a combination of rail, river and road transport which had been used to service the Assam tea industry was utilized but this could only provide 600 tons per day. By 1943, this figure had been raised to 2,800 tons but this was still insufficient to cope with the rising scale of operations. This logistical problem was not finally overcome until 4,700 trained railwaymen were brought over from the United States together with many powerful new locomotives which enabled the daily throughput to rise to 7,300 tons.[26]

When I mentioned these statistics to Yoshihiko Futamatsu in our correspondence[27] he immediately asked for further details and I referred him to the appropriate source.[28] He subsequently wrote to say that he now better understood the difficulties which needed to be overcome by the British in order to satisfy the needs of their forces which were similar to those faced by the Japanese. He also felt that while the British succeeded in raising their throughput to the desired level the Thai-Burma and internal Burmese railway systems were never able to meet the Japan's military needs. This, he thought, was a major factor in Japan's defeat at Imphal.[29]

The roles of Futamatsu and his friend and colleague Renichi Sugano in these events will now be examined. The former, born in 1912, studied engineering at Kyoto University where he specialized in bridge construction. After graduating in 1935, Futamatsu was employed by Japan National Railways until 1940. He was then called up and became a *gunzoku* (a Japanese military auxiliary) with the rank of Captain and a role as a consultant civilian railway engineer. This led to him being attached to the HQ of the 9th Railway Regiment where he met Sugano for the first time.[30] The latter, born in 1919, entered Military Academy in 1938 and graduated two years later. He was then appointed as a Company Commander in the 1st Battalion of the Regiment with the rank of Captain.[31]

Subsequently, both officers took take part in the invasion of Malaya in December 1941. However, while Sugano landed directly on the Peninsular, Futamatsu arrived in French Indo-China prior to the start of the war and then moved into Malaya via Thailand when the fighting began.[32] Sugano's unit had the task of making temporary repairs to the track and bridges immediately behind the advancing troops while Futamatsu worked with the 4th Special Bridging Group which followed up constructing more permanent structures. When the Malayan campaign ended both were at first involved in the renovation of the colony's rail network. Futamatsu subsequently joined the Southern Field Railway Group based in Singapore and was soon to be concerned with planning various aspects of the proposed Thai-Burma Railway. At about the same time Sugano moved into Burma where his Battalion helped to restore the damaged railway track before being re-deployed to Banpong in Thailand.

By then the HQ of the Southern Field Railway Group had been moved to Thailand where Futamatsu and Sugano were able to renew their friendship. However, now promoted to Major, Futamatsu was largely engaged at a strategic level. Likewise, Sugano, now also a Major in command of the 1ˢᵗ Battalion, was involved in the more practical work of constructing the track. Thus, the extent of their contact is not clear but certainly became less once the line had been completed. By this time, Sugano was permanently based in Burma, while Futamatsu enjoyed a much wider brief. His exact status – although always senior – is not known until March 1943 when he was made personal adviser to Colonel Imai who was in charge of a new *gunzoku* formation with special responsibility for bridge-building.[33] This is partly explained by the peculiar nature of the Japanese military system: the need to always maintain 'face' and the complex relationship between engineers and regular soldiers. This is well illustrated by the impractical suggestions made by one visiting Staff Officer which were initially agreed but later quietly circumvented.[34] These were tactics which Futamatsu was reluctantly obliged to accept and he also understood the need for the Railway to be built to replace the dangerous shipping route to Rangoon.[35] He seems less sure about the concept of employing POWs to help construction for he does not fully agree with the suggestion that their dispersal from Singapore would help the Japanese administration to provide an enhanced level of food and other supplies.[36] However, he does consider that it was both legal and proper for prisoners to be made to work and felt that it was differences between Western and Japanese cultures and attitudes that made the imposition of physical punishment such a bone of contention between the two sides.[37]

This reluctance to condemn Japanese policy may be thought to be compounded by his criticism of many POWs who were accused of being 'negligent' and thus excuses the engineers who 'scolded' them.[38] Futamatsu also points out that Japanese discipline was traditionally physical with inferiors being customarily punished by kicks and blows from their superiors. The fact that this system was applied to prisoners as well as Japanese troops was, he felt, quite understandable.[39] This view, not shared by many prisoners, is further undermined by his belief that their Korean guards were 'good-natured people' which was not the experience of many of their captives.[40] The lot of those he describes as 'coolies' was, he admits, much worse than that of the POWs. This was because they were frequently provided with only very small rations of what were often the wrong foods for their difference religions and virtually no systematic medical attention. In Futamatsu's words: '...one was forced to divide them within their huts: at times it was no different from driving them into their graves.'[41]

Both prisoners and local labourers suffered in varying degrees from a wide variety of diseases including malaria, dysentery, cholera, bubonic plague and beriberi.[42] These problems were made worse by the heavy rainfall – one of the highest in the world[43] – and paradoxically at times by a shortage of drinking water for much was contaminated by mud, rotting vegetation and excrement. This meant that all water needed to be boiled which, in the circumstances, was frequently very difficult.[44]

The combination of heavy rainfall, contagious diseases, malnutrition and mountainous, jungle terrain made the building of the Railway exceptionally difficult. Nevertheless, Japanese determination and ingenuity, plus their ability to ignore the cost in human lives, ensured that it was completed in a particularly short time. On the other hand these massive problems, allied to a significant shortage of equipment and materials, meant that, '...we ended up with an imperfectly-constructed railway with no prospect of maintaining transport viability'.[45] These technical deficiencies were then to be exacerbated by the growing scale of Allied bombing and even though a system of rapid repairs was successfully introduced throughput failed to keep up with demand.[46] Futamatsu later learned, perhaps with some envy, the progress of the Indian Railways (and availability of transport aircraft) and concluded that their success in carrying and supplying British forces was a major factor in the battle for Burma.[47]

Any attempt at assessing the writing and beliefs of Futamatsu must take into account his upbringing and the fact that for most of his life he only had access to Japanese sources. While this changed in the post-war years his knowledge was constrained in many ways and his contact with former POWs only came about when he was approached by Geoffrey

Pharaoh Adams (at my suggestion) during his visit to Japan in 1981. This led to a subsequent introduction to James Bradley and Futamatsu was then given copies of their works which he has quoted extensively in his biography.[48] However, in spite of these links he still does not seem to have been aware of the immense literature in English and it was only through my intervention that he learned of the existence of such a relevant study as Slim's *Defeat into Victory*.[49]

These omissions in Futamatsu's background knowledge appear to have made it difficult for him to make informed, impartial judgements and he remained convinced that the United States and Britain started the Pacific War. As a consequence he continued to believe that the Geneva Convention – even if it had been signed – would not have been relevant to the employment of POWs in Thailand. However, he makes no comment on the suggestion that following the deaths of a number of Japanese prisoners at Featherston Camp in New Zealand in February 1943 the Military Authorities felt justified in adopting an even harsher regime for its work-force building the Railway.[50] He also seems to have been equally content for the prisoners at Selerang Barracks to be forced to sign a declaration that they would not attempt to escape even though this was later used to justify the execution of those who were captured after seeking freedom.[51] While he argues these points with some force his only comment on the execution of Chinese Merchants without trial after the fall of Singapore was that it was: '..a well justified necessity'.[52]

Many of the items outlined above are further expanded in Futamatsu's account of his war service which follows. Apart from considerable additional material this provides a distinctly Japanese point of view, free from the Western preconceptions, which may have inadvertently distorted this Preface and other studies. Futamatsu was, of course, originally writing for a Japanese readership and had no wish to offend, but I am convinced that his work accurately reflects his recollections and genuinely-held opinions. At only one point can I detect a deliberate distortion and this appears to be for personal or prudish not political reasons. This item concerns the setting up of a 'field hospital recuperation centre' at Hin Dat Hot Springs in which he fails to mention that its real purpose was to provide a 'comfort station' for the benefit of Japanese troops and Korean auxiliaries.[53]

With this minor exception Futamatsu's study not only gives much insight into the construction of the Railway from one at the very centre of events but it also supplies a unique counterweight to the many and varied publications produced by Western authors.

The defeat at Imphal and the subsequent retreat of the Japanese army placed great strains on the Railway which was intensified by the increasing level of Allied air attacks. As many locomotives were destroyed by this bombing campaign more were ordered from Japan and in the Summer of 1945 Futamatsu was sent to Saigon to arrange for those just landed to be moved to Thailand.[54] He was still there when on 15 August 1945 he heard the Emperor announce his decision to surrender.[55] Soon afterwards he was able to return to his unit in Bangkok and was then to share their internment in a number of different camps.[56] Western readers may be interested to learn that these new prisoners then occupied themselves much as British POWs had done in Germany and Italy though not in Japan. These activities included educational and occupational courses: the manufacture of many articles from local materials and numerous theatrical productions which ranged from serious drama to song-and-dance concerts.[57] It is not clear to what extent Futamatsu joined in these events – he seems to have been mainly concerned with studying English in private; he was fortunate in being released after less than a year in captivity.

Following the Japanese surrender a system had been created whereby any individual suspected of a war crime could be nominated by the persons involved or their friends. In this event potential witnesses would be asked for their opinion and a case would be prepared if a consensus seemed certain. Thus, when Teruo Saitoh, second in command at the Bridge Camp, was accused of minor infractions by some former prisoners at Tamarkan he was exonerated by evidence provided by Philip Toosey and his adjutant David Boyle.[58] In fact, neither Futamatsu or Sugano were named as offenders in any respect so were repatriated to Japan on schedule – Futamatsu in July 1946 and Sugano in January 1947.[59]

Following his return Futamatsu settled in Tokyo and resumed his career as an engineer with Japan National Railways. In 1961, he took early retirement and moved back to his family's Tokugawa built home in Kyoto and then joined the High Speed Railway Company for whom he helped to design the new Kobe rail network. At a later stage, in 1974, he set up Central Consultants Inc. in Meguro-Ku, Tokyo, and continued to advise on many engineering projects until the late 1980s.[60] Sugano's post-war career was quite straightforward. After his repatriation he moved to Shinjuku-Ku in Tokyo and there established a photographic business which was to occupy him for the remainder of his working life. Over this period he also maintained a great interest in his wartime experiences and played an active part in the 9th Railway Regiment's post-war association,. This he represented on at least four occasions when visiting Thailand and Burma;[61] he was also a key figure in arranging for Locomotive C5631 to be returned to Japan. This was the first engine to travel the completed Thai-Burma Railway and is now preserved at the Yasukuni-Shrine in Tokyo.[62]

This brief outline and analysis of the life and work of Yoshihiko Futamatsu is based on a number of sources including his written works, our mutual correspondence and a series of interviews undertaken when I was teaching at a number of Japanese Universities. Of these the most important by far was his account of his wartime experiences published originally in Japanese, and now in English, under the title: *Across the Three Pagodas Pass: The Story of the Thai-Burma Railway.*[63] This would not, of course, have been of any significance but for the efforts of Ewart Escritt. His translation of this memoir into English now makes it available to a wider range of readers around the world who would otherwise have had little opportunity of evaluating the non-Western viewpoint for, as noted earlier, there are few comparable works in English to which interested parties could refer. Thus, for the first time, posterity has been given the opportunity of reaching a balanced judgement on a highly controversial subject.

◘

Ewart Escritt produced his translation during the 1980s. He and his proposed publisher at that time – The Athlone Press – then agreed that while this was a literal (word for word) study which faithfully reflected the Japanese original it required suitable annotation, revision and editing to make it more understandable to potential readers. The precise nature of these changes would inevitably have been a matter of some discussion but Escritt's death in 1991 ended this possibility so it has fallen to me to make any necessary amendments. It should be stressed, however, that this final version is fundamentally that created by Escritt more than twenty years ago and that these alterations are essentially of a minor character. In addition, the passage of time has seen much more information becoming available and it is hoped that its inclusion will add further value to the translation. As a result of these modifications it is believed that this revised edition will place Futamatsu's writing in a better perspective and be a fitting tribute to Ewart Escritt's scholarship and memory and at the same time make the text attractive to a wider readership.

Following his work on Futamastu's text Ewart Escritt felt it would be useful to provide a personal Introduction which would aid the readers' understanding of his study. In his opinion this required an outline of many background topics as well as details of Futamatsu's career, views and philosophy. The most important of these concerned the planning and construction of the Railway and Escritt was anxious to point out the limitations which Futamatsu experienced in his choice of route. Escritt also wished to refer to certain aspects of Japanese culture, mentioning good and bad individual behaviour and the nation's constitution which gave critical power to the military authorities. It was they, rather than any parliamentary body, which then made the decision to employ prisoners-of-war irrespective of the legal niceties if it would assist the Japanese war effort. This was, of course, against the provisions of the Geneva Convention – which are included in full[64] – not signed by Japan but also in breach of the earlier Hague Agreement which she had.

Escritt then provides some details of the labour that was utilized in the building programme and comments on the Japanese lack of medical care for their own troops as well as for prisoners and locally recruited men. He continued by emphasizing the value of discipline, loyalty and personal relationships in the difficult circumstances of the construction process and how secret radios brought hope and comfort to many in near despair. These were banned by their captors and discovery would have led to severe punishment. Escritt mentions a numbers of cases which involved the *kempeitai* but many brave individuals were never deterred. A further danger arose from the growing number of bombing raids made on the Railway: the details of several of these are included: one of which records the death of Major Paddy Sykes at Nong Pladuk.[65] Those prisoners who survived their work on the track as well as these other perils were then to face a final challenge as the Japanese guards planned their elimination if Allied forces were thought to be approaching.[66]

In his Introduction Escritt also provides a brief account of his own wartime career and of the parts played by many individuals. Amongst these was Boon Pong,[67] Pharaoh Adams,[68] Jim Bradley[69] and C.H.D. Wild (whose eloquence saved Bradley from execution)[70] and, inevitably, Philip Toosey under whom he served in many camps. However, it was Escritt's relationship with Futamatsu which forms the most important aspect of his Introduction. This is typified by an exchange of *Haiku* (a three-part poem of seventeen syllables) which demonstrated their mutual regard.[71] Although not an essential prerequisite to the reading of Escritt's translation this background information will undoubtedly provide the general reader with a better appreciation of the role and achievements of the Thai-Burma Railway. It may also help to increase their understanding of Japanese attitudes and resulting policies as well as more fully explaining the background to the suffering of those who worked and died during its construction.

In my revision of this translation I have followed Ewart Escritt's decisions in a number of ways. Futamatsu's English is somewhat archaic and in places it may be difficult to understand his exact meaning. Nevertheless on balance I, like the translator, felt that retaining his style more accurately reflects the Japanese text so I have made only marginal changes. It would also appear that Futamatsu wrote a number of his chapters as separate entities so that some contain a degree of repetition. While these could have been omitted or limited both Ewart Escritt and I believed that this would seriously disturb the flow of the narrative so we agreed to leave the text as the author intended. A final point concerned the number of substantial quotations from the writings of ex-POWs Adams and Bradley and of the American pilot, Carl Fritsche, which were included in the Japanese original. These were employed by Futamatsu to supplement his own impressions of events so although they may be thought to be too extensive they have also been retained in full.

With these minor comments, criticisms and reservations I commend Ewart Escritt's translation of Futamatsu's work in the belief that it will make a significant contribution to our knowledge of the real events and consequences of the building of the Thai-Burma Railway during the Second World War.

Peter N. Davies
School of History
University of Liverpool
December 2012

INTRODUCTION
Ewart Escritt

A horror story of brutality, inefficiency and inhumanity may be described by a writer from a totally different culture in terms which we in a Christian society must find inadequate. It is fascinating to uncover, so far as we can, the reasons lurking behind such apparent inhumanity and to describe the actual situation in which these things took place.

Futamatsu himself was a dedicated professional railway engineer and also, like his CO, fair-minded, always ready to see both sides of an argument. During the Pacific War he was not greatly affected by the militaristic propaganda with which the Army flooded the nation in 'the dark valley' of the 1930s. His commander had read engineering at Tokyo Imperial University, but of course, as a regular soldier, he had to comply with superior orders which in theory emanated from an Emperor who was still divine.[72] I suspect that Futamatsu hero-worshipped his Colonel, and the Colonel certainly recognized his subordinate's professional skill. Their association ripened into warm friendship.

The Thai-Burma Railway was a necessary concomitant in the Japanese Army's assault through Burma into India, one which came to the fore as a result of the US Navy's successful action off Midway Island in the Pacific in 1942 when most of Japan's aircraft-carriers were sunk or damaged. The British Far East Naval Squadron took control of the Indian Ocean, in particular of the Andaman Sea off the coasts of Malaya and Burma, so it became vitally necessary for the Japanese Army to develop an overland trucking route across the Three Pagodas Pass and on to Moulmein in Burma, to facilitate their invasion of India.

Looking ahead to the possibility of some such eventuality, Imperial Japanese Army General Headquarters in Tokyo had taken on a civilian railway engineering expert in 1939. Using Thai maps, Kuwabara proposed the building of a railway to connect Thailand with Burma. He calculated that it would take two years to complete. Officially 'The Railway to link Thailand with Burma', it became known as the Thai-Burma Railway.

Plans for a railway from Thailand through to Burma had previously been investigated by German engineers working for the Thai government in the 1890s, and independently by the British early in the twentieth century. One line of entry involved a route from their colony, Burma, to reach Pitsanlok in northern Thailand. The other involved a railway from Thailand through to the Andaman Sea coast in Burma. IJA GHQ chose the latter (which the British had abandoned as impossible to execute) despite the facts that the climate, health conditions and distance involved were against it. Local Thai had grave doubts of its success.

Uniquely among civilized nations Japan declined to ratify the Geneva Convention for the treatment of prisoners-of-war. Since the early 1930s militaristic propaganda, in the dark valley of that decade, insidiously boosted the medieval concept *bushidō*, 'the way of the warrior'. Forgotten was the chivalry of the Russo-Japanese War of 1904–1905 when a beleaguered Japanese general surrendered with all his men and returned to Japan with honour after the war. Now, in the 1940s, an enlisted soldier pledged to commit suicide rather than surrender in battle, and if hit by disease to lie at attention in his quarters. No dressings were issued to them or to their prisoners apart from quinine and creosote pills: hideous tropical ulcers resulted in seventy amputations, done by Australian, British and Dutch surgeons with what limited equipment they had managed to carry in their packs on the march.

Such, in practice, was how the Japanese Army interpreted the way of the warrior. These prisoners were sub-humans who had surrendered in battle. The Japanese could not ratify the Geneva Convention because it was impossible, they said, for Japanese soldiers, sailors and airmen to surrender. Given that they were not engaged in a situation of forlorn hope, this theory held water in the Malayan campaign. At the surrender parley at Bukit Timah General Yamashita asked General

Percival how many Japanese prisoners the British were holding. 'Not one', was the subdued reply. And in their campaign across the Pacific islands the magnificent bravery of the American marines was matched, some might say obscured, by the wholesale suicides of the Japanese defenders, military and civilian alike. On the island battlefields there, a Japanese soldier would feign dead, holding a concealed hand-grenade, to take one marine with him into oblivion. In their 'octopus pots', the Japanese equivalent of the marines' foxholes, they would wait for their enemy to get close and then destroy him with a grenade.

But, if when all seemed lost, they were faced *en bloc* with defeat, they tended to be lost, typically looked for a higher order, and sat on the fence. When the atomic bombs dropped, I was ordered on 17 August 1945 to Bangkok from the remote foothills near Nakhon Nayok where the Japanese were preparing their obligatory 'last stand for a decisive battle'. My job was to act as Staff Captain 'Q' on Ex-PW HQ we set up to get ourselves out. The twenty thousand fully armed soldiers in Bangkok under a one-time head of the *kempeitai* had not surrendered because the C-in-C of the Southern Army in Saigon, Field Marshal Count Terauchi Hisaichi, was a hard-liner who would not accept a merely broadcast message from his Emperor. I had commandeered a Japanese soldier with a jeep and told him to drive me to the Japanese HQ. A priority was to find staging camps in which we could house ex-prisoners from the worst cholera belts on the railway, and by good luck my driver had found me the empty Law University, across the padang by the Royal Palace. Like my nineteenth-century college, Keble, it was built on the corridor system but unlike Keble it had only one latrine. So I asked the General for a working party of soldiers to dig latrines. It sounds foolhardy but after three years we knew our Jap. The General hesitated, passed the buck, and told me to take my request to the colonel commanding prison camps in Thailand. My driver took me a hundred yards down the same road, and I presented Colonel Nakamura Shijō with his general's superior order, a *meirei*. In ten minutes I had my squad and they worked like blacks on the job. This small episode illustrates a facet of the Japanese character not always appreciated in the West.

The Count's final surrender filtered through to us in Bangkok on 8 September. The Emperor's brother, Prince Kanin, had been flown out from Japan in late August to give him a personal order face to face.

Futamatsu is guilty on occasion of chop-logic, that form of disputacious argument endemic in Japanese philosophical passages. Examples occur, for example, when he tries to gloss over the reason why the Japanese Army could not allow his Government to ratify the Geneva Convention for the Treatment of Prisoners-of-war, and in another passage when he attempts to leave it as an open question whether the Army committed violations of the Convention or not. Again, he disputes unconvincingly the post-war stigma of 'Death Railway'. However, he does rehearse articles in the Convention which were violated, but tends to argue that the terrible conditions in which the railway construction took place constitute for it a special case. And he tends also to regard as 'retaliatory action' any attempt to bring offenders to book in the War Crimes Trials.

He was born in 1912. He graduated in engineering at Kyōto University in 1936, going down in that year into Japan National Railways' head office as a civil engineer in their construction bureau. He was called up in 1941 into a specialist bridging company of *gunzoku* (civilian auxiliaries of Japanese nationality) and served with a railway regiment on the West coast line of Malayan Railways on bridge repair, notably across the Krian River, during the campaign to capture Singapore. In June 1942, he was seconded, in the rank of Captain, to the HQ of 9 Railway Regiment with responsibility for survey of the projected Thai-Burma Railway and for design of bridges up to the frontier at the Three Pagodas Pass. He became professional railway engineering adviser to the regimental commander, Colonel Imai Itaru, and on the railway's completion in October 1943 he commanded a battalion, in the rank of Major, on line-conservation on the Thai side, patching up rail track and repairing bridges which increasingly had come under RAF and USAAF attack. In August 1945, he was sent to Saigon to expedite transport to Thailand of replacement locomotives exported from Japan.

After the Japanese surrender he was ordered back to Thailand, and was interned in military prisoner-of-war camps at Nonhoi near Bangkok and later near Nakhon Nayok, which is 40 km from Prachinburi station on the north-east line of Thai Railways. In April 1946, he was moved to a camp half-way between Nong Pladuk and Banpong, and was repatriated in July 1946.

He re-entered Japan National Railways, from whom he retired in April 1960 at the age of forty-eight in order to become chief engineer on subway works on the Kōbe high-speed railway. Subsequently, he worked with a consultant engineering company in Tokyo and Ōsaka.[73]

In the Japanese Army a railway engineer is a specialized sort of engineer. The commander of a railway regiment is normally a graduate in engineering of a reputable university and the officers, warrant officers and NCOs are specialized technically. During the Pacific War army ranks were as follows, in downward order of rank: *shōgun* (army commander), *taishō* (general), *chūjō* (lieutenant-general), *shōshō* (major-general), *taisa* (colonel), *chūsa* (lieutenant-colonel), *shōsa* (major), *taii* (captain), *chūi* (lieutenant), *shōi* (second-lieutenant), *minaraishikan* (cadet officer), *juni* (warrant officer), *sōchō* (CSM, staff-serjeant), *gunsō* (serjeant), *gochō* (corporal), *heichō* (lance-corporal), *jōtōhei* (superior private), *ittōhei* (first-class private), *nittōhei* (second-class private). An RSM was a *juni*, a brigadier was *ryodanchō*, not of general officer rank but an appointment for a senior colonel. Collective nouns were *shōkō*, commissioned officers, *heitai*, soldiers, *heisotsu*, private soldiers. Strictly speaking, each of the above ranks was prefixed by *rikugun*, Land Army, to distinguish it from *kaigun* Sea Army, i.e. Navy. During the Pacific War there was no separate Air Force. The Army had its own aircraft, the Navy its own separately, and rivalry between the two arms was carried to ridiculous extremes.

The railway had its starting point at Nong Pladuk (80 km from Bangkok on the southern section of Thai National Railways), its terminus Thanbyusayat (about 50 km from Moulmein on the India National Line to Ye on the Burma coast), with main construction bases at Nong Pladuk on the Thai side and at Thanbyusayat on the Burma side.

The line ran from Nong Pladuk 50 km to Kanchanaburi (always abbreviated by Japanese railway engineers and by prisoners-of-war to Kamburi,) crossed the river Mae Khlaung at Thā Makham, and continued thence alongside the river Kwae Noi upstream as far as the Three Pagodas Pass, descended thence along the upper valley of the river Zami and crossed the Taungnyo mountain range to Thanbyusayat, at which point it converged with the India National Railways line to Ye on the Andaman Sea coast. In the event it ran for 415 km through mountainous jungle, rose to about 275 meters above sea level and was built with prisoner-of-war labour using picks, changkuls, cold chisels and mallets, gunpowder, saws, derricks and pulleys, with local dredgers and cement-mixers for concrete well-crib bridge-piers and bridge-abutments.

The route followed that used in antiquity by Burmese raiders who came over the Three Pagodas Pass and crossed the Mae Khlaung by a liana and bamboo footbridge at Ban Thā Manao near Lat Ya before moving on to assault Ayutthaya, the ancient capital of Thailand.[74]

Railtrack gauge was set at one metre, a gauge common to southern region railways making it possible for trains to run straight through to Singapore, again from Phnom Penh in Cambodia and Moulmein in Burma, and again as far as Rangoon. Planned transport volume was three thousand tons a day each way. Rails were shipped up from dismantled Sumatran and East coast Malayan Railways. The line had also a theoretical purpose of developing a commercial transport route between Burma and Thailand. Construction materials available in the area with other necessary materials were to be supplied by the Thai and the Japanese governments. It was to cost 700 million yen.

Military construction forces were laid down as one railway HQ, two railway regiments, and one railway materials depot, with auxiliary units as needed, i.e. *gunzoku* (of Japanese nationality) and *heiho* (of non-Japanese nationality, in the railway's case Koreans). Labour needed was specified as local coolies and prisoners-of-war, as appropriate.

For Kuwabara's projection in 1939 IJA GHQ had had prepared aerial survey maps to scale 1:20,000, which on the Thai side covered the Kwae Noi but the Kwae Yai (the Mae Khlaung) only as far as the immediate Thā Makham area.[75] It followed, therefore, that as this emanated from the highest authority Futamatsu had no option but to plan the main river-crossing at Thā Makham instead of the traditional crossing at Ban Thā Manao near Lat Ya. The latter would have elongated the line by about 25 km but would have eliminated the need for a cutting near Chungkai and a plank viaduct beyond it which together cost the lives of many prisoners.

The situation he faced was made the more difficult by the criminal negligence of the Thai Government's contractors who failed to press ahead with the lorry highway which was necessary in this monsoon climate. The most elementary exercise in work-study had evidently not been done by them. At the time Futamatsu was unaware of the Thai contract. When I told him about it after the war, he commented that the narrow jungly track via Lat Ya to Ban Thā Manao (mis-named

Ban Thā Dan by the engineers) was then still the narrow jungly track described by Pavillard in his book, *Bamboo Doctor*.[76]

Errors in place-names inevitably arose because of the difficulty of transliterating Thai script into Japanese syllabics. In this instance Ban Thā Dan is much further upstream, is in hilly country and has no river-crossing.

In the Imperial War Museum in London there is a Japanese railway engineer's trace of the Thai-Burma Link Line. It is in scroll form reading from right to left but has been folded and there are cracks along the folds. It is also rubbed and stained so that some *kanji* (ideographs) are illegible, others hard to decipher. It was found at Kamburi after the Japanese surrender by an agent of Standard Vacuum Oil, who passed it to his Bangkok manager, Nai Tack Fee, who gave it to his opposite number in Asiatic Petroleum Company (Royal Dutch Shell), C.F. Colchester, who had worked on the railway as a prisoner-of-war, and he presented it to the Imperial War Museum in 1954.[77] From internal evidence, it was made for the transport section of 5 Company of 3 Battalion, 9 Railway Regiment.

On this trace only the main Bangkok-Singapore line is marked as a 'line in operation' and the Moulmein-Ye line as 'uncompleted'. The Moulmein-Ye line was in fact completed in 1925. It was described in *Railway Gazette International* (3 April 1925) as being 89 miles long, made through difficult country with annual rainfall of 367 inches. There were 200 bridges. No roads existed and heavy material had to be conveyed up tidal creeks in country boats.[78] The line had been surveyed by 1898. On Waterlow & Sons' map of Burma railways of that date the track is marked as 'surveyed', with stations planned at Moulmein, Pa-auk, Kawthut, Taungbon and Yemyoma (terminal, i.e. Ye). From Pa-auk runs a 'suggested' track through Ataran and Thanbyusayat to the Three Pagodas Pass.[79] Probably the first general reference to the Moulmein-Ye line is in *The Encyclopaedia Britannica* of 1929 in which the map of Burma shows it as an existing railway.[80] From internal evidence the trace in the IWM must have been drawn no earlier than August 1944.

At this time Thailand, *Muang Thai*, the Land of the Free, was a constitutional monarchy, Pratet Thai, controlled by a military dictatorship under Field-Marshal Phibun Songkhraam. When the Japanese Army marched in on 9 December 1941, he had no option (after a token show of resistance) but to capitulate. To the tourist it is the land of Buddhism, of brilliantly-tiled pagodas, of national observances and ceremonial dancing, of historic ruins, of elephants, often gorgeously apparelled, and of lovely women (particularly if below the age of thirty). The Thai are sticklers for prestige.

Yellow-robed priests with shaven heads are a common sight, begging as mendicants under the eaves of houses, haughtily giving no thanks for oblations, treated like buddhas. In modern times, after that brief interlude under Japanese occupation, the Thai have switched from their former anglophile culture to a brash American substitute.

It is essentially an agricultural economy. Educated Thai are generally less proud of their modernity than of their wild forests and mountainous terrain, of their teak and of the long rivers on which it is logjammed down to the sawmills.

In the history of the railway, for various reasons several towns and villages have their importance. Nong Pladuk, for example, an insignificant cluster of dwellings, was the initial starting-point of the railway. But of the considerable complex of sidings, workshops, foundries, godowns, military barracks and prisoners' compounds, not a trace remains today. All signs of the railway's worst bombing raid are wiped away. Two kilometres from Nong Pladuk is Kommā where is Wat Kok Mor, the lovely Buddhist temple near which Nong Pladuk's dead were buried. The wat remains, but the dead have been exhumed and today lie in the large cemetery at Chungkai.

In the Pacific War, Kamburi (Kanchanaburi) was at first a Japanese airstrip and finally a prison camp in which officers were segregated when the Japanese began to fear a paratroop invasion. It was seldom out of railway records. Here the Japanese erected a monument 'to ease the souls of the prisoners' who became victims of their captors' own neglect and brutality. It was dedicated in March 1944. On a marble plaque on a concrete pillar set on the large plinth of one of the four corner buttresses was engraved in English:

IN MEMORY OF DECEASED PRISONERS OF WAR 1944

The vast Allied cemetery here had been the scene of annual ceremonies held by the Thai, British and Australian governments to commemorate these men, held in the same spirit as the epitaph on the cemetery on the slopes of Garrison Hill at Kohima in Burma:

> When you go home
> tell them of us and say
> for your tomorrow
> we gave our today

The real name of Chungkai, known to every ex-prisoner on the railway, is Khao Poon. Here, too, is a very large cemetery, but the place is also infamous for a cutting through a rocky hill. The line of the projected railway route curved round at the waterside at its foot. In the normal way one would plan a tunnel here but the regiment's men had no tunnelling experience so Futamatsu had to plan a cutting which in the event proved to be 100 metres long, maximum depth 40 metres, and about ten thousand cubic metres of rock had to be excavated, a cutting which cost the lives of many prisoners.

Further along is a high cliff on the North bank, the '103 km' point (calculating from the village of Nong Pladuk where the 0-km post had been set up on 5 July 1942 to mark the point at which the Thai-Burma Railway was to branch off from the main Bangkok-Singapore line on Thai National Railways). The cliff face rose about 50 metres up from the water and continued along for about 200 metres, the wall-face rising perpendicularly and topped by a luxuriant growth of trees and shrubs. There being no straight alignment at riverside level, it was decided to make a direct run halfway up the cliff face and build a plank viaduct. This, too, cost many lives.

Konkuita in the jungle was the site of the joining-up of the Burmese and the Thai sides of the railway construction. No. 5631 tank engine, decked with the Thai and the Japanese 'poached egg' national flags, brooded nearby in a cutting, an AA-gun post was set up, and the GOC presided at a ceremony at which the two regimental commanders drove gun-metal dog-spikes into an ebony sleeper to fix the final rails. One of the many legends tells how an Aussie prisoner prized out these 'gold' spikes and sold them for a large sum to a lurking Thai. Each commander was presented with a commemorative replica, which was cast with the date shōwa 18nen 10gatsu 25 nichi along one side,

25 October 1943. One is preserved as an heirloom in Colonel Imai's family. For engineers a bronze medallion was struck to commemorate the occasion.[81] The site of the ceremony is now buried deep under water in the Khao Laem hydro-electric dam, which is 90 metres high, 910 metres water surface-level 155 metres above sea level. The dam covers 42 km from its most southerly to its most northerly points. Power-turbines, capacity 300 megawatts, are in tunnels in the Khao Laem mountain with spillways for rivers. The Kwae Noi had to be diverted for about 500 metres during construction.[82]

The Three Pagodas Pass has the central pagoda marking the frontier boundary, the other two being in Thai and Burmese territory respectively. Each is about 6 metres high. They are now a shining white trio, having been restored after the war, but I have seen a colour photograph of them as they were when the railway was built, the steps crudely roughened by time, lichen-covered, lacking part of their finials at the top, encroached upon by saplings and trees. Their Thai name is *phra chedi sam ong* which means 'the three religious spire-shaped temple towers'. The village near the pass is called Paya Thonzu (*thonzu* is a religious numerative, *paya* means 'pagoda').

All these places were emblematic of a hideous task, hideous alike to prisoners and coolies and engineers. The Japanese made up many plaintive songs like these:

> We are men drenched in soaking rain,
> gritting our teeth, gritting our teeth ...
> But if you wait, Spring comes again,
> and boats come up again.

> Left behind at home my darling child no doubt has grown.
> How is my wife's health? Has anything changed?
> We shiver in our dreams.

> Even when the wind drops, tigers lurk in rubber groves.
> Leaves fall and scatter. Why do they scatter?
> News, news of our homeland –
> Shall we hear soon in August?

Why do stars loom low on a Panga Forest night?
Now in our dreams we think, think, think of home,
and wait for a boat to load, to greet a boat.

In rubber groves in Panga Forest our final lodging to die,
Sparse shade, leaves and branches overhang,
Even today showers impend.

If you visit our comrades' honoured graves
(mists crowding in, dimly dawn comes calm in the forest)
railbed grows chilly, mists penetrate your body ...

We made a banner of remembrance of our comrades
who refused to die defeated, it was soiled by rain,
it was a collection of autographs, and we set it up
on top of a hill.[83]

In Chapter 30 Futamatsu remarks that 'those who have to spend a long time in the jungle realize that their object in life becomes that of staying alive', and that 'the curfew orderly made men forget the toils of work and when night fell the fields and hills of home floated under their eyelids, and in their dreams they saw their family friends'. Officer prisoners and senior NCOs were lucky in one respect, that they had, or developed, a strong sense of responsibility for their men, doubly lucky when men of their own unit were in the same camp. Indian Army officers were unlucky because their men were all segregated from white men (and pressurized to join the INA, the Indian Army of Independence). The Dutch, as the RAPWI (Returned Allied Prisoners-of-War and Internees) handbook told them after release in 1945, had a strong sense of survival, had an overpowering urge to look after themselves. We found they tended to jump queues at the cookhouse, a memory which caused an amusing incident when MV *Orbita* carrying British ex-prisoners home in October 1945 was passed in the Mediterranean by a Dutch liner. Her identity was announced over the tannoy and a spontaneous roar went up from *Orbita* of '*Eten halen*', the Dutch phrase for our cookhouse call of 'Come and get it!'

That too many Australian officers were privately ashamed of themselves for being undemocratic, *scilicet* being officers, was completely cancelled out by the astounding way an Australian soldier did everything he could to help his cobbers.

But in the jungle along the river-banks lurked unseen a remarkable neolithic archaeological find. In 1943, a Dutch archaeologist recorded in his brief diary, 'March/April 1943, at Bankhao, found palaeoliths', in fact pebble tools and polished adzes. Luckily this prisoner survived. He was Dr H.R. van Heekeren, and in 1960 his Government proposed to the Thai Government a joint Thai-Danish Prehistoric Expedition. They found a large number of sites in caves and on mounds in open spaces, unearthing over forty skeletons of which ten could be determined as female and twelve as male. Twenty-six of them could be determined as under thirty years of age, eight below forty, only two over forty. They were found at levels varying between 75 and 180 centimetres. Associated finds were earthenware vessels, personal ornaments and ritual objects. The most frequent finds were stone adzes, but there were also barbed harpoons, barbed arrow-heads, spearheads, and a fishhook made of animal bones, and a knife blade made from the shell of a freshwater mussel from the river. Stone bark-cloth beaters and baked-clay spindle-whorls showed that these people wore clothes, and baked-clay pellets were possibly used as missiles with a pellet bow for hunting small game. Around one skeleton's neck shell beads were found in the form of small buttons with a perforated hole in the middle, arranged in two rows along with cylindrical stone beads. Arca shells perforated for suspension and animal bones perforated longitudinally seem to have been used as ornaments. The finds were those of an area inhabited by a Neolithic people c. BC 2000, probably living in small settlements on mounds near the River Kwae Noi, with an economy based on some agriculture and domestication of pigs and cattle augmented by hunting and fishing. Their pottery shows well-developed manufacturing techniques and their tools reveal a differentiated inventory of stone, bone and shell manufacture. Their stature was nearly the same as that of today's Thai, but their life-span was short, averaging at death below forty years. They buried their dead in the settlement and the abundant presence of pottery and other burial gifts suggests a belief in an after-life.

But in 1943, above ground in the camps, on sleepless nights when, carried away by intolerable homesickness, a man went outside when the guard was not looking, above the jungle trees the Southern Cross twinkled in the night sky. In Chapter 30 Futamatsu also describes how his 'surroundings were spread out in a hushed silence like that on an ocean floor'. The tokay's cry rang out. When would this railway at last be opened to traffic?

Had he but known them, he might have echoed in his thoughts songs sung by Japanese soldiers in their fruitless, battered exposure on Guadalcanal Island:

> No matter how far we walk
> we know not where to go
> trudging along under dark jungle growth.
> When will this march end?
> We hide in the dark during the day
> and dare to move only at night,
> Deep in the lush jungle of Guadalcanal.
>
> Our staple food, our rice, is gone,
> we eat roots and grass.
> Along ridges and cliffs we lose our way,
> leaves hide the trail.
> We stumble and get up, fall and get up…
>
> We are covered with mud from our falls,
> blood oozes from our wounds.
> We have no cloth with which to bind our wounds,
> and flies swarm to the scabs,
> Yet we have no strength to brush them away.
> We keep on falling down, we can't move.
> Many times have I thought to kill myself.

The railway achieved prominence in the West initially as the result of debriefings of prisoners whose unmarked ship, the *Rakuyo maru*, in transit from Singapore to Japan, was torpedoed by an Allied Forces submarine which rescued them. This was reported by Sir James Grigg,

Secretary of State for War, to the House of Commons on 17 November 1944.[84] John Coast, R. Norfolks, gave the railway its soubriquet 'Death Railway' in his *Railroad of Death* (Commodore Press, 1946). He became press officer, FO, Bangkok, and later press attaché to President Soekarno of Indonesia.

The Geneva Convention for the treatment of Prisoners-of-War has over thirty-five articles but in the context of the Thai-Burma Railway eight stand out in particular.

1. They must not be employed on unhealthy or on dangerous work.
2. Daily work must not be excessive. They should be allowed a rest of twenty-four consecutive hours, preferably on Sundays.
3. They must at all times be humanely treated and protected, particularly from acts of violence, from insults and from public curiosity. Reprisals against them are forbidden. They are entitled to respect for their person and honour.
4. Their food ration shall be equivalent in quality and quantity to that of depot troops of the detaining nation.
5. Clothing, underwear and footwear shall be supplied to them.
6. Each camp shall possess an infirmary where prisoners shall receive attention of any kind of which they may be in need.
7. They shall be allowed to receive individually parcels of foodstuffs and clothing.
8. Intellectual and sporting pursuits shall be encouraged so much as is possible.

An important life-line for prisoners was a chequered one, secret radios. It was a complicated story. The Naval Barracks at Kranji on Singapore Island had not been entered since capitulation, and a party of prisoners was sent, with Japanese permission, to clean the place up. They found the electric light could be made to work, so the Japanese, while the devastated city lighting system was being restored, kept the party there on the cleaning job with a Japanese guard. In a small storeroom leading out of the transformer room the party found shelves stacked with radio valves of all sizes. These they 'won' and hid. There was some intercommunication between various prison-camp areas on the Island, contacts such as ration parties, exchange of scarce resources and so on, always with a Japanese guard accompanying them. In the secret radio context there were three in particular, first the main camp at Changi, second the Kranji cleaning party, and third the camp near Bukit Timah on the golf course where prisoners were navvying for Japanese shrine-carpenters who had been sent from Japan to build a shrine like a small temple, the Shōnan Shrine, to ease the souls of Japanese soldiers killed in the Malayan campaign to capture Singapore. At the Ford factory at Bukit Timah the Shrine party found some 50-gallon drums of petroleum jelly, needed with Japanese approval by Roberts Hospital at Changi. The Kranji party managed to smuggle out a good-stock of 1½-volt valves which the Shrine Party in turn managed to smuggle into Roberts Hospital inside a petroleum jelly drum. Meanwhile the Royal Corps of Signals had been alerted at the start of the exercise and their artificers got busy making miniature wireless sets concealed in the bottoms of officer-type water bottles, to be activated by small 1½-volt batteries. From then on, each party sent from Changi to Thailand carried with them a wireless set and batteries, both ingeniously concealed in various 'obviously necessary' utensils.

Independently of the Kranji development Captain John Beckett, 2 Cambs, built a secret set in Sime Road PW camp on Singapore Island in 1942, but on arrival at Chungkai in Thailand with a box of components he was at a loss how to know how to operate in jungle conditions. Luckily he came across Lieut. Tom Douglas, RCOS, who in civilian life was a BBC engineer and expert in wireless construction. With Beckett's components Douglas built several sets in officer-type water-bottles. Their efforts are described in detail in *The 18 Division Booklet*, issue for 1988–1989, pp. 5–11.

The first upset in a Thailand camp occurred when a *kempei* (Japanese secret policeman) grew suspicious, overhearing a prisoner's casual talk which suggested that he knew something of what was happening in the outside world. At first the *kempei* thought someone must have smuggled into camp copies of the forbidden *Bangkok Chronicle*, an English language periodical for that polyglot city, edited under Japanese supervision by pro-Japanese Thai. Without warning the camp guards, *kempei* made a snap search for the periodical during which a wireless set was discovered and three prisoners were beaten to death. From that point onwards security drill for wireless sets was made extremely rigorous.

Only selected officers and warrant officers were entrusted with the news from New Delhi and they were always given it a fortnight late. The prisoner had to say that any item overheard by a *kempei*, Japanese guard, or Korean *heiho*, came from 'an educated Thai on a ration-detail' down in the local town. The dangers run by Boon Pong, as I mention later, became even more obvious when he was smuggling 'canary seed' into a camp up country.

There were some narrow escapes by the courageous men operating these sets. At Thā Sao, Captain Biggs, RCOS, who had carried a set up in October 1942 in Lt-Col McOstrich's party from Singapore, had the set concealed in a blanket on his bedspace and the batteries and earphones in two haversacks hung up on pegs. One day when Biggs was down at the cookhouse as messing officer, Colonel McOstrich was told by the Japanese that a search was about to be made. With great presence of mind another prisoner said he urgently must go to the latrine, was given permission to do so, and warned Captain Biggs who immediately returned to the hut and stood at his bedspace. As he arrived the Japanese discovered the earphones and set up a great hullabaloo and chattering as they examined them. Biggs swept blanket and set off the bedspace behind him and pushed them with his foot under the sleeping platform. The Japanese excitedly searched his bedspace and found the batteries, chattering and crowding around. Biggs stooped down, lifted set and blanket up off the floor and replaced them on his bedspace. The Japanese then searched underneath the sleeping platform and found nothing. Biggs explained he was hoping to light his end of the hut with the batteries and incredibly the Japanese bought the story. It was lucky they were *kempei*: the camp staff would not have done so, batteries being permitted only for use by Japanese camp staff.

Charlie Mott, one of Chennault's Flying Tiger pilots, was associated with radio set batteries. He was shot down when raiding Tak airfield in Burma and 8 January 1942, and after hospital operations in a Japanese military hospital in Bangkok was put into Nong Pladuk prison camp with a pair of shorts and slippers. We rallied round (I gave him a blanket) and he quickly established himself in our society – he had played chess for his State, would lie on his blanket and play eight of us simultaneously on home-made chess sets. Our RASC drivers took to him for his engineering skill and elected him to be the Officer in charge of 62 Truck & Motor Pool of about 200 RASC and other drivers hauling rations up to camps as far as the Three Pagodas Pass. When the Japanese motor-transport got as far as Thā Sao, a prison camp radio set was carried, in a tin covered with rice to the camp perimeter fence and Charlie ran leads from a lorry-battery insider the Japanese MT compound. The contact worked spasmodically for about a year.

The worst example of *kempeitai* reaction took place at Kamburi in September 1943 when a wireless set was discovered. Seven officer-prisoners were brutally beaten with heavy bamboo rods over a period of three days as a result of which two of them, Captain Hawley, SSVF, and Lieutenant Armitage, RA, died. The seven prisoners' terrible ordeal included vicious kicking and punching of body and face, intermittent beating with the buckled end of leather belts, and immersion overnight in a water-filled ditch. The kit and personal effects of the two dead men were never found, presumably destroyed by these bullies, who buried the bodies behind the camp guardroom. When the Japanese, fearing a paratroop landing, segregated all officer-prisoners into a single camp at Kamburi at the far edge of the padang alongside the railway, the padang which in the earlier stages of the occupation had been a Japanese airstrip, the problem arose of how to transfer stocks of about 300 1½-volt batteries accumulated in the Thā Makham and Chungkai camps. Fortunately it had been decided to dismantle the Thā Makham huts and to transfer the big bamboo hut-poles to Kamburi for building new huts there. Liaison was established with an officer-prisoner whom the Japanese had detailed to come over from Chungkai, with a Korean *heiho* as guard, to visit sick prisoners at Thā Makham. The Chungkai batteries were put into a big army pack with fruit for the sick and placed on top, and the prisoner carried them, under guard by the *heiho*, passed the Japanese guard-room at Thā Makham. Here they were secreted away and the same night some bamboo poles were selected and filled with batteries and these poles were marked. The following day when the official party of prisoners came over from Kamburi with a lorry, the officer-prisoner in charge of the party, the only one in the party in the know, packed the marked poles first at the bottom of the lorry with the rest on top, and so brought them under armed guard past the guardroom into the officers' camp. When a set was eventually completed it was built into the structure of one of the clay ovens in the camp cookhouse.

The obligatory 'last stand for a decisive battle' referred to earlier, occasioned the move from Kamburi to the foothills north of Nakhon Nayok where they were to tunnel into the rock for the Japanese defence redoubts. Colonel Toosey was in charge, under escort of a Japanese staff-serjeant, of the first party.[85] I was in charge of the second party after the lapse of a week in July 1945. Nakhon Nayok lay in a large tract of country virtually depopulated of Thai inhabitants by a virulent strain of cerebral malaria, that form of the fever which leaves the sufferer screaming until he dies in a sudden rigour. Contact with Thai underground freedom fighters was thus impossible to establish, and it was decided not to attempt to transfer batteries until later on. The Japanese commander of the officers' camp at Kamburi, a quite remarkably vicious sadist, Captain Noguchi Hideji, who amongst other things had confiscated the prisoners' musical instruments, had himself travelled to Nakhon Nayok, and an officer-prisoner who had been compelled to act as his batman took the opportunity of secreting in his baggage a wireless set strapped to a cornet which Noguchi presumably intended to play. When the Emperor made his surrender broadcast, Colonel Toosey had what must have been the ineffable pleasure of requesting Noguchi to supply batteries for the wireless set Noguchi had no idea he himself had brought to Nakhon Nayok.

My own involvement in the railway began in the late afternoon of 5 February 1942 when the final detachment of 18 Division, diverted from Basra in the Gulf for political reasons, was about to land on Singapore Island after low level attacks by Zeros which sank one ship and killed two men of my own company manning a machine-gun post on my own ship whose defence, brilliantly organized by Colonel Thomas, 9 RNF, put three Zeros into the sea off Keppel Harbour. We landed in the dark two nights before the Japanese themselves crossed the Straits and landed on the north-west coast of the Island. On 18 June 1942 my company, 54 Infantry Brigade Gp Coy, RASC, CO Major R. S. Sykes to whom I was adjutant, was the first to travel overland from Singapore to the head of the Gulf of Siam, detraining at Banpong on 23 June to develop what became the Thai base workshops and stores of the railway. I remained at Nong Pladuk until 26 January 1945 when all officers were segregated into a camp at Kamburi, and remained there as a hut commander until late July when I was sent to Nakhon Nayok. When the atomic bombs were dropped on Hiroshima and Nagasaki I was ordered to Bangkok to act as Staff-Captain 'Q' on the Ex-PW HQ, as I mentioned earlier. That job completed, I flew to Rangoon on 29 September and embarked in MV *Orbita* on 11 October, disembarking at Liverpool on 9 November.

◻

In the interval between April up to August 1943 the railway engineers' task, and therefore the prisoners' task, was to crowd in a volume of work calculated by Futamatsu at over 20,000 cubic metres of spoil a day and 10 metres length on bridge-building. The prisoners' daily stint was increased, double-shift work was introduced and the working week was made into a ten-day 'week'. Heavy pressure was put on them, they were beaten with heavy bamboo rods, kicked and shouted at … 'supeedo', 'hurree uppu', '*baka yaro*' (idiots), '*chikushō*' (miserable animals). All this work, the roadbed, the steel bridge, culverts, wooden bridges over minor streams, rail-laying as far as Wanyai and on to Kinsaiyok, was done by what the Japanese called 'human wave' tactics.

The Speedo was the prisoners' version of the Japanese *kyūsoku kensetsu*, rush-construction. The volume of work may be guessed from facts such as that 688 bridges had to be built of which seven were steel with concrete piers and bridge-abutments. Six of them were in Burma, over the Zami, Apalon, Mezali, Winyaw, Khonkhan and Myettaw rivers, and one in Thailand over the Mae Khlaung river. Few of the others were over a hundred metres across but they included the 200-metre plank viaduct at Arrow Hill. For small spans of 10 metres and larger spans of 70 to 80 metres 'text-book' methods were used. For girders on wooden bridges 30-cm squared timbers were used on top of the foundations made by pile-driving. Prisoners recall heaving on a rope 'fishing' for a heavy plumb-bob from the derrick, dropping the plumb-bob as a pile-driver, the sweating men singing '*valdhai la valdhai la*', the Volga boat song. Clamps were used to bolt up timbers, a low safety-factor for such foundations. However, when the bombing started, their construction being simple, they collapsed but being simple could be repaired rapidly, a nightmare job vividly remembered by prisoners. From early 1943 Allied reconnaissance aircraft flew over and were greeted in camps by the Japanese special bugle-call:

To which I set a metric song in the Japanese manner, '*bakugekiki tonde kuru*' which means 'the bombers come flying'. In June 1944, the base at Thanbyusayat was bombed but intensive raiding began with the opening-to-traffic of the railway. The six steel bridges in Burma were all damaged by bombing, some in up to seven attacks. In Thailand the Mae Khlaung bridges were attacked ten times between 29 November 1944 and 28 July 1945 by both USAAF and RAF in B24 Liberators, the most successful attack being that of 13 February 1945 when three of the eleven spans fell and most of a rebuilt wooden bridge destroyed.

At Nong Pladuk on the night of 6/7 September 1944, B24s attacked railway sidings at Kommā half a mile from the camp. A petrol train and some ammunition were completely destroyed in a blaze of fiery light visible 50 miles away at Kamburi, but one bomber undershot his target and dropped two sticks across the camp, one of which fell on the central hut causing over 400 casualties including 90 dead and those who subsequently died of wounds. Many men had taken the meagre protection of shallow ground depressions and drains, but most were in their huts in accordance with Japanese standing orders for air-raids. Sjt Watanabe Masaō, admin NCO of the camp, went at once to the bombed area, carried to the hospital hut one of the first casualties, and assisted generally in directing prisoners to drains while the raid proceeded. Again at Nong Pladuk, during the evening meal on 3 December 1944, three formations of B24s raided the camp in waves from about 7,000 feet. The first wave pattern-bombed the workshops and godowns next to the extensive sidings outside the camp, the second covered the bombed area with incendiaries, the third in error bombed the prisoners' cookhouse and an adjacent hut, killing several prisoners including Major Paddy Sykes, RASC, my CO, an outstanding figure in the camp, loved and respected.

The Japanese were uneasy in the presence of madmen and avoided them. Two Argyll & Sutherland Highlands private soldiers created a phantom dog which they took everywhere with them, threw sticks for him to catch, good-dogged him for bringing them back, gave him drinks of water and imaginary food, waited while he pee'd against posts. The Japanese soldiers and the Korean *heiho* regarded them as mad, and kept away from them. Some dug-out regular soldiers among the prisoners at Nong Pladuk thought a young gunner officer was a fool or a madman who unfailingly on his own initiative insisted on marching out with the camp working parties past the camp guard-house, gave the guard a 'two-fingered' salute, marched them back again at the end of the day with his haversack bulging with the results of barter with Thai women lurking in the bushes at the place of work. Lieutenant Harold Payne, 137 Army Field Regt, RA, was to me one of the minor heroes of the railway. In my mind's eye I see him today, in his battered slouch hat and tattered scarf, stomping out past the guard to the strains of Colonel Bogey, called by the Japanese 'The River Kwae March', played with verve by 'Ace' Connelly, a pre-war bandsman and jazz-player, now the prisoners' 'Ace' cornet-player.

Successively British CO of prison camps at Bukit Timah, Thā Makham, Nong Pladuk, Kamburi and Nakhon Nayok was Lt-col Philip Toosey, DSO, RA, whose decoration in the field was for engaging enemy infantrymen over open sights in the battle on Singapore Island, and even so extricating his twenty-five pounders. He became one of the most distinguished among several remarkable camp-commanders whom even the Japanese admired for his courage in standing up to them in the prisoners' interests.

A different sort of courage was displayed unobtrusively by a middle-aged Thai at Nong Pladuk, the wife of K.G. Gairdner, a civilian internee in Bangkok, who through his compradore, K.S. Hong, got a note signed 'V' through to Major Sykes on a ration detail in Banpong. Sykes replied as 'V/V'. Gairdner went on supplying monthly small packet drugs and 200 to 400 ticals, subscribed by him and fellow-internees. By 1943 when the effects of the Speedo were plainly beyond control, 'V' arranged a loan of 12,000 ticals. The notes had to be in

20 ticals, these being the highest denomination issued to us by the Japanese. This not inconsiderable load was concealed in a sack of tapioca flour which the messenger, this time Milly Gairdner, passed to Paddy Sykes in front of a Japanese guard.

Another heroine was Madame Millet, wife of the French consul in Bangkok, untiring in her efforts in raising subscriptions for prisoners' welfare, for obtaining supplies of medicines, and carrying V/V's intelligence notes on trips to North Africa via Saigon.

My own private hero was Captain Charles Wylie, 1 Gurkhas, after the war a member of the team who conquered Everest. I was listed to take a party up-country to replace sick and dead prisoners. At the time a very severe attack of amoebic dysentery made me take a precautionary visit to the squatter-latrine, and I passed copious blood which would not stop flowing. The British camp medical officer said I must be replaced and sent to the hospital hut. Hearing this, Charles Wylie at no notice volunteered to take my place on a party which proved to be destined for one of the cholera belts. Typically of the man, he said he had no recollection of the circumstances when I wrote to him after the war to thank him for an act which probably saved my life.

To prisoners the best-known hero was Nai Boonpong Sirivejjabhandu, GM, known to them as Boon Pong. The Speedo greatly increased the number of prisoners brought up from Singapore. Gairdner kept the Nong Pladuk area as his responsibility but asked E.P Heath of the Borneo Company and R.D. Hempson to take responsibility for camps up-country. Heath asked his friend, Nai Clarn of Anglo-Thai Corporation to ask his friend Nai Boon Pong of Kamburi to act as courier to hand over clandestinely-procured money and medicines, at great risk to his life from the *kempeitai*, which he did as far as Thā Khanun. He became a legendary figure to prisoners. He also supplied camps with 'canary seed' (batteries for secret radios). Hundreds of survivors owe their lives to his help.[86]

I ought to mention a particular Japanese hero, an aircraft navigator called Sakurai. Major-general Shimoda Senriki, on a reconnaissance flight as GOC on 26 January 1943, crashed into a teak forest on the slopes of the Mayan Tong mountain, and eleven of the crew were killed outright. Sakurai, however, managed to live only on water for a month, and although severely injured succeeded in struggling out of the jungle where he was found by a search party on 23 February.[87]

Two other heroes of the railway, whose exploits are described in Chapters 29 and 32 in Futamatsu's book, were Lieutenant Pharaoh Adams, RASC, and Lieutenant Jim Bradley, RE. Adams drove 100 head of cattle, beef on the hoof, for ten days over 120 km of swamp, jungle, mountain and stream to Konkuita, as described in his book, *No Time for Geishas* (Leo Cooper, 1973). Bradley with nine others escaped from Songkurai. Five of them died in the jungle before reaching the Andaman Sea coast but the survivors were recaptured, condemned to execution, and sent back to Singapore for court-marshal. Their object had been to tell the outside world about the treatment of prisoners-of-war. *Towards the Setting Sun* (Phillimore, 1982) is his unemotional, historically accurate account, written at his wife Lindy's insistence as a catharsis to exorcise the nightmares to which his experiences had made him a nightly sufferer. He was deeply indebted to Captain C.H.D. Wild, Ox & Bucks LI[88] whom the Japanese called *nemuranai se no takai hito*, 'the tall man who never slept', who was always alert, night and day, to his fellow-prisoners' interests. Wild, fluent in Japanese, was summoned to attend Bradley's execution as one of the official witnesses required by Japanese military law. He so moved the Japanese colonel by his intervention describing their true motives in escaping and declaring it would be a blot for eternity on the escutcheon of *bushidō* to execute such brave men, that the colonel burst into tears and countermanded the execution.

Futamatsu was presented by authors Adams and Bradley with copies of their books and his request for permission to include quotations in his own book was given by both authors. They may have been puzzled at times by some passages and by some omissions. Japanese authors tend to give the gist of much of what they purport to quote, at times quote verbatim, and omit passages in the middle of quotes for no apparent good reason. At the bottom of such omissions often lies an aspect of Japanese politeness. It becomes a question of readership. Who are expected to form the author's main readership? Futamatsu's book was primarily written for a Japanese readership and he is at pains to leave out some passages likely to offend such readers.

Lieutenant Adams recalls an occasion, shortly after the opening-to
-traffic ceremony on 25 October 1943, when an eastbound train
stopped at the sidings at Konkuita. 'It was filled', he wrote, 'with
Japanese sick and wounded; they had been shut up in those steel 10-ton
trucks for many hours, without food or water, and their wounds, all
serious, untended since boarding. The prisoners-of-war were moved to
pity and many went forward to offer them water and even a cigarette in
some cases. The now useless warriors of the Emperor lay in their own
filth, and all were nauseated by the stench of their foul matted bloody
dressings. Little wonder that the Japanese High Command were callous
to us prisoners if they could treat their own kith and kin thus.'[89] In the
autumn of 1944, I had a similar experience when supervising a squad
of prisoners repairing the embankment just outside Nong Pladuk station. The cha-wala was just brewing up tea in the old oil-drum used
for the purpose, when a Japanese eastbound train of enclosed steel
rice-cars drew up alongside. It was filled with Japanese soldiers, some
mere youths, all badly wounded, with a lieutenant and a corporal in
sole charge. My party saw these wounded men, untended, many with
dysentery, some already dying, lying in blood and filth. To a man the
prisoners swarmed alongside helping the soldiers to sip mugs of tea,
some wiping their faces clean of sweat and dirt. I sensed danger, the
corporal looked furious, my Korean *heiho* from the camp looked res-
tive, so I engaged the lieutenant in conversation, his replies being in
very good English. Suddenly I realized it was Inoue Tōjō, my college
contemporary. I do not know whether he recognized me but I could
see he was almost sinking to the earth with shame. He shouted to the
corporal not to interfere. I went on talking to enable him to recover
some of his devastatingly lost face, without revealing my own identity.
The signals on the line showed green and this horrible incident closed.

After the war Thai National Railways set up a C56 tank engine at
Thā Makham station in commemoration of the war years on the railway, which had brought prosperity to a previously under-developed
area and greatly boosted Thailand's tourist trade. To the Japanese, the
construction of the railway, despite its calamitous ending, has been
claimed as ranking among world engineering feats with the building of
the Panama Canal, and after the war two C56 tank engines were repatriated: C5644 makes tourist trips on the Ōigawa Railway Line, where

1

it originated: the other, C5631, which was present at the ceremony on 25 October 1943 at Konkuita, was set up on a metre-gauge set of rails in a corner of the Yasukuni Shrine, the temple in Tokyo which is dedicated to Japanese war-dead. It is kept in apple-pie order by the C5631 Preservation Society, whose members, on a monthly rōta, grease and oil it and polish up the paint.

The Bishop of Singapore made the final summing-up, 'We must forgive, but not forget.' Not all prisoners-of-war were angels, not all Japanese soldiers sadistic villains. A few of these risked suspicion of being disloyal, by helping prisoners in various ways. In my own case, a Korean *heiho*, at a time when prisoners for security reasons were forbidden in the Nong Pladuk camp to learn Japanese, taught me the two Japanese syllabaries (they have no alphabet). He risked torture by *kempei*. I was dubbed by dug-out regular officers as Jap-happy, a form of Jap-happiness which in the long run enabled me to abstract straightforward news items from the Japanese camp commandant's newspapers, surreptitiously brought to me by my own CSM, Frank Stadden, who worked in the Jap office. He then pressed them and returned them. By reading between the lines, we were able to follow, for example, the stirring movements of the American marines in their systematic recapture of the islands in the Pacific. When a news item ran, 'Our heroic Japanese soldiers made a strategic withdrawal from Colombangara', it was a pound to a penny the marines had re-taken Colombangara.

When the atomic bombs dropped prisoners had varying degrees of unease about the reaction of the Japanese Army to the Emperor's broadcast, many believing that *bushidō* extremists would try to kill them. This was particularly the case in a country under the influence of Count Terauchi but if orders to kill prisoners existed, in Thailand at any rate it appeared that the *kempeitai* had filleted them from the offices of the various HQs. It was left to the British Division of the International Prosecution at the International Military Tribunal Far East, B & C Offences, to reveal what may be the only unfilleted document.[90] It was found by ex-prisoner Jack Edwards at the Kinkaseki Mine in North Taiwan. The document emanated from the Taihoku prisoner-of-war camp and was addressed to the commanding general of the Taiwan *kempeitai*. The document is listed by the British Division as Document No. 2071 (certified as Exhibit '0' in Document No. 2687). It describes the reply to Taihoku's query about 'the extreme measures for prisoners-of-war' and runs as follows:

The time and method of this disposition are as follows:

(1) The Time.

Although the basic aim is to act under superior orders, individual disposition may be made in the following circumstances:

(a) When an uprising of large numbers cannot be suppressed without the use of firearms,

(b) When escapees from the camp may turn into a hostile fighting force.

(2) The Methods.

(a) Whether they are destroyed individually or in groups, or however it is done, with mass bombing, poisonous smoke, poisons, drowning, decapitation or what, dispose of them as the situation dictates.

(b) In any case it is the aim not to allow the escape of a single one, to annihilate them all, and not to leave any traces.[91]

The timing of this document (1 August 1944) has added point to those who know that in the summer of 1944 senior officer-prisoners secretly ordered named officers to act as key personnel in a putative mobile infantry brigade. I myself was nominated as Staff-Captain 'Q' to serve, as I discovered later when I arrived, under Major R.A.N. Davidson 4PWO, Gurkha Rifles, as DAQMG and Lt-col C.E. Morrison, 1 Leicesters, as DDST.

Detailed documented accounts exist of the militaristic take-over as a criminal course since 1931. One could say, with Ienaga Saburō in his book, *The Pacific War*, that a Great East Asian War lasted from 1931 to 1945. He argues that the use of prisoners-of-war on forced labour was only one aspect of the Army's general violation of International Law. The effect of the take-over led to inevitable side-effects such as training to breed vicious fighters with a penchant for brutality against enemy prisoners. The tendency of Japanese to react to constant pressure with an explosion of irrational destructive behaviour was only too well-known to prisoners in Burma and Thailand. The conduct of the Japanese Army in the Pacific War was far inferior to their disciplined behaviour in the Russo-Japanese War.

Eight captured USAAF men were vivisected in May and June 1945 at Kyūshū Imperial University in experiments to test human limits of resistance to pain. For example, a prisoner had saline injected into his bloodstream to find the quantitative limits before death occurred. Air was injected into another prisoner's veins to ascertain the volume at which death occurred. In the case of another prisoner his lung was excised to find the limits to which the bronchial tubes may be cut before death occurs.

The brilliant novelist, Endō Shūsaku, in his book *The Sea and Poison* (1958), confronted the problem of individual responsibility in wartime in a study of a doctor who had been ancillary to the test team and on return to civilian practice in peace-time was dogged by his. sense of guilt. Endō's translator, Michael Gallagher, comments that his thesis is that the West is informed by the faith (he is a Catholic) even when formally rejected: the East is informed by a kind of pantheism so that the East knows no tension of opposites like good versus evil, flesh versus spirit, God versus devil. The East, he argues is a 'concave' world which has no God, the West is a 'convex' world which has acknowledged the existence of God.

In Tokyo many *kempei* deserted their units, panicking at the Emperor's broadcast but not omitting to fillet HQ records of prison camps like Ōmuta in Kyūshū or the interrogation centre at Yokosuka near Yokohama. This overall display of docility is in marked contrast to the spirited dynamic resistance movements in Thailand and Burma during the Japanese occupation. But harsh treatment of Japanese by the Russians in Manchuria had its counterpart in Japan during the predominantly American occupation with GIs frequently accosting women in the street, or actually assaulting them, assaults resulting in women committing suicide or becoming street prostitutes. Victims of robbery by GIs were rarely able to recover their property or receive compensation.

B and C Class War Criminals included men who had no real chance of defending themselves and were executed. An example of mistaken identity (taking the charitable view) when the wrong man was to be put to death was Captain Wakamatsu Shiguō, commandant of Kilo

100 camp in Burma and later of the hospital camp at Nakhon Pathom in Thailand. According to testimony by prisoners at both those camps he was a humane man of principle, kind to prisoners and exerting his jurisdiction by protecting as far as he could the men under him. At Singapore in September 1945 Major Robbie Robertson, RAE, confirmed these views in his defence, and related how the *Moji maru* transport in which he himself was a prisoner was bombed in the Andaman Sea. In her stern she was carrying explosives, a fire broke out, and a Japanese officer left his cabin and with no regard for his own safety threw the explosives overboard. This was Captain Wakamatsu, under whom Major Robinson later served in Kilo 100 camp. The court commuted Wakamatsu's death sentence to life imprisonment on 13 August 1946, yet despite this he was hanged by the Australians on 30 April 1947 at Singapore, an act of retaliatory judgement without retrial. His story, first told to me by Robbie Robinson, was set out in the *Asahi* newspaper on 4 October 1982.

The militaristic take-over of 1931 re-asserted the right, written into the Constitution of 1898, of giving the war ministers in the Cabinet direct access to the Throne. In 1913, the Constitution had been changed to allow retired officers to serve, but in 1936 the regulation was changed again making the Army and Navy ministers men on active service only. Thus the Army could topple the Cabinet by refusing to nominate a serving officer to serve as minister.

In 1940, Army Minister Lt-General Tōjō Hideki transferred Lt-general Nakamura Aketo, commander of Yamashita's 5 Division, 'for violating orders to avoid a clash in advance of the Japanese takeover of French Indo-China'. Nakamura emerged as commander of the *kempeitai* and by 1945 commanded all 50,000 forces in Thailand, the General with whom my encounter has been described.

Japan's last war? It is possible that the economic development of the Pacific Basin, with its transfer of world dominance from the Atlantic to the Pacific, would leave Japan powerful enough to influence a consolidation of Australasia, China, and ASEAN (Indonesia, Malaysia, Singapore, Thailand, The Philippines), and realistic enough to remember that in war the winner does not take all.

After the war Futamatsu published *An Account of the Construction of the Thai-Burma Railway* in 1955, and my correspondence with him since 1979 culminated in his illustrated pamphlet, *Recollections of the Thai-Burna Railway* in 1980. The tale had come full circle from marines in the Pacific to his recreations of the railway. As a Buddhist, he might stress how we all are recreated in an unending series of afterlives leading (we hope) to a predestined nirvana. For Christians, life after death goes on 'out there' in a heaven each individual imagines for himself. For the Agnostic, Flanagan and Allen sang of the dawn which comes again after dreams underneath the Arches:

> We are men drenched in soaking rain,
> Gritting our teeth, gritting our teeth …
> But if you wait, Spring comes again,
> And boats come up again.

He had been distressed by inaccurate, biased articles and books by Australian and Japanese journalists, and by the brilliantly acted but grossly distorted denigratory account of Japanese railway engineering talent put over in the film version of Pierre Boulle's novel, *Le Pont de la Rivière Kwai*, which has been widely shown in Japan under the title *Bridge built in the Battlefield*. Ex-prisoners-of-war, to whom a preview was given, tried to get excised some of the worst errors, but to no avail. Futamatsu determined the time had come for a definitive history to be published while Japanese and Western survivors were still alive and could verify his statements. His book was published in 1985, a greatly more detailed work than his earlier two pamphlets – an objective, unbiased account, historically accurate, *Across the Three Pagodas Pass: the Story of the Burma-Siam Railway*, of which my edited translation follows.

Boulle's 1952 novel contained fewer impossibilities than did the 1967 film, but none-the-less the two principal characters, Colonel Nicholson (played by Alec Guinness) and Colonel Saitō (played by Hayakawa Sessue) are caricatures of type-cast Indian Army officers and of Japanese officers passed over as unfit for front-line service. Boulle was unaware that a railway engineer took precedence over a mere prison-camp official. The bridge in the novel was a wooden bridge and so was the bridge in the film which was built in Sri Lanka. In the novel it was not blown up. The real bridge over the Kwae Yai was a steel bridge with eleven steel spans of 20-metre pony-type Warren curved chord half-through trusses. It was, of course, blown up, but by bombing and not by sabotage.

Personnel employed on the railway included about 11,000 Japanese military, 61,106 prisoners-of-war, and 182,948 Asiatic coolies. Of the prisoners-of-war 12,399 were recorded as having died before leaving Thailand and Burma, and it has been estimated that over 90,000 Asiatic coolies died on this work.

My translation is edited to remove a few redundancies, to simplify a few tautologies and to omit detail such as the initial formation in Japan of *gunzoku* railway engineering units, of small interest to Western readers. The translation is followed by a fuller bibliography than you normally find in works for the general reader.

To the Western reader the intrinsic quality of the book lies in four directions. First, the author is at pains to present the truth in detail about the construction of the railway. Second, he tries to present a case, unconvincingly, for playing down what lay behind a Western journalist's slur, 'the death railway'. Third, he describes the real reason why the Japanese did not ratify the Geneva Convention for the Treatment of Prisoners-of-War, but works the case round to a doubt in his own mind as to how far the Japanese Army violated its clauses. Fourth, justifiable professional pride in the techniques and skills of a civilian railway engineer makes him sceptical of the professional regular soldiers' attitudes.

Futamatsu printed twenty-eight small photographs in his original Japanese text. They cover the following places and persons: Railtrack over Krian River: Seletar airfield burning: railway stations at Singapore, Nong Pladuk and Banpong: the 0-km post at Nong Pladuk: looking at the Mae Khlaung crossing-point in July 1942: the plank viaduct at Arrow Hill: the Mae Khlaung steel bridge: the same after being bombed: Colonel Imai Itaru: jungle along the Kwae Noi: labouring at earthworks: air photographs of the steel bridge: Kamburi and Kinsaiyok areas: hut construction: work with elephants: The Three Pagodas Pass: C5631 engine decorated for the joining-up ceremony: the cemetery at Kamburi: the memorial monument at Thā Makham (six photographs are ascribed to Sugano Renichi, six to Geoffrey Adams).

His sensitivity is illustrated by his reply to a *haiku* I wrote on receiving a copy of an autographed photograph of himself taken at Wanyai camp on 12 November 1943. He is immaculately spruced up in formal uniform but I was immediately impressed by his youthful look. The *haiku* ran:

Wanyai no
Futamatsu kakka
Seinen yo

Which I translate as 'Senior Officer Futamatsu at Wanyai … but he's only a youth!' In his reply he quoted a *haiku* he himself had written on an occasion, in the Wanyai area, which is translatable as follows:

In my mind's eye I see again
Peacocks flying over the river at dawn
In the jungle valley.

The remarkable sensitivity of well-educated Japanese in poetical contexts was particularly well illustrated by Sir Laurens van der Post in his article in *The Times* of 25 January 1989. Describing the Emperor's reluctance to go along with the Army's determination to act in a way which led to the air attack on Pearl Harbor, he used 'the most powerful weapon at his command in speaking of his own distaste for war in the symbolism of a favourite poem of one of the great transitional emperors, Meiji'. Emperor Meiji's poem runs:

Yomo no umi minna
harakara to omou yō ni
Naze namikaze no
tachisawagaruramu?

A friend of van der Post has translated this difficult poem: 'If all oceans are really brothers, why then are the wind and the waves raging?' Laurens van der Post goes on:

In the dead silence that followed among the Chiefs of Staff, Hirohito went on to say that this poem was an expression of peace and that he had always cherished it and sought to guide his life by it. I believe it was with a heavy heart, full of regret and a sense of doom, that he stayed at the head of his people in the war that followed. The great Admiral Yamamoto warned against the attack on Pearl Harbor. 'You will go only to awaken a sleeping giant.' Moreover the Emperor's way was also the way of the noblest Japanese spirits.

Ewart Escritt
Oxford
February 1990

To the memory of those
who did not return

ACROSS THE THREE PAGODAS PASS

By

Futamatsu Yoshihiko

TRANSLATOR'S
ACKNOWLEDGEMENTS

In accordance with Japanese custom given names are printed after family names.

My thanks are due to Geoffrey Adams, Dr Louis Allen, Jim Bradley, MBE, Burt Briggs, Cecil Colchester, Rose Coombs, MBE, Professor Peter Davies, Dr Christopher Dowling, Carl Fritsche, Dr James McMullen, Charlie Mott, Harold Payne, OBE, Dr Bryan Powell, Roderick Suddaby and John Ullmann for their help at various stages in the writing of this book.

I also wish to thank Lindy Bradley who typed my manuscript.

PREFACE

It is a long time, forty years, since the end of the Second World War, and with the lapse of time what happened in it is like a distant historical fragment of a past which people have now forgotten. With the end of the war we Japanese set up a new constitution which outlawed war, sought peace and declared that Japan would never again go to war.

But how can the present generation who have no war experience understand what war is? By the same token, how can they bear malice, how criticize, how amend the real truth? To them it is the responsibility of those who did experience it to tell them the reality … they can describe it and it is plainly their responsibility to do so. One must admit, however that they are getting few in number.

When our army made their strategic attack on India, they planned a railway for military purposes to transport supplies overland. After the war, the construction of this railway was the background to the film *Bridge built in the Battlefield* (Japanese title of *Bridge on the River Kwai*), and the prisoners in it were supposed to be those who sang the theme song the 'River Kwai March'. Moreover, because so many were sacrificed, the slur, 'Death Railway' was slammed on it. Full details of the actual conditions of its construction do not now exist. The film is full of errors, and to have dubbed it 'Death Railway' is clearly far from the reality.[92]

Its construction involved an unusually difficult operational sequence in military action in a war area. To use prisoners-of-war and their help to complete the task constituted a unique phenomenon in a world railway construction.

In mountainous terrain in a jungle belt pivoting on the Three Pagodas Pass on the Thai-Burma frontier, construction meant enduring a climate of sweltering heat and heavy rainfall, meant battling with epidemics of serious diseases such as malaria and cholera, and mastering nature in the form of jungle for a distance of 415 kilometres and in the space of one and a half years completing the task: the solid fact, in my opinion, is that the Japanese left behind them a record of considerable enterprise.

I myself was a railway engineer in one of the railway construction units and I know the true facts about the construction of the railway. I can describe their significance; it is meaningless, I think, to go on dwelling on the deaths and destructions one-sidedly.

In April 1981 Mr Geoffrey Adams, an Englishman who had worked on the railway as a prisoner-of-war, visited Japan and came to see me. He left with me a copy of his record of experiences of the war years entitled, *No Time for Geishas*.[93] These recollections were those of a British prisoner-of-war of the actual conditions, but they were an impartial, coolly-written account. Then again, later on in 1983 Mr James Bradley, a former prisoner-of-war who made an escape, wrote about his experiences, and sent me a copy of his book, *Towards the Setting Sun*.[94]

Mr Adams makes the following statement in his memoirs:

> We British hate war, but you can't deny it exists. It benefits no-one and we must hold ourselves aloof from it. To leave behind a record of my experiences of what it was like in those days is, I think, something that will acquaint the coming generation about what war really is. I do not forget the suffering my experience of war entailed, but we must forgive the men who caused it ...

I can agree with Mr Adams' opinion and so, taking advantage of their permission, I can quote from time to time from both these gentleman's memoirs and from my own experience, give my book the title of *Across the Three Pagodas Pass*, and record one aspect of the history of the construction of the Thai-Burma Railway. This record transmits historical truth. For those who seek peace, if I hold firm in telling them something about the struggle, I shall win an unanticipated pleasure.

Futamatsu Yoshihiko
July 1985

Chapter 1

DEPARTURE FOR THE FRONT

The policy of continuing the war between China and Japan was not approved by America and, with their anti-Japanese freezing of assets as well as of oil in the southern zone, our country was increasingly under coercion. Diplomatic relations between Japan and America becoming difficult, secret preparations were pushed ahead in case by any chance it came to war. So far as we knew at the time diplomatic negotiations between Japan and America were believed to be succeeding.

Gunzoku, civilian auxiliaries of Japanese nationality, were called up nation-wide, higher management, junior management and other employees according to the district where they were born. Special Railway Bridge Unit was formed of *gunzoku*, as an auxiliary of a railway regiment. In the battle-zone, a railway regiment's role was to work on the enemy's railway lines and to administer the rear organization. In the event of an outbreak of war in the southern war theatre (to which we suspected we were due to join, being equipped with light summer clothing) the whole force to which we were attached had a complement of about 2,000 men. I was attached to unit HQ and in addition to me there were thirteen *gunzoku* senior officials in the four working companies. There were about seventy junior officials of NCO rank and altogether about 500 *gunzoku* were attached to the HQ and working companies. The unit was due to be sent to the Malayan front as a part of the Expeditionary Force with the Imperial Guard Division, who were nick-named '*Miya*'. Junior officials wore swords at the hip but ordinary employees had side-arms only and did not have rifles. Because we *gunzoku* for the most part had no experience of military training (the junior officials did not even know how to salute) we were all at sea and confused.

In the afternoon of 24 October our transport, the *Hakuroku maru,* slipped her moorings in the port of Ōsaka. She passed through the Straits of Shimonoseki, moving out to the open sea and that evening passed in the offing at the western tip of Kyūshū through the chain of five islands and we saw from the ship the last trace of Japanese land like the shadow of a sea-borne bird. No-one would have believed that we were to live abroad for over five years. We had contracted at our enlistment for repatriation every two years.

We entered some part of the South China Sea, seas became rough, and the ship tossed about left and right as if she were tipsy. In heavy seas the convoy ships which formed our fleet went out of sight. We passed close to Taiwan and began to feel hot. Our ship was heading for the southern region.

Chapter 2

IN INDO-CHINA

On the anniversary of the Emperor Meiji's birthday, 3 November, we reached the waters off the southern coast islands and the following day entered the port of Haiphong, at that time a French possession in Indo-China (now North Vietnam). It was known as 'Indo' for short. Near the ship were cargo-handling lighters (sampans) and a crowd of peddlers' little boats. Their Annamese dress was new to me and when I heard them talking I realized I had indeed come to a foreign country and for the first time I set foot on foreign soil.

Even at night the heat did not abate. On the lovely lakeside of Granlac the chalkstone buildings were reflected in the quiet waters of the lake. One walked down tree-lined streets and in the French manner cafés lined the sidewalks. There were *petits fours* cakes which were sweet-tasting, and we enjoyed a helping.

In mid-November we were transferred from Haiphong to towns along the line of the transverse railway called The Phut & Embai Line. The train crossed a high steel bridge over the River Songkoi called Bon de mer. The bridge served two purposes, first as a bridge route: second, when there were no trains it isolated the railtrack which provided unusual facilities. At Embai there was military training every day.

My unit was the first to go to Saigon. On 25 November we entrained at Haiphong station. From the carriage window you could see the South China Sea. Somehow the atmosphere was tense, but one still sensed no indication that one was at war. The train arrived at Saigon on 28 November. Saigon was called the Paris of the Orient, a beautiful town which Frenchmen took to their hearts. On the main street under the rows of trees in Maronie there were cafés and at teatime a band performed a musical programme. The leaves in the line of trees shone through and through in the hot southern sun, trembling and whispering in the breeze. I remember my first taste of snails as the French cooked them. I bought clothes to combat the heat, short-sleeves, divided *hakama* (trousers), lightweight gear suitable for the southern region. Even so, the sword at one's hip was somewhat of a nuisance.

At the end of November, together with Matsudaira, the railway chief official at HQ, I went to Cambodia to survey their railways. When we essayed to go into Phnom Penh station, a section of track on the line over the frontier had been damaged and the Tsūjima Battalion of 5 Railway Regiment was standing by charged with the duty of re-connecting it. The section of damaged track between the Cambodian line and the southern part of the Thai line was said to be on the Thai side of the frontier. Unit commander Major Tsūjima was worried because our survey showed the frontier area was dangerous. Even up to this moment we could not forecast when war would start for Japan; we were hoping that there would be an agreed settlement in the negotiations with the Americans. Still, hour by hour, we lived in the shadow of war.

On 1 December our survey unit travelled from Phnom Penh on the Cambodian line, our object being to utilize an efficient transport capability for which we had to verify the viability of the railtrack. To safeguard our secret undercover movements, we were disguised as ships' passengers and tourists. By chance a Frenchman who was travelling on our train saw us and my chief, Matsudaira, told me to keep him under observation. I invited him to the dining-car, having recourse to my sole stock of French, *bonjour* and *merci,* gave him several cups of coffee, trying to make him feel at ease and not get wind of our survey. This was an unexpected tough job added to a difficult survey job.

The following day we arrived at the station on the frontier. From the station the frontier was two to three hundred metres to the North, and a bridge was being built over a small river.

The station-master treated us in a friendly manner but we didn't understand a word. We talked to yesterday's Frenchman and he ended up by being interpreter in buying some lovely silks. We asked the station-master to be our guide as we thought we would like to go and see the bridge at the frontier. He led us to the river-bank and we all got into a boat pointing downstream, but when we got close to the bridge we saw on both banks machine-gun emplacements sited menacingly. At the moment when he led us to the boat on the river-bank a couple of Japanese soldiers had come and asked to go with us. They were without badges of rank and weren't carrying swords. The boat was handled by the stationmaster, going downstream in mid-river, because that was thought to be the frontier-line. He was worried he might be shot at if he went over it. Apart from being in the narrow confines of a boat it was a small boat and he was crossing the bridge-route. It's odd, but our bridge survey was accompanied by bursts of laughter!

That evening at the shelter we were stopping at, these two infantry officers greeted us and courteously offered their help at the frontier station. It was surprising that they were travelling at the frontier as ordinary soldiers without side-arms. They were people from an advance party and it looked as if the moment to occupy Thailand had come as they were reconnoitring the frontier. From such circumstances one supposed it was inevitable that hostilities would break out, and I was not sure whether I felt belligerent or not – on arrival at Saigon my own bridge unit was also an advance party.

On 4 December a warning order came from 2 Railway HQ that, '4 Special Railway Unit must wait for their advance into Malaya until X and Y hours.' Chief Official Nishijima, who happened to be present, was looking for a pretext for advancing into Malaya, a British possession, but an essential pre-condition was lacking – he had been told that X, Y and Z days had to seem likely to happen. To me it was a quite intractable problem but indicators were appearing moment by moment that we were being dragged bodily into war.

Chapter 3

OPENING OF HOSTILITIES

On 8 December 1941 I was at the HQ's lines-of-communication hotel in a corner of Rue Catenar, Saigon. At the hotel entrance an Imperial Guard Division sentry stood on guard. In the garden red canna flowers basked in the morning sun, blooming in a blaze of colour. I went into the hotel lobby and listened to a radio broadcast in Japanese. It was nine o'clock in the morning. The broadcast was serious.

The source was an IJA GHQ communiqué. What we heard was that the Imperial Japanese Empire was involved at midnight in a state of war following the joint American-English proclamation of war on Japan, and in an instant our feelings became taut and tense. The successful surprise attack on Pearl Harbor was reported. As I stood there in the lobby, I heard the news repeated, that the American-British declaration marked the start of the war for Japan. When the negotiations with America were broken off, this had meant war. This news came as a shock. Since our departure from the homeland the unit had been reorganized and up to embarcation was under strict orders to keep secret that it was an undercover transport unit and so we made a showy departure for the front and each individual was furnished with a copy of a meaningful label: but we really knew it meant war. On the Cambodia frontier the circumstances made everyone tense. One began to unravel that mysterious order of a few days ago. One renews his decision to give selfless patriotic service and even if one became a victim there's nothing he can do about it but resign himself to the thought that in the end he returns as a hero to the Yasukuni Shrine. We had tended so far to lose our bearings, got needlessly worried. The unit commander addressed us and boosted our morale.

We soon became front-line troops at Phnom Penh. At the crossing-point on the Mekong river our trucks had to await their turn on the ferry. At Phnom Penh was the royal palace and the streets of this Cambodian capital were newly completed. At city centre there was a star-shaped market where they sold big spiny-lobsters and big crabs, an impressive sight, but we had no time for sightseeing. News came that in the offing at Kuantan on the Malayan Peninsula the battleships *Prince of Wales* and *Repulse* of the British Far East Squadron had been attacked and sunk by Japanese naval aircraft.[95] There came also a report that the Japanese Army was making a lightning conquest of Malaya. That Japan at the start of hostilities should win such victories delighted me, it was a heartening thing, but thereafter one did not expect anything quite so dramatic.

On 12 December I went from the unit to the Bangkok HQ in advance, having been given responsibility for liaison and for fixing up billets. More and more joining in warlike activities unilaterally, I became unexpectedly cool in what really was audacious activity. Because my duty lay in the rear echelon, where there was no fighting, I did not give a thought to the risk of being killed. For some days before leaving for the front I had been excessively busy. I had even begun to get acclimatized to the heat of the southern regions and, sleeping at night, I recalled winters at home. I waited for seventeen days and then left Phnom Penh HQ, riding in Lt-Colonel Mayama's car. We went North along the River Mekong, passed over the frontier and broke into Thailand. On the highway into Bangkok the traffic was congested with Japanese Army lorries. The rule of the road varied in Indo-China, Cambodia and Thailand and across the frontier traffic accidents occurred, even a head-on collision. But the highway on both sides was broad, with no ups-and-downs, and essentially ran straight ahead. Apart from low scrub and coconut palms, it was an unpopulated stretch. That evening we passed a hamlet called Don Muang,[96] a resort in the northern suburbs, and in the distance could see pagodas in the sunset sky. This was Bangkok. I felt deep emotion as my war ensued from that point. I recall the triumphal entry into the streets of Bangkok, at the crossroads with the Anung Sawari Pagoda bathed in the setting sunlight. In Bangkok there were then several hundred Japanese expatriates – and what can such an event, the outbreak of war on 8 December, have meant for them! Originally in business in the commercial district and later with 9 Railway Regiment's Sakamoto Battalion, there was, I recall, Mr Chikawa Saburo – who was an experienced interpreter: he wrote:

> We broke in and through the Japanese embassy opened negotiations with the Thai Government following what might be called a peaceful occupation. In other parts of Thailand occupation forces bided their time, fully prepared for a show of force if that became necessary. The planned outbreak of war on 8 December being imminent, Prime Minister Phibun of Thailand initially concealed his view that a weakness showed up in the Japanese Government's high-handed demands. Our ambassador tried to probe Phibun's real views. In fact, to the Japanese embassy the decisive issue came when a signal had been put out in the embassy garden for the reconnaissance aircraft sent over quite soon from Main Southern Army HQ. On 7 December the embassy had got ready, against a show of force, a vessel standing by at a Bangkok wharf into which our women and children were put on board. Civilians in the prime of life were concentrated in the embassy to resist their adversaries, the Thai Army, when the Japanese Army moved in. On the vessel light machine-guns and other weapons were put on board in secret, and at the embassy itself the entrance had barbed-wire entanglements set up as a barricade. All this was completed by midnight. So on 8 December our occupation force began their assault, the landing campaign was put into execution, there was spasmodic resistance from the Thai Army at its bases on the southern waterfront of Bangkok, at Chumphon in the South and elsewhere. Phibun called a conference, consented to a peaceful occupation, called off the Thai forces' resistance, the embassy and our compatriots were safe and the Japanese Army of Occupation welcomed.

Shortly after I entered Bangkok an attempt was made to find residences of British subjects within the City limits: they had all evacuated pell-mell, inside their houses no furniture, clothing, etc. was to be found, not even a single sheet of paper! At the residence of Ambassador

Crosby was found his signed notice ordering them to evacuate with each individual's life and property his own personal responsibility. England, without any sort of previous notice, in an unexpected coup had declared war. Allowing for the time difference, the Japanese Army, with a previously announced declaration of war, made landings and surprise assaults on Singora and Kota Bharu in the northern part of the Malayan Peninsula. In fact, in an article in the Singapore special edition (October 1979) of the British magazine, *After the Battle,*[97] Prime Minister Churchill, in the opening paragraph of his diplomatic document, transmitted to the Japanese Government what amounted to an ultimatum. The passage runs: 'To have opened hostilities without giving any previous notice is a matter of regret. Here, England declares a break-off of diplomatic relations with Japan.' Former prisoner-of-war, Mr Adams, in his recollections states: 'England was involved in an endless war.'

Whether one likes war or finds it repugnant, a situation in which one was inevitably drawn into is clearly what happened to England. Japan, post-war, in the context of the New Constitution of 1946, declared she abandoned war, but there is no guarantee that she would not withdraw her declaration. Settlement of a dispute between two nations ought to be done by peaceful negotiation: as for the use of armed might, steering clear of it would be the right course. Formerly naturalized Japanese, one found in travelling around Malaya, were employed as guides, and one, living in Kota Bharu, waiting for the outbreak of hostilities, is said to have been plastered in the early hours by a Japanese projectile. His girlfriend had moved back into Singapore and in the end when Japan suffered defeat in 1945, she had difficulty supporting herself. Here is an example of how a Japanese who held office on a battle-front reacted to the realities of battle.

It was on 25 December when our bridging unit was moving to Bangkok that there was an intelligence report that a car accident *en route* had caused casualties. Without even entering the front line one wonders whether one can be rated as a battle-casualty. The unit was concentrated at the Macassar Railway Workshops. We *gunzoku* were expecting to be in the front line, we were quite busy, but we felt a certain amount of tension.

On 30 December the unit travelled in a goods train which had been got ready at Bansoe station and went South on the South Thailand

Line. It crossed a high steel bridge over the River Menam and moved on from Bangkok. It passed through Banpong and in the Peburi district crossed over the River Mae Khlaung which runs South into the Gulf of Siam. We passed Chumphon, Prachuab Khiri Khan and other places and went on through a station, whose name escapes me, into a plain which had much cactus and one wondered whether it was really an extensive paddy-field. It was dotted with coconut palms and water buffaloes were at work.

On 31 December the train continued South and in the afternoon entered a ravine in the hills where it came to a complete halt. The train-driver said the planned haulage limit for rolling stock had been grossly exceeded and in this section of track the engine failed to take the incline. The unit commander ordered everyone to alight and 'Shove the train!' was his command. It was a novel, an unheard-of situation. That night was New Year's Eve, 1941.

When the train stopped at a small station the buildings shone cheerfully in the moonlight, and was that not a moment to see the New Year in? The melody was heard, 'Auld Lang Syne', which one used to hear as if 'the firefly's light was on the window-pane'. In the battle-zone we were homesick at the thought of ringing out the Old Year, and the sound of instrumental music evoked in us sentimental feelings. At first light it was New Year's Day, 1942. The train pulled into Hat Yai, the station at the junction in southern Thailand.

We were ordered to alight, and everyone set about assembling machine-parts when the sound of an explosion was heard. 'Enemy planes!' was the alarm and we got out of the place, scattering like little spiders out of a cocoon. In a flash we heard the noise of sweeping machine-gun fire. We all felt more and more we were riding into the battle-line, that our lives were in danger.

The sky was clear on New Year's Day. We greeted a very hot New Year but there was no time for rest. We had to push on.

Chapter 4

THE RIVER KRIAN

On 8 December the Japanese Army had landed at Singora and Kota Bharu on the Malayan Peninsula. The invasion force, successful in their landing and surprise attack, immediately crossed the frontier and assaulted the British possession of Malaya. The brigades, which set up the route to the whole of the Malayan coastline, on their way South pushed aside the resistance of the British Army's defence-position at Jitra, north of Alor Star, and towards the end of December reached the line of the River Perak. On 1 January Ipoh caved-in and our Army closed-in on the line to the north of Kampar.

Our bridging unit used Malayan Railways after a surprise infantry attack and pursuit and got into Sungei Patani on 2 January. The airfield was bombed, the enemy destroyed his railway-lines with mines: it became pretty dangerous. On 4 January the unit was ordered to the Krian River railway bridge and told to prepare temporary bridge-girders. The bridge was 100 km from Sungei Patani going South and while the girders were being put up the retreating enemy's time-fused charges blew up three trusses, a 40-metre gap. At the same time the road downstream of the bridge was also damaged so a temporary bridge had to be put up.

During their retreat the British Army held us up by destroying the highway over bridges regardless of size. Our infantry drove on in pursuit and to the bridges which enemy field engineers had collapsed repairs had to be made. The advance continued and on both the Perak and the Krian rivers the demand was for installing temporary bridges quickly. All of us *gunzoku* gave demonstrations of our skills and pressed on with the work, everyone in high spirits, having been accorded such an opportunity of taking an active part in the Japanese Army's invasion of Singapore.

The bridges covered about 200 metres in total extent and their construction-framework comprised three 40-metre-span trusses. In addition, two 40-metre-span trusses had also fallen down in mid-river together with their bridge-piers. In re-installing the fallen trusses there was no margin to spare in the time available and so we had to make wooden temporary bridges downstream. The river-bed was over ten-metres deep, covered with mud, and because it was near to an estuary the ebb-and-flow of the tide affected water levels. After technical engineering tests we pushed in stout timbers about 20 metres long to make bridge-piers, and made wooden girders 4 metres long to fit one span, and lowered the railtrack surface as much as possible, work which proved inadequate, so we had to work to a gradient below normal percentages to secure the track.

On 6 January the pile-driving job started. All the unit's working companies in turn were apportioned to it, with 2 and 3 Labour Companies laying and securing the roadbed and then laying the railtrack, 4 Company assembling materials together with a Materials Company formed specially from 1 Labour Company.

Since the job was below surface pile-driving meant that we had to erect a piling frame. It was a painful job, and because it took time to commandeer boats for pontoons it was 9 January before piling got out to mid-river. In the assembling of materials the business of buying and fashioning stout timbers was difficult and in the end, to get the right coverage, we had to log rubber-trees in a plantation. Later on, stockists of timber girders and metal fittings were sent promptly from Thailand. The rails to be used were shunted into a sidings near Nibontebal station.

Since enlistment these men, with their special skills, casual labourers, carpenters attached to the Labour Company, in spite of criticism by all the regular soldiers that they had become slack in military discipline, demonstrated in their work the strength of their several crafts.

The work progressed smoothly. There were nearby rubber plantations on both banks of the river, backed by the dense bush of the jungle.

12

On these dense forest-green the southern countries' sun blazed down, glittering, dazzling. In the dry season in Malaya in January midday heat exceeds 30 degrees Celsius. The river current was affected by tidal ebb-and-flow and the water-level rose and fell, and in consequence the turn-round in a single day gave two metres of fast current per second. It was the same in mid-January, and by then we had two or three hundred coolies, a workforce which crowded the banks. We *gunzoku* were quartered in an evacuated private house on the riverbank near Nibontebal town.

From dawn to sunset the noise of pile-driving echoed across the river surface and the bridge-building work reached its peak by mid-January. It turned out that the job was under the supervision of Colonel Imai, commander of 9 Railway Regiment, who worked with Staff Officer Hongō of 2 Railway Control. I was responsible for starting the work off and explained to them the circumstances of the construction site. It was now that I met Colonel Imai for the first time: several months later I was sent to the Thai-Burma Railway construction team and had not thought I should be able to meet him a second time.

Although they had broken into Malaya only at the end of January the Japanese Army took Gemas, were pushing on South and, according to an intelligence communiqué, were pressing on even as far as Malacca on the West coast. On the Krian river we finished making the girders on 27 January and the job of laying the railtrack was hurried forward. There was now no need to worry about air-raids destroying what we had done, so it was possible to finish the temporary bridge by the end of January, the stipulated period.

On 30 January a test run was made for a train to run over the temporary bridge. I set up a test-engine on the decking, it moved along the bridge, confirming that trains could cross without mishap – despite the creaking of the girders one kept on hearing! To a man the Labour Company shouted, '*banzai*!', and in the heat of the day on the new bridge they had built the echo of that shout filled brim to brim the approaches to the River Krian.

That same night, for the assault on Singapore, the first train crossed the bridge to the clatter of a full complement of artillery shelling. The men assembled on the approaches to the bridge repeated their shout of *banzai* at the top of their voices. All those on the bridge-construction

13

job were united in the joy they felt in the satisfaction of having been part of the campaign to capture Singapore. I thought that with that tumultuous *banzai* ringing in their ears everyone would appreciate the strength of *gunzoku* techniques exemplified in this task.

About this time the Supreme Commander, Lt-General Yamashita Tomoyuki, was in position at Kluang, expecting his van to get within hailing distance of Singapore Island when they got into Johore. His Malayan assault force comprised the Imperial Guards and three advance brigades from 5 and 18 divisions, about 50,000 officers and men.

Several years later, in March 1983, I visited the Krian River bridge after forty years. The building where our quarters were, I was amazed to find, remained as it used to be. There were the River Krian rice-paddies and the bridge we had repaired. I recalled the scene, the banks crowded with coolies and our men of the Labour Company and the sound of the *banzai* – even today I hear it and am filled with deep emotion. Forty years on the current flowed as it used to do, quietly one was sheltered in the green shade of trees on the river bank.

Chapter 5

THE MALAYAN CAMPAIGN

For us who had left our homeland in October 1941 and come to the southern region, the opening of hostilities had begun in Saigon on 8 December. Many *gunzoku,* those who doubted whether war would ever start, were considerably disturbed on the day when it suddenly did break out. We disliked war and as members of an Army company called a bridging unit were apprehensive because, being in the end belligerents, we could hope for no advantages when hostilities ended. We were not ourselves in front-line battle-action but, writing this after forty years and reliving the life of being at war, I too, what with the sickness and the bombing, really do not know how I escaped death time and time again,. When they departed for the front, how many of our comrades could have known their lives depended on surviving the bombing or defying the demon of disease, how many could have forecast what lay in store for them?

In the early hours of 8 December the Japanese Army's 5 and 18 brigades, officers and men of detached units, landed in the teeth of the enemy in surprise attacks on Singora, Patani and Kota Bharu. Companies of 5 and 9 railway regiments also succeeded in their task of capturing the railway which ran inland of Kota Bharu and Singora. From Hat Yai, 5 Brigade got across to the Malayan frontier and pursued their attack down the West coast. The railway regiments followed up in pursuit, capturing engines and rolling-stock and set about securing installations along the railtrack. The enemy, with no airfields left in northern Malaya, destroyed his defence-line at Jitra near the frontier, was unable to hold out against a precipitous assault, went on withdrawing and at the end of December finally fell back to Taiping in the South. The main force of our Army thrust along the highway opposite Taiping on the road to Singapore City, made lightning attacks using bicycles in what were called bicycle units and broke through the enemy's position. By demolishing highway, railway and bridges the enemy made their withdrawal in this way by blocking our transportation facility.

The unit who landed at Kota Bharu pushed on South along that part of Malayan Railways which runs down the East coast, finishing up at Gemas. Other units cut through thick jungle to the upper Perak River, mounting a fierce attack, and planning to secure the Kuala Kansar highway bridge. At the end of December our forces reached Ipoh town and on 1 January confronted the enemy in his in-depth position in the Kampar area, but thanks to a tank unit we were able to crush him.

Using boats in the Telok Anson area a Japanese unit effected a landing and immediately closed in on Kuala Lumpur, the capital of Malaya. Carrying on South from Ipoh, the main body of 5 and 18 divisions cleared away the enemy's resistance on the Slim River at Trolak, moved on from Mersing and made a powerful assault on the Malayan capital. Some of them advanced on Muar from Malacca on the West coast and then from all directions moved South of Kuala Lumpur town in the Kluang and Gemas areas.

By the end of January the enemy's battle-line in the Malayan Peninsula collapsed and the British, Indian and Australian forces had withdrawn into the Island of Singapore. Army Commander Yamashita advanced his HQ to Kluang, 100 km South of Gemas. On 31 January the vanguard of the Japanese Army was able to move at last into Johore Bharu on the Southern tip of the Malayan Peninsula. From the frontier in the North to Johore Bharu is 'the little gap' of 1,000 km, the breakthrough had averaged 50 km a day, and now with The Straits within hailing distance for us the enemy was defending Singapore Island. Major-general Heath, the commander in northern Malaya, reviewing this battle, makes the following remarks in his memoirs:[98]

The defence of northern Malaya was defective in various aspects. The spot where the enemy landed was near an airfield which was quickly completely overrun and so the situation developed ... Actually, to have complete defence-works was impossible. The construction of the Jitra position was postponed, making it too late for the period within which it could have been fitted-out. British construction-methods, too, involve a great deal of sprucing-up compared with those of the Japanese. Confronted by the climatic features of the southern regions, the enemy's soldiers had the benefit of preparation and training. The British were in the long run incapable of brave battle-spirit bolstered by patriotic devotion. With the loss of the battleships *Prince of Wales* and *Repulse* we lost control of the seas and with our airfields taken by force one after another we lost mastery of the air. One should not be surprised that the Malay Peninsula in such short time fell at last into the enemy's hands, Notably in the defeats at Slim River and Trolak the Japanese Army's plan for the capture of Singapore was rigorously pressed through.

By early February the Japanese planned to take Singapore with three divisions, 5, 18 and Guards, and these were concentrated on the southern coast at The Straits. Bit-by-bit their preparations for the assault were being achieved.

Chapter 6

THE FALL OF SINGAPORE

In the early hours of 8 February 1942 the Japanese Army's 5 and 18 divisions, who had been awaiting their opportunity to invade the Island's North coast by The Straits at Johore, crossed The Straits in the dark in small boats and made a decisive landing in the face of the enemy, a landing achieved bit-by-bit under enemy shell-fire. The Straits echoed with their voices encouraging one another. Their campaign to take Singapore Island was beginning.

The surviving British, Indian and Australians were now all on the Island, and the GOC commanding its defence, Lt-General Percival, had been strengthening its defence-works, but part of the British 18 Division reinforcement had still not arrived. The Island had lost mastery of the air and day-after-day the streets of the City were exposed to bombing, bombing on streets which sustained damage and had no military equipment.

An officer of a British reinforcement group landed on the Island on 5 February. His company was in the supply and barracks corps (the Royal Army Service Corps). He was Lieutenant Geoffrey Pharaoh Adams, and in his book, *No Time for Geishas* (1973) he tries to recount how it happened. I quote from it:

In February 1942 we were approaching Singapore in our transport. Lying off Cape Town in South Africa we had heard that two British battleships had been sunk. The ship altered what had so far been her course and we proceeded in haste to Singapore. I am a butcher's son,

18

volunteered for the Army, became a lieutenant and because of my trade was posted to the Royal Army Service Corps. When we left England in December 1941 America was a neutral power *vis-à-vis* the war with Germany, but on 8 December when Japan started the Pacific War the joint Allied Forces group was formed. At this point my first acquaintance with Singapore came into my thoughts and I knew nothing of the fighting in Malaya, so I could guess what might happen when we reached the Island a few days before the Japanese Army landed on it.

On 3 February, our MV *Félix Roussel* had an air-raid but we had strict orders to maintain a low profile. With our convoy ships we navigated the Sunda Strait. The duty officer had just announced over the tannoy that 'the birthday party for Lieutenant Adams will start at noon' when an air-raid warning reverberated throughout the ship. Our escort battleship HMS *Exeter*'s AA-gunfire beat off the enemy planes. I had not been expecting to be given a birthday party – a war experience for a young man still growing up! While we were moving along the swampy shore of Sumatra there was a second raid and again in the Banka Strait 27 aircraft came into attack, but as before they were foiled by AA-gun fire and no damage was done. However, we did not think we should get into Singapore harbour unscathed.

On the morning of 5 February, cutting through a cloud of black smoke on the horizon, *Asahi* planes were seen climbing into the sky. Bearing in mind our course aiming directly to Singapore, somehow it seemed a bad luck omen! Whether we got through or not our transports still lay outside Singapore harbour: just when we were getting close to its mouth with the Rhio Archipelago in the offing, suddenly enemy planes came in to attack. From high altitude bombs were falling one after another to split the convoy, then they started to attack us at water level with a damaging high-speed dive-bombing attack. Each ship's AA-gun fire fought its defensive engagement and four enemy aircraft were shot down, but the convoy, except for one ship, was only slightly damaged. Our ship was hit amidships: a bomb set the officers' mess on fire, machine-gunners abaft the funnel were blasted by enemy bullets, and a bomb made a direct hit on a lifeboat, killing Corporal Hadley of my company and several others. The *Empress of Asia*, before whom we were next in line, was set on fire, was unable to steer, and sank, the *City of Canterbury* received some damage and together with our ship was barely able to scrape into Keppel Harbour.

On 6 February after our landing, what we had already seen from the seaborne aspect was the cloud of black smoke coming up from various places in flames in the City. The streets were being mercilessly destroyed by the enemy's shell-fire and by bombing. Immediately on our landing a staff officer came from Malaya Defence HQ to liaise and he said sarcastically, 'At this juncture what have you come for?' I was dumbfounded. I didn't understand at all what he meant.

We needed maps so we asked for street maps but were told they had been abandoned in a goods wagon a month ago in Kuala Lumpur station. We took delivery of a few single-sheet naval charts but for use on land they were no good. Next day we were busy under cover refurbishing our arms. It was a tense situation. I myself had not expected to take part in the action so soon. In India our course had been changed and we had had to change the loading of freight in Bombay Harbour.

I was ordered to reconnoitre our forward position and took along a squad as advance-party. The meeting-point was in Tampines Road and I took a 3-ton lorry, and a motor-cycle which I rode. Just as we were getting near the rendezvous we were attacked by several enemy planes. A bomb fell in our rear and we were attacked with sweeping machine-gun fire: it seemed as if we were targets for retaliation! However, it was all over in ten seconds but we had had a narrow escape from death. You could see the South shore of Johore clearly. On the far shore of The Straits the enemy's Imperial Guards Division had the Island sewn-up tight with a hostile force of 10,000 officers and men.[99]

Our own projectiles were flying over our position all the time. Shells from the heavy coastal defence artillery seemed to us to make a noise like that of an express train hurtling through a station. Our own shells were comparatively few and intermittent and we were a little downhearted. In the sky Japanese and their allied aircraft mixed together flew around like an air-circus without colliding, flying left-right, up-down, it was marvellous. We moved into a rubber plantation. It was hot, sticky and damp and horse-flies and mosquitoes attacked us, and we were at a loss what to do. That night I had an attack of fever and was evacuated back to a field-hospital tent. For two or three days I was unconscious in a high fever. A wounded soldier back from the front line told me that the Japanese had landed at midnight on 8 February. On the morning of 13 February, with a medical officer's consent, I came out of hospital at my own request.

Major-General Heath commanded the spearhead of the defence forces in Malaya with 3 Indian Brigade. Compared with the Japanese the British were inferior in equipment and weaponry and the Indian troops lacked fighting-spirit, showed an uncooperative attitude, things which worked to the disadvantage of the British. Thus the position at Kampar could not be supported, the defence-line at Slim River was ripped apart, Kuala Lumpur was abandoned. Our Army went on losing time and again and the final battle-line on the Malayan Peninsula, on Singapore Island itself, was thrown away as a result. I gradually began to understand what that staff-officer had meant, cursed because 18 Division had not arrived in time. In our attempt at reinforcement we had not appreciated the Malayan topography and the 18 Division's troops had not been acclimatized to monsoon weather: to attempt an effective reinforcement was dicey. Our air force had been evacuated to Sumatra so mastery of the air was at the mercy of the Japanese: airfields on the Island had been quickly bombed and their usefulness impaired, our fighter-planes were caught on landing-strips. In extent, Singapore Island resembled Japan's Awaji Island. Outside the City area it was largely jungle, apart from land newly cultivated for rubber plantations. The connection between the Peninsula and the Island was by causeway at Johore Bharu. From Johore to Singapore City was 72 miles. This Island formed the base for British control of eastern waters and a governor-generalship had been established. A resident defence-force was in position and Keppel Harbour and the naval port at Seletar had their defence-works The Island's chief defence consisted of high-calibre heavy artillery facing out to sea:[100] no special care had been taken against attack from the North down the Peninsula, and even what the GOC set up as thought necessary was far from what was needed.

On the other side, the Japanese Army which invaded Malaya comprised three divisions only, but they were picked troops, well-equipped, and with ample training in hot climates and southern region topography. Their technical units were well-organized, engineers, railway engineers, well-trained to give technical superiority, gunners, tank drivers. General Yamashita's men were prepared to lose their lives in a spirit of loyalty and patriotism, and their fighting spirit kept up their sustained, determined attack. I don't know whether this is a narrow view or not, but in my opinion the British Army lacked the enemy's striking power.

General Percival, who had allowed the Japanese to land on the Island at midnight on 5/6 February, made his final stand on the high ground at Bukit Timah, and from 10 to 13 February the Japanese concentrated their attacks on this position, the dominant Japanese air force augmenting the assault by fierce bombing of Bukit Timah heights and of the City streets..

Wishing to get back to my own company I left the hospital and found my way to 18 Division HQ, on which shells frequently fell. On 12 February part of the Japanese Army got close to the northwest suburbs. The City's supply-reservoir was seized, the pipe-line breached within the City area and the flow of water began to be suspended; the situation was that the livelihood of the 160,000 citizens was threatened. Food supply also was a problem, sanitation deteriorated, and we were worried that there might be outbreaks of infectious diseases. On 13 February in the middle of my meal a dud shell fell, dangerously injuring some men. On 14 February I saw soldiers killed by a direct hit. In the late afternoon of 15 February the bombardment started to let up a little. An order came to destroy stocks of alcoholic liquors in the godowns. When Hong Kong fell the Japanese soldiers who took it committed acts of violence and so, considering such acts, it was thought that a similar situation called for the destruction, bottle after bottle, of whisky and brandy. Meanwhile from the front line came a rumour floating around that a cease-fire parley was taking place. In the gunners' positions they began blowing up their gun-barrels with gunpowder. One could see gun-barrel fragments whirled up high in the evening sky. I was ordered to return to my own company, an order having been circulated that we should formally surrender immediately after return to our units. The cease-fire order was issued for 8.30 pm on that day.

So in the end, after useless fighting, we had ended up by surrendering. We were ashamed and worried,. What would happen after surrender I had no idea. I wondered whether we should be repatriated, but no one knew what status we would have.

The fall of Singapore was a great blow to the Allied Forces. To England it was the death-blow to colonialism in the Orient, and to the outside world the white men's superiority-complex was lost. Japan's strategic predominance was set in motion with some initial difficulty in practice. The people of SE Asia confirmed their faith in freedom and independence: they hoped to be able to escape from the constrictions of the historical past. With the surrender of Singapore I had become a prisoner-of-war and so became the unwilling servant of the ruling country, Japan, for several years thereafter living a distressful life. I did not think they were an entirely hateful people, these Japs who had captured us, and one thought that these Englishmen, their prisoners, were not wholly good either – not all angels. In disputes between nations and in the defence of freedom and independence one cannot deny there's a danger that they fall into the situation called war. At such a time, I thought, one must face up stoically to whatever hardships had to be borne.

Chapter 7

SURRENDER

On 10 February 1942 the Japanese Army had confronted the British Army on Bukit Timah heights on Singapore Island. The Army Commander in Malaya, Lt-General Yamashita Tomoyuki, despatched to Lt-General A.E. Percival, the British Army Defence Commander, a note demanding a parley. The text had been written in English by Lt-Col Sugita, Intelligence Commander at HQ, and was dropped by aircraft into the British lines. The gist of it was that General Yamashita expressed his respect for the gallant fight put up by British Army troops but that, encircled as they were, it made good sense to make a cease-fire in the battle and to advocate a surrender as men would be uselessly, and increasingly, sacrificed: if by any chance this advice was not followed, in a general offensive even more would be lost. The note ended: 'The truce-bearer must hoist the British flag and a white flag, and must proceed on foot along the road leading to Bukit Timah.'

On 15 February the truce-bearers as instructed hoisted the white flag and a Union Jack, and accompanied General Percival along the road to Bukit Timah. In a room in the Ford factory, which was on the hill above the troops' position, the two generals conducted their parley. Their conversation at the parley was printed in a special 'Singapore' issue of the English post-war production, a monthly magazine called *After the Battle* (November 1981).[101] It was described from beginning to end and said that General Yamashita conducted it calmly in a gentlemanly manner: General Percival, who was urged to accept unconditional surrender when pressed for a prompt answer was said to have turned rather pale and in a low, small voice answered, 'Yes.' General Yamishita is said to have threatened him but in fact this was not true: he spoke in an ordinary conversational tone and is himself on record as saying, 'I did not take up a positively overbearing attitude', a statement quoted in an article in *The Southern Cross*, a bulletin of the Singapore *Nipon-jinkai* (the Association of the Japanese). At the parley three stipulations were agreed: 1. Item, that there should be a cease-fire and that both armies should not alter their battle-line. 2. Item, that until the morning of 16 February the Japanese Army should not enter the City. 3. Item, that the British Army, until relieved by the Japanese Army, should ensure the keeping of public peace and order. Under the British Army's cease-fire stipulation, all troops were ordered to cease fire by 8.30 p.m.

The City pipelines were now empty of water. The British Army was short of ammunition, loss of military strength was severe and altogether they were unable to continue the struggle. On the other hand, too, the Japanese Army was also short of ammunition and they were approaching the point of finding it impossible to sustain their attack.

Later on, at the time of the ceremony of signing the Japanese surrender at Singapore in September 1945, the Supreme Commander of Allied Armies in SE Asia, Admiral Mountbatten, had the victorious Union Jack unfurled on the national flagstaff in front of Government House in Singapore. It was the identical Union Jack which General Percival at the time of the surrender in February 1942 had taken to Bukit Timah on a truce-bearer's shoulder. It had been secretly hidden by an officer and kept hidden all that time. It is an episode which tells the story of Englishmen's disposition to revere their national flag.

Lieutenant Adams who surrendered at Singapore gives the following account in a memorandum written on the day of surrender:

At night on 15 February I could not sleep. We had been routed at war and had surrendered and the realization of what I supposed I had been waiting for proclaimed itself. In a leaden gloom I remembered things about my home, wondering whether people there had changed. Sleep was impossible, I kept silent, unwilling to talk.

Thereafter for four years I, the writer could not even in a dream recall what I thought would be my experience.

In his memoirs Lieutenant Adams goes on:

On the morning of 16 February, just as we were finishing breakfast, a Japanese serjeant came in with half-a-dozen NCOs. They were the first Japanese I had ever seen. The serjeant shambled up and addressed in queerly-enunciated English. The meaning of what he said was, 'You men are prisoners-of-war of the Imperial Japanese Army. You are to comply with our orders.' The way he pronounced 'r' and 'l' affected his accent and made it sound funny. Even while he was saying this, we were looking at his unseemly garb which struck us as odd. The black pupils of his eyes behind his spectacles, the flat nose in his small face, the bulky uniform the more-than-mouthful of teeth and so on, to us fully resembled the 'Jap' of popular cartoons. He had long trousers and a khaki jacket against the heat, and looked like an old farmer with his long leggings and pigskin boots. He had a serjeant's badge of rank on his chest, a sword dangled at his hip from a leather belt, he had a revolver at his right hip, from his shoulder dangled a pair of field-glasses. The Japanese Army's five-pointed star was on his helmet. His subordinates looked the same, a queer sight. At the back of their helmets they all had dirty pieces of cloth as awnings against the sun. The NCOs had put cloth puttees wound round their legs and they had black-soled rubberized boots with forked big toes. Somewhat meagre to look at, these little men, one could not really believe it was Japanese troops like these who in battle had harassed our Army whose bravery was to no avail. In front of their left hip they fastened their ammunition-pouches, a bayonet hung down on the left side. On the bayonet-frog was fixed a 'god-charm'. A sweat-towel was tucked into their belts. These troops also had old-type infantry rifles, on the barrels of which dirty letters of some kind were written and a Rising Sun flag stuck in. At the hands of such troops our Army had been defeated – it was a mystery how such a thing could happen. But that was that *had* happened: within a little over two months from the opening of hostilities, within that short period, a military force using an army with the .38-model of a reconstituted Mauser rifle and a navy modelled on our own navy, Imperial Japan (this backward country!) mastered the Pacific Ocean region and on top of that ended up by occupying Singapore, Britain's greatest base overseas.

The English, against the reality, equate the stock Japanese of the cartoons with the real Japanese, compounding an offensive sin against the truth. And, Japanese are liable to be under the impression that all British officers have deep red walrus moustaches.

The Japanese serjeant could talk to us from the start because he could speak English. The greatest difference between us was that none of us could speak Japanese. He asked whether any of us could speak Japanese and the answer was that none of us could. He then asked who was our commanding officer and the senior colonel stepped forward. He told him to salute: what a disgrace for a British Army colonel to salute a serjeant! The serjeant said, 'Everyone lay down what arms he has, and get a move on!', waving his revolver and pointing to the colonel to give the order to disarm. We finished throwing down our arms in about ten minutes and then proceeded on foot directly to the Bukit Timah road and were concentrated in the grounds of the Island's airport. On the Bukit Timah road into the City there was their army on the march, infantry units, tanks, one-after-another in battle-order. To the citizens alongside the highway it was a pity that the scene they had been accustomed to was solely that of their masters, the British, hitherto. But now on many buildings Rising Sun flags were hung out and a feeling of allegiance to their new masters was openly displayed.

My internment ended quickly as I essayed to go by myself into the City on a motor-cycle, by-passing the sentry. Here and there in the streets the embers of war conflagrations were still smouldering and fumes arose from them. Here and there you could see corpses in buildings which had been destroyed by bombing and the artillery duel: this was what I saw on the way. Chaos and misery combined. Piteous bodies of horses strung up like lumps of meat on the barbed wire, remains of cars and lorries were to be seen in profusion. I tripped and fell off my bike, whereupon some Japanese who were passing by kindly helped me off the ground and said, 'Are you out of Gold Flakes?' I thought they were kind-hearted men. It was evening when I entered the City streets but there was no electric light so it was pitch-dark inside buildings. My search was not being a bit useful because looting had already taken place and there was nothing of value to be seen. I returned to the airfield camp, the sentry did not question me and opened the gate for me. In the sky above the streets of the City pitch-black smoke was swirling up in the gloom of dusk. I was concerned about people whose houses had been burnt out in Singapore, but I also wondered what state the people in my own country were in now.

On 17 February Lieutenant Adams and all the surrendered men were moved into Changi military barracks. These British troops who had surrendered expected to be treated in accordance with the Geneva International Convention Agreement. However, since the Japanese Government did not acknowledge that Japanese troops could become prisoners-of-war, the Convention was never ratified. At the outbreak of hostilities both the British and the American governments demanded that Japan would treat men who became prisoners-of-war in accordance with the Geneva Convention. The Japanese Government appreciated the purpose of this proposal but could not envisage a situation in which Japanese troops would need to be treated as prisoners-of-war. Japanese troops were taught the rule that 'it is not allowed to be captured alive' and an individual captured by the enemy is ashamed and is treated with scorn for having taken such cowardly action. This is the reason why Japanese soldiers repeatedly berated men 'who had committed the error of becoming prisoners-of-war'. This led to acts which at the time were regarded as ill-treatment by prisoners. Lieutenant Adams in his memoirs well understood the reason for such acts and recalled the feelings the Japanese soldiers with whom he came into contact ... 'they did not always deny ill-treatment'.

As for the British Army prisoners in Changi concentration camp, Indian sepoys, who up to that point had fought as allies, had them under surveillance. Partly under coercion the Indians had participated in the fighting, but after the fall of Singapore the Japanese Army's firm strategy was to support the movement for the independence of India, and Japan cooperated partly in making them betray England.

Later, bad elements among the Indians made Subhas Chandra Bose their leader, under Japan's patronage. He set up an Independent People's Army (the INA) and they chanted, 'Asia for the Asiatics!'

Chapter 8

SHŌNAN, 'LIGHT OF THE SOUTH'

In March 1942 the military government gave Japanese-occupied Singapore its new name Shōnan, Light of the South. The Mayor inaugurated this great recognition of the gallantry of Japan's warriors, and 25 Army Military Government took over the administration of Malaya and Singapore. After the occupation there was an anti-Japanese movement fomented by a large number of disreputable overseas Chinese merchants who were executed, for the most part without trial: this gradually stopped the unrest and public peace and order were restored.

In Changi a new commandant, Major-General Fukunaga Kyōhei arrived to administer the Shōnan prisoner-of-war camp. To prevent escapes the new commandant demanded that all officer-prisoners should sign a written pledge not to escape, so that re-captured escapees could be executed. The officer-prisoners used the International Prisoners-of-War Convention as their pretext for refusing to sign. They had no case for utilizing it because Japan did not ratify it. General Hattori felt that the local company of guards could not deal with his instructions to the letter so his chief-of-staff concentrated the prisoners in a single barrack square at Selerang, and kept them so crowded together that normal living conditions were impossible to sustain. There was now the risk of lives being lost and the Changi prisoners all gave in to the chief-of-staff's demand and signed. It was at this juncture that the Thai-Burma Railway was about to be built as an overland trucking route to Burma and as a source of manual labour in the Thailand-Burma area prisoners-of-war were to be used, sent up from Changi [as a matter of fact a large number had been sent before Selerang: editor].

Since the occupation of Singapore Lieutenant Adams and his group had been living in the Shōnan prisoner-of-war camp, starting their new way of life in it. In the southern region the native peoples had been liberated and the Japanese ideal of a Great East Asia Co-prosperity Sphere was preached and realized. Our Army had Japanized Singapore as Shōnan City. Concurrently, a monument in mourning to the souls of the departed heroes of the campaign, the Shōnan Shrine, was constructed. It was put up on the heights of Bukit Timah on the outskirts of the golf-course near the McRitchie reservoir. 15 Independent Engineering Regiment, Yokoyama Unit, were assigned to do the job and to conscript prisoners from the Shōnan camp as labourers. About a thousand prisoners including Lieutenant Adams were moved to Bukit Timah. To build the Shrine in the Japanese manner special materials were sent from our mother-country together with specialist shrine-carpenters. The prisoners' job was to make the roadway to the Shrine, to build a bridge over an arm of the reservoir, and to make the ceremonial staircase for worship. For this work Lieutenant Adams and his men were marched out daily from Bukit Timah camp under instruction by Serjeant Inotani of Yokoyama Unit. In Changi, the prisoners took their instructions from their own officers, enjoying a kind of freedom, so this was the first experience of Adams and his fellow-prisoners of working under instruction from Japanese NCOs. In July Yokoyama Unit were transferred to Burma for the campaign to attack Imphal. 5 Engineer Regiment, Tamura Unit took over from them. In the campaign to take Singapore Tamura Unit had given heroic support for the men of 5 Division at the crossing of The Straits at Johore. The regimental commander, Colonel Tamura Yasuji, was a gentlemanly man who in his handling of the prisoners looked after their welfare. The Sikh guards of the Changi camp were replaced by Korean *heiho* (auxiliaries not of Japanese nationality), Lieutenant Kanada being in charge of them. Compared with the Sikhs they were good-natured people. Korea had been claimed by Japan as a possession but, going back into past history, China under the Manchūs had Korea as a possession and the Republic of China took it as being under their rule.

Both from the guards and from Japanese soldiers prisoners got violent treatment, but the prisoners saw the Japanese doing the same, high-ranking men striking and kicking lower ranks as a punishment. I agree the prisoners justly felt contempt and shame when exposed to it. However, the men in Tamura Unit, with their commander's special concern for the prisoners, were told to treat them mildly in their contacts, and so in general they were treated with genial friendliness by the Japanese soldiers. According to Colonel Wild at the War Crimes Trials, Tamura Unit in their defence of Kojima in the Pacific gave a particularly favourable example of the way in which they treated prisoners-of-war, no evidence was attached to them of suspected war crimes and at a early stage they were repatriated. They had made no distinction between friend and foe in their treatment of prisoners, this was appreciated, an example to talk about.

In the task of building the Thai-Burma Railway, described in the next chapter, there were still more differences of opinion: there was both cruelty and distress in the work and so on top of the issue of humanity there was also the issue of how the prisoners were in fact treated. In the War Crimes Trials in Singapore we thought that some of the soldiers involved received retaliatory one-sided punishments. However, there were few examples, I think, of cordial treatment of prisoners comparable with that given by Tamura Unit. It is obligatory on me, one of the participants, to describe the real conditions on the Thai-Burma Railway. It acquired a bad reputation as 'the death railway' simply because of an estimated number of deaths.

For the prisoners building the Shrine, the commander of 53 Brigade, 18 Division, was the senior prisoner-officer, Brigadier Duke. (Futamatsu's text prints 'Major-General'. In the Japanese Army a brigade, *ryōdan*, is commanded by a full colonel, called *ryōdanchō*, not a general officer.) In Tamura Unit his adjutant was Lieutenant Nakano, the liaison officer was Major Hashimoto, and Adams recalls Matsuzawa among the regimental officers. He writes, 'Within my association for four years of prisoner-of-war life, my recollections of these few months only are pleasant and unforgettable', and he goes on as follows:

Our job was to build steps up a hill slope, the road for worshippers. The squad leaders on it were Corporal Kamimura and Superior

Private Tamahiro, who hailed from Hiroshima Prefecture and were men of genial character, ruggedly honest, and as Japanese soldiers go were splendid fellows. Corporal Kamimura shaped up his cap to a point and so was nicknamed 'The Gnome' as he looked like one of Disney's Seven Dwarfs. Private Tamahiro could speak little English. His nickname was 'Ten men' because he always asked for ten men on any job. These two men were kind to the prisoners, and they all worked with a will on the job. They didn't understand what the prisoners were talking about but from time to time gave them cigarettes or their packed rations. When a senior officer came on an inspection they kept watch so that the prisoners did not incur censure. These men were kind to the prisoners but I do not suppose for a moment that they showed any disloyalty to *tennō heika* (The Emperor). Camps varied. In some no humanity was shown to prisoners. By contrast, when a black market in petrol was being investigated, the Tamura Unit commander took special precautions to delay the *kempeitai* (Military Secret Police). Brigadier Duke expressed his thanks for Colonel Tamura's kindness. Boiled rice as a staple diet was of course deficient in vitamins and there was a good deal of malarial fever. Prisoners-of-war had a daily wage allowance, officers 20 cents, NCOs 15 cents, private soldiers 10 cents, Sick men, by official Army regulations, had no allowance, so on Brigadier Duke's proposal part of the daily allowance was kept back for the sick.

About this time news from the outside world was circulated from some source. On 2 May the battle of the Coral Sea, and on 5 June the battle off Midway Island were severe blows to the Japanese Navy, and it appeared that an Allied Forces counter-offensive had begun. Here at Bukit Timah the graves-marker for Tamura Unit's war-dead was being constructed and every day offerings of flowers were dedicated. The lovely fellowship of comrades-in-arms was there to be seen. Near this monument to the dead a cross was put up for the Allied Forces' battle-casualties, all the time flowers and cigarettes were dedicated on the cross as well.

In September when the Shrine was nearing completion a rumour gained ground that they were to augment the labour force on construction of the Thai-Burma Railway very soon. For Adams and his fellow-prisoners the day finally came for their move from Changi to Thailand. They said goodbye to the kind men of Tamura Unit, and The Gnome and Ten Men came to Singapore station to see them off. None of them knew what hardships awaited them.

Chapter 9

THE THAI-BURMA RAILWAY

In the Spring of 1942, with a pause after the occupation of Singapore, the campaign to occupy Burma went ahead. As Rangoon was the supply-base for Burma, for Southern Region Army GHQ there arose the urgent problem of the safety of the supply route by sea. In Burma the British-Indian Allied Forces had given in to the Japanese Army's offensive in a crushing defeat, but because of submarines from the British Western Fleet operating in the Andaman Sea off Burma the Japanese maritime supply-route was threatened, so the overland part of the preparations for the campaign to recapture Burma on the way to India was pressed forward. This year in June in the battle off Midway Island the Japanese Navy lost from its main force four aircraft-carriers sunk, a heavy blow which destroyed the hope of any defence in the Andaman Sea. The safety of transports out of Singapore to seas off Burma had become a problem. Southern Region Army used the plan for an overland route to Burma, taking advantage of the study made in 1939 at *Daihonéi* (Imperial Japanese Army HQ in Tokyo) to find what use could be made of a railway out of Thailand into Burma. In their survey, construction of a railway would need 'two railway regiments taking about a year'. Major-General Hattori Shimpei, commanding Southern Region Army's 2 Railway Control, resolved in February this year to make a survey on the ground of this railway project. On receipt of his order, Staff Officer Irie, together with Railway Official Nishi-jima surveyed the area from Kanchanaburi up to the Three Pagodas Pass on the frontier. They judged that the volume of work needed was much greater than in the original estimate, and calculated that it would take over two years. It therefore became urgent for the construction to start promptly, so without waiting for *Daihonei*'s orders the General assigned in March 1942 the main construction units, namely 1 Railway Materials Workshops, 5 Railway Regiment, and 9 Railway Regiment.

The railway's starting-point was at Nong Pladuk, 80 km from Bangkok on the southern section of the Thai National Lines, with terminus at Thanbyusayat, about 50 km from Moulmein on the India-Burma National Line to Ye, the construction bases being Nong Pladuk on Thai-side and Thanbyusayat on Burma-side. A plan for a railway had previously been investigated by the British early in the twentieth century. One line of entry involved a railway route from their possession, Burma, to reach Pitsanlok in northern Thailand. The other involved a railway from Thailand to reach the Andaman Sea coast. The former involved crossing a high mountain-range and would take a long time. The other, by comparison, had the demerit of elongating the interval even though it crossed a low mountain: to all concerned the long gap between the two capitals, Bangkok and Rangoon, was the bugbear. Climate, too, and health conditions were unfavourable, and to increase production-volume one could not expect financial efficacy. In the end the British had abandoned the idea but this was the plan the Japanese Army decided to adopt despite its inherent difficulties. Local Thai were said to have grave doubts of its success.

This railway, as joining Thailand with Burma, was officially called 'The Thai-Burma Rail Link'. It ran from Nong Pladuk 50 km to Kanchanaburi, thence ran alongside the River Kwae Noi upstream as far as the Three Pagodas Pass and crossed the frontier moving northwest to reach Thanbyusayat, a distance of 400 km in all. The Three Pagodas Pass is 275 metres above sea level (Futamatsu's text prints 400 metres a.s.l. but British Royal Engineers in 1946 measured it as 275 metres a.s.l.). On Thai-side the extent of the line was over 300 km, on Burma-side 100 km. Gradient was under 10/1,000: there was no need to make a top class road. It was, however, in an area where our heroic soldiers had to plunge into dense jungle, and because there was a complex ground-levelling in many small ravines an immense volume of work was forecast. Climatic conditions were those of the region near Tenasserim in the world's heaviest rain-belt which brought an unimaginable volume of rain in the rainy season. In this mountainous country endemic malaria was expected to hinder the work. Accordingly, distress in the work of construction was forecast. The demand, for strategic reason, for maintaining an overland route to Burma made necessary a daring conquest of that distress. Further, because the route's transport-construction materials and the labour force were inadequate, the toils of construction units were expected to multiply. In June the formal order came from the Southern Army to prepare the Thai-Burma Rail Link Line. The basis of the plan was as follows:

Railtrack gauge: one metre

(This gauge is common to all Southern Region railways, making it possible for trains to run straight through from Bangkok to Singapore, again from Phnom Penh in Cambodia and Moulmein in Burma as far as Rangoon).

Railtrack:

Railroad load liability under 15 tons per wheel axis.
Gradient maximum 25/1,000.
Line curvature minimum 200 metres radius.
Track surface 4 to 5 metres wide.
Roadbed a good 15 centimetres deep.
Sleepers timber, over 15 per 10 metres.
Rails weight over 30 kilograms per metre.
Intervals between stations within 10 km apart.
Station length over 200 metres, for efficient working.
Planned transport capacity 3,000 tons per day each day.

From April 1942 1 Railway Materials Workshops were set up at Nong Pladuk and at Thanbyusayat and stocks of construction resources and mechanical parts began to be assembled. The job of constructing, maintaining and safeguarding the line was assigned to 5 and 9 railway regiments: 5 Railway Regiment on Burma-side being the construction unit from Thanbyusayat (who later transferred this duty to 5 Special Railway Installation Unit) and Thai-side 9 Railway Regiment as construction unit from Banpong. The men of 9 Railway Regiment were transported from Rangoon via Shōnan in May, then by sea to Bangkok and thence arrived at Banpong. 9 Railway Regiment's 1 Battalion finished their job of running Sumatra's railways in May and took post in Banpong entrusted with preparation of a quantity survey of the route. The regiment's main body then moved into pre-arranged billets.

The route ran on level ground from the minor station of Nong Pladuk, which is about 5 km from Banpong station on the southern part of Thai National Lines running to Singapore, about 50 km from Bangkok. It then ran along the North bank of the River Mae Khlaung (also known as the Kwae Yai, the Big Kwae) to Kanchanaburi, west of the town, crossed the Mae Khlaung in the neighbourhood of the Thā Makham and turning left ran along the Kwae Noi (the Little Kwae), a tributary of the Mae Khlaung, at which point it entered the jungle belt. Along the Kwae Noi it crossed many mountain streams, then ran north-west up to the Three Pagodas Pass. Thence, crossing over the Apalon, Mezali, Zami and other rivers it reached Thanbyusayat. On Burma-side it extended about 100 km. Going North on the Ye Line it is about 50 km from Thanbyusayat to Moulmein.

The area from Kanchanaburi in Thailand to Apalon in Burma is topographically complex in deep jungle, a belt where no human beings lived permanently, with no highway for vehicles to get through. On Thai-side it was possible to transport things by boat on the Kwae Noi for about 150 km, as far as the Thā Khanun area, but on the Burma-side the water-courses were transverse, so we needed a lorry highway. According to the survey on the ground by 2 Railway Control it was obvious that work on construction 'by two railway regiments taking a year' would be far from what the task would demand. It was now expected to take twenty months to the end of 1943. The big problem was how to procure and move supplies of food and fodder and of resources like tools and timber. Furthermore, in the depths of the jungle drinking water has to be conserved, hygiene kept under control, medical supplies to protect the sick being the subject of scrupulous care, The labour force, prisoners-of-war from the battlefields of the southern region, and the employment of hired local coolies, had to be taken into account. As regards employing prisoners-of-war on this construction work, whether it was a violation or not of the

International Prisoners-of-War Convention, not to employ them on military operations, I do not know.

Exact records of construction are no longer in print, so here follow, in round numbers, estimated mechanical parts data:

Rails: 32,000 tons,
Timber poles: 650,000,
Ballast: c. 400,000 cubic metres,
Bridge timber: c. 60,000 cubic feet,
Cement: c. 1,000 tons,
Explosives: c. 300 tons.

Also mechanical items as follows:

Engines used: *Class C56 pony tank engines*: c. 35 made in Japan, they were shipped over and reconstructed to one-metre rail-gauge and to wood burning. They were made for the Ōigawa Railway Company by Kishaseizō Kaisha in Ōsaka.

Thai, Malayan and Burmese engines diverted and used on the line: a total of c. 50.

Wagons: c. 400, gauge modified and couplings improved ... these shipped from Japan.

Military materials:

Covered railway wagons, type-100: c. 50,
Flatcars, type-97: c. 600,
Lorries: over 300.

Apart from these, locally requisitioned *motorboats, sampans*, etc. totalled over 700, and also 400 *elephants* with their mahouts were enlisted and set to work. Among the materials rails diverted from Burmese and Malayan railways which were worn out were replenished by exports from Japan. Timber for *sleepers* was procured locally by lumbering.

The Japanese Army units concerned were the central HQ, 1 Railway Materials Workshops, about 1,000 men, and 5 and 9 railway regiments, about 5,000 men, Special Installation Railway Unit, about 1,000 men, a Signals Unit, a Sakui Unit, Labour Unit, about 1,500, a grand total of over 9,000. Units directly in support included an Anti-infection Water-supply Unit, a Commissariat Unit, a Field Hospital, etc., about 1,000 men and in addition, if you count them, the people needed to run prisoner-of-war camps, which must make a grand total of over 10,000.

Of prisoners-of-war employed as labourers total numbers by country were 30,000 British, 13,000 Australians, about 18,000 Dutch and about 700 Americans, an estimated total of 61,800. Of these over 13,000 were victims of death by illnesses, or over 22 per cent. About 3,500 were buried at Thanbyusayat, and about 8,400 at Chungkai and Kanchanaburi. Coolie labour gangs, Indonesians, Malays, Indians, Burmese, Chinese and Thais, comprised about 100,000 people, of whom about 70,000 worked on Thai-side, 30,000 on Burma-side, Half of them died, after the war about 8,000 were repatriated, and the balance, 28,000 of them, are recorded as not knowing where to go. This total of victims said to have been 50,000 is no falsehood: there was a dead man for one in every hundred sleepers. At the best season for work, each day a gang of a hundred men marched out a kilometre to the work-site. Over 50 km a day were worked so one could estimate that every day there were over 50,0000 labourers on the job. 10,000 Japanese Army victims from bombing and from accidents after the line opened for traffic added up to a big casualty percentage, and post-war the line bore the reputation of 'The Railway of Death'.

The railway was started in June 1942, to be finished at the end of 1943, but *Daihonéi* ordered the period to be shortened by means of high-speed construction methods, *kyūsoku kensetsu*, which the prisoners called 'The Speedo'. With the advent of the monsoon and with the period planned to be curtailed by over two months, the prisoners and coolies had a hard struggle, working day and night, and it was October 1943 before the line could be opened to traffic. The line's construction extended over 415 km, a marvellous record, and this railway's overland route and the opening of the Panama Canal in the USA can be measured up as work records in engineering. And it is an odd precedent that in the middle of a war it was completed with the help of prisoners-of-war. One ought not to forget the large numbers of prisoners and coolies with whose help it was done, men whose bones lie buried in the jungle; respect is due to them and we offer our sincere condolences.

The railway involved many men working in mountainous jungle where signs of human habitation were rare: our soldiers faced sweltering heat, struggled in heavy rain, were continually threatened by the demon of ill-health, making it a hard struggle to stay alive, but they performed automatically their feat of endurance. However, without in the end accomplishing their mission of creating a sufficiently successful supply-route to Burma, engineers could say the whole thing could have been abandoned, with advantage involved as we were in the disastrous defeat of Japan. It is a sad circumstance for those concerned with its construction. It is a truly regrettable thing that the actual wartime railway is a nightmare whose traces one wants to forget.

In March 1983 I had the opportunity of revisiting the railway. The sections of track for 130 km from Nong Pladuk were as they were in those days, and the line's terminus at Namtok station was unchanged. The bridge over the Mae Khlaung at Thā Makham stood on a rice-paddy ridge and below me the waters of the Kwae Yai flowed on, and on the luxuriant green of the far bank right up to the frontier the range of hills loomed up into an azure sky, and I was able to recall that past for which I had looked forward so much to revisiting. The railtrack west of Namtok as far as Thanbyusayat had been taken up and you could not see the roadbed. Also, upstream on the Kwae Noi at Namuchonyai the Khao Laem dam had been built, and at Konkuita the place of the joining-up point had met the fate of being submerged under water. The site along the line as far as Namtok had been beautifully developed with people living on it. I saw that the railway zone had developed a service to the community, but I confess that as one concerned in the line's construction I felt a little disappointed.

Chapter 10

PREPARING CONSTRUCTION

In our bridging unit we heard of the fall of Singapore at Nibontebal. The temporary bridge over the River Krian gave us pride and satisfaction during the occupation of Singapore. Since our departure for the front, for the first time we felt happy, feeling at ease in that Malayan Spring. The feeling of seasonal contentment with the dry season was very slowly ending. The rainy season was approaching, squally periods grew longer, and the green of the mass of trees grew daily in luxuriance. After the occupation of Singapore public peace and order in Malaysia were stabilized and the Japanese Army's Military Government saw to it that popular sentiment also became peaceful. British rule was replaced by a new administration which was adapting itself to the situation. Even at Nibontebal, which had been evacuated, the women and children were coming back home, and in the town the feeling of tranquillity was like floating on calm water. Even around our quarters the chanting voices of children began to be heard, singing songs in Japanese. We, too, said our few words in Malay: the outlook of the populace had become gentle and quiet.

In the towns shops opened up for trade. A Japanese Army military scrip circulated at Malay-dollar equivalents: price-values were not clear but Japanese people could shop. Somehow one got used to the tastes of unusual fruits in the Malay Peninsula, of durian, mango. All this comes back into memory, somehow or other one grew to enjoy the way of life in the southern region. On the other hand, victims of endemic diseases like malaria and dengue fevers appeared and the military doctors were

41

kept busy. Under the Military Government throughout Malaysia the railways and bridges damaged in war action began to be restored. The bridging unit had instructions to repair railway bridges and each labour unit moved onto its construction site. Unit HQ moved to Taiping and I was stationed at Nibontebal, as an advisor on Krian River rail bridge restoration, attached to 3 Labour Unit who were in charge of the work. The bridge had been bombed and the third bridge-pier in mid-river was under water: the truss we had made had fallen. In order to re-float it and the bridge-pier whose weight had sunk it deep into the mud on the river-bottom, we continued to utilize the buoyancy of the tidal ebb-and-flow by making a big wooden Noah's Ark. We launched her in May from the river-bank and christened her the *Konno maru*, named after the commander of the Labour Unit.

By this time construction of the overland Burma supply route, the Thai-Burma Railway, had started, railway regiments had moved into Burma and were embarking on its construction. From their station in southern Malaya our 5 Special Installation Railway Bridging Unit and a railway regiment were moved into Burma for this task, and 5 Special Railway Bridging Unit took the restoration work in hand. To take in hand this task, I and the Bridging Unit commander, Murahashi, had made an official trip, as fellow-experts, from Kuala Lumpur to Shōnan. We had been thinking of returning from the trip to Ipoh, this being unit HQ, and I was awaiting orders to transfer to 2 Railway Control. However, in the middle of the trip the order was extended for men with railway construction experience to help in survey and selection of route. From Railway HQ I was the one selected and joined the Thai-side construction unit. I felt anxious ... having gradually got used to responsibility in Malaya and from there moved to a completely strange Thailand, unaided and feeling insecure: I had to deal with a fresh responsibility. However, I'd been selected as an engineer and set out determined to use the very best techniques. With my fellow-experts we made a foursome, Ikegami Saburō, Sogara, head of the control group, Kataoka Shōfutoburō, and Satō Shinzei, a congenial group.

From this time there followed for us a period of about two years on construction of the Thai-Burma Railway. Today, forty years after the war, I have renewed my acquaintance with Englishmen who worked on it in those days. I have read their interesting accounts, written by men experienced in this work, and have interpolated quotations from their books in my present work, and I have revised my opinions about the causes and effects of this railway, not frivolously, and present them in their sequences.

On 10 May 1942 we *gunzoku*, who were to be transferred to 2 Railway Control, set out from Ipoh. Since our departure for the front we had developed a liking for the mountains and rivers of Malaya but were now to be separated from them. The previous year, when we were stationed in Malaya, trains travelling North passed over the frontier to Hat Yai, but international express trains through from Malaya to Bangkok were hardly running from May onwards: these trains previously carried a very great number of passengers. We arrived at the Bansoe switchyard north of Bangkok in the early hours of 13 May. We went on street tramcars out of Bansoe, asking where 2 Railway Control was. From dawn the weather in the city cleared up bracingly but it quickly became hot. After two nights and two days in the train we had got tired and suffered terribly. To us, the yellow robes of the priests were strange and we were surprised that so many people went barefoot, but they overflowed with vitality. While what they said about losing independence was untranslatable. We found that one of the city sights was the National Stadium near Chulalongkorn University, equipped for an Olympics meeting. The entrance was adorned with the Olympics symbol.

Major Hikiji, an old acquaintance at Control, with railway officials Nishijima and Itabashi were already waiting for us. We were at once invited into the office, on the walls of which was length of aerial photos pasted up all round, 10 metres of them. Major Hikiji told us this mosaic of topographical photographs showed the course of the Thai-Burma Railway as it was so far, making up a stereoscopic map on the reduced scale of 1:20,000. I began to examine the mosaic (the combined set of aerial photos joined up but without an actual ground map). In the middle area was a river spread out like a while cloth curving about as it flowed. Even though you could say that on the map it ran along like a street you could see no sign of human habitation. Only the contour lines of the river-course were marked in. We knew our task was to lead the survey into what looked like an impenetrable jungle belt and immediately we felt uneasy. How could we get into that jungle and how was it possible to survive in it? There seemed to us no way one could face up to such a terrible life. It was a monstrosity. Railway official Nishijima told us he had reconnoitred the area and gave us various details about it.

On the photographs the source of the River Kwae Noi was shown as being in the Three Pagodas Pass area. The river was narrow, about 10 metres wide. There was plenty of water, even in the dry season it did not dry up, but in the rainy season when rain fell on the headwaters the river-water rose several metres in short time. Trees and undergrowth on its banks stood about 20 metres high and under the trees the jungle's luxuriant growth impeded one's entry. Animals and pythons lived in the devilishly thick bamboo-clumps, peacocks flew around. Over the mountain recesses you could sometimes get a glimpse of a tiger. In the river there were crocodiles. Upriver from Kanchanaburi there was no way through for vehicles and the only way open was for boats on the rise and fall of the River Kwae Noi. To get through the jungle it was best to ride on an elephant. Topographically, altitudes did not vary much but it was like a maze. In the rainy season the rainfall was beyond imagination, the river flooded in an instant and was dangerous. Population was scarce, and because individuals carried malaria-germs, we could not mix. This intelligence report by Nishijima made us more and more uneasy. Knowing that subsistence in the jungle endangered one's life we secretly had to face up to it with tragic resolution. Even with aerial photography one could picture the maze-like topography, extent of jungle, and its depth. It became clear this was a zone which must be unexplored and had no signs of human habitation: strategically it had to be done but we forecast the distressful nature of this zone for railway construction. Notwithstanding the respect due to those whose courage had determined to make this construction, one harboured grave misgivings about a plan alleged to take two years to complete.

On the other hand, if we could do it and complete the plan, what could be described as the boiling-over of the spirit of the Japanese Army would be recorded, and we determined to do it.

In two or three days we moved from Sumatra to Banpong to conduct the survey under 9 Railway Regiment's direction.

Chapter 11

BANPONG

It was May 1942, six months after hostilities had broken out. Thailand had declared war and permitted passage though her territory, adopting a helpful attitude, and to that extent she co-operated overall in the Japanese Army's transportation. Trains for military duties ran from Indonesia and Cambodia, and from Malaya, and movement of troops to Shōnan had become a comparatively harmonious practicality. The Thailand National Line's southern part gave on to the Bansoe junction in Bangkok, crossed Rama I bridge over the River Menam in the city and going South into the northern part of the Malay Peninsula reached Hat Yai. From the junction with Malayan Railways western line at Batam Bazaar on the frontier the line made possible unbroken transportation from Bangkok right into Singapore. Banpong station is about 80 km from Bangkok on this southern line. Construction of the railway began here. Its small station was the point of entry, and Japanese Army units on construction work and a labour force were moved into it, the labour force being prisoners-of-war to be employed as navvies and brought up from Malaya. Together with Nong Pladuk, 5 km east of Banpong, it became the construction base with huts, provision and fodder, a temporary 'anchorage' for groups passing through. Huts were built on the outskirts of the town in the Nong Pladuk direction. Materials were stockpiled meanwhile and the stockpiles grew taller and taller.

West of the town flowed the River Mae Khlaung which ran through about 50 km of the prefecture whose office was in Kanchanaburi town.

From the front of Banpong station the highway to Kanchanaburi extended straight to the North. In front of the station was a small inn on the highway and in it 9 Railway Regiment's 1 Battalion (Sakamoto Unit), who had moved up from Sumatra, set up their HQ provisionally. On 20 May I reported to this HQ. Sakamoto Unit had been moved into Malaya at the outbreak of hostilities and had been restoring the captured Malayan Railways. Since March they had been running Sumatran railways. In May, on orders to prepare the construction of the Thai-Burma Railway, they had moved into Banpong as the regiment's advance party. Under Major Sakamoto the unit commander were his Adjutant, Lieut. Takabayashi, Admin. Officer Lieut Kuribayashi, Paymaster Lieut Hijikata, and his Medical Officer, Lieutenant Hirota: these were the principal regimental officers. Sakamoto Unit as advance party were responsible for survey, on the Thai-side, of the proposed track of the Thai-Burma Railway. Under the direction of the unit commander, 1 Company (Sugano Unit) were responsible for hut-building and 2 Company (Sudō Unit) for clearing the line of the route. For the survey itself a special survey unit of NCOs was formed, NCOs who had experience of railway route survey. In charge of it was 2/Lt Mōri, a young man who had held office in Korean Railways and who, as it happened, was a graduate of my own university.

The inn became our quarters for the time being. Its woman-owner, a hospitable, good-natured person, received us kindly and warmly. There were bed-bugs in the bedroom on the upper floor (but we kept quiet about it) but the restaurant on the ground floor was an airy dining-room, a lively place because customers always congregated in it. The highroad ran in front of the inn and there was an unceasing coming and going of people and vehicles. The town's population was some thousand souls but the station which took you to Kanchanaburi had much traffic and on the highway in Banpong there was a varied row of shops and stalls where you could buy foodstuffs and there were crowds of people eating, day and night without a break, a scene no different from that in Bangkok. We could not read what it said on the shop fronts but the merchandise showed what the shop's trade was in. There was a market in the middle of the town and peasants from the suburbs came in every day to buy vegetables and fruit. It was a busy scene. Here and there in the town were open spaces and as the Japanese

46

Army units arrived they set up temporary huts and the population's accommodation began to multiply in no time. From their point of view people in the town began to look forward to the railway construction: somehow everything overflowed with activity.

The townspeople, who were not far behind Bangkok-style in manners, still dressed in varied Thai styles. Men wore short-sleeved white tunics with black *panung* or underskirts. Women wore similar white tunics with skirts of various colours from hip to thigh. Compared with the men's dress, women's dresses were short. Under a little cap the women wore palm-leaf hats over short hair. All wore no shoes and that they went barefoot was a little odd. Middle-aged women chewed tobacco and betel-juice, had quids in their mouths, and the red smear round their mouths did not look nice. Many boys wore no clothes and played games naked. One often saw uniformed soldiers and police undressed. Officials wore uniforms with many badges and with decorative buttons. Somehow civilization and the underdeveloped seemed mixed together.

The Thai are Buddhists, and in every town and village is a Buddhist temple. In Nakhon Pathom, which is no great distance from Banpong, there is a splendid Buddhist pagoda. At Banpong itself there is a temple with beautifully-coloured tiles, and Buddhist priests with shaven heads and yellow robes were a common sight. Priests are treated with respect and they themselves are haughty. Because it is customary for priests to be treated like buddhas, as religious mendicants it is not their custom to acknowledge offerings with a bow.

The people's culture and education were good but their houses were not. In those days the attitude of mind of the Thai, who in a Japanese connection had the advantage of being on the victor country's side, was nevertheless one of unease. They say the Thai army was the most powerful in the world ... and Japan, who had defeated England, seemed to rank number two.

At Nong Pladuk, 5 km east of Banpong, the railway materials godowns and workshops units were being set up, and they began assembling construction materials as at Banpong. Huts were built at both places for Japanese units, and the railway sidings in which materials were stacked were enlarged. The huts they made used *atap* for the roofs, a simple job, literally:

On bamboo posts our roof
miscanthus-thatched ...

The bamboo used for posts and beams was 10 cm in diameter and about 10 to 15 metres long, joints being fastened with ties and again fastened with cords of bark. For roofs we used *atap* which is made of the leaves of the nipa palm. The pieces of thatching were repeated at 30 cm intervals, and the pitch of the roofs on over 30 *atap* sections allowed rain-water to run down them quickly. The height of floors above the ground gave satisfactory ventilation and furthermore its height of 60 cm kept off verminous insects. Instead of bed-board we used split bamboo. Each hut was 5 metres wide, about 40 metres long, and accommodated over 50 men. The materials were local and a hut could be built quickly in a couple of days.

There was a continuous spell of fine weather and the *atap* roofs could dry out. The stars in the night sky made a beautiful sight, but the rain returned and there were roof leaks. Drifting rain collected under the floors, so we had to dig deep ditches round the huts. We grew used to living in huts and became quite at home and comfortable.

The bugle call for reveille could be heard shaking the *atap* on the walls each day when our day started. This was called the land of perpetual summer but the temperature first thing was low and it was passably cool. As the sun rose up so promptly did the temperature. When the sun began to get brilliant over the tree-tops, roadside stalls were put out and *samlor* tricycle-cab men began to ply for hire. Mixing in with the crowds who came to market were yellow-robed priests under the eaves of houses, religious mendicants. At 8 a.m. the national flag was run up on the flagstaff in the garden of the police-station and the national anthem was played. People both at home or walking in the streets, or just resting, stood still, even the Buddhist priests, they all revered their national flag. For the Thai this was the moment to feel pious.

The labourers marched out when the sun was rising and in no time at all the outdoor temperature rose to over 30°. The arid atmosphere made us sweat and get quickly into the shade to get dry again. In the afternoons the shrilling of cicadas was deafening, but at dusk a cool breeze gradually came in on the rows of houses in the streets. With the drop in temperature cool air embraced us, from the bushes came the shrilling of insects, and in the distance came the monotonous beating of the big drums in the special dance around the national flag. Late in the evening the Southern Cross Constellation began to rise above the horizon, and our thoughts of our distant homeland came racing into our minds.

By the time we began to get used to life in this country we began to feel less worried about our health. To keep out the *anopheles*, use of veils and of mosquito-nets was strictly enforced. However hot it was, exposure of hands and legs was forbidden as a safety-measure. Food and fruit bought on the wayside were delicious but dirty. However, for us nice-tasting fruit and unusual cookery sometimes overcame appetite and curiosity.

After our arrival in Banpong about a month elapsed. Then 9 Railway Regiment's HQ, their 2, 3 and 4 battalions and supplies and work-shop unit arrived in succession, and arrangements for getting ready the construction were put in train. In our case, we had a look at the topographical map of scale 1:20,000 and the problem was that, so far as the results of Nishijima's survey went, several potential starting-points had to be looked at. The responsibility for the survey weighed heavily and because it all depended on my guidance I lost my self-confidence and felt somewhat uneasy. However, on 5 July 1942 we inaugurated the start of the trace to be surveyed at Nong Pladuk, and the Thai-Burma Railway's starting-point on the Thai-side was reckoned officially as the guide-post (the 0-km post). That day the sky was clear over Nong Pladuk. From a cloudless deep blue sky light poured down from the dazzling sun, and step by step up crept the heat. To attend the inauguration Commander Sakamoto and I stood facing Nong Pladuk station. There were paddy-fields from Banpong as far as Nong Pladuk and on the paddy-ridges here and there coconut palms stood up and made a southern country landscape. Beyond the paddy-fields distant hills could be seen shimmering in the hot air. The farmers driving water-buffaloes were not thinking about war and things like that. At Nong Pladuk many sidings were being built on which store-wagons for railway-construction materials were stockpiled, the loads were piling up. The prisoners-of-war made cheap labour. The scale of railway construction starting from this base was very plain to see.

The 0-km guide-post, a new 10 cm squared timber post with '0' written on it in bold *sumi* (Japanese ink) was planted between the two railtracks on the up-line to Bangkok. Soldiers positioned at the guide-post held it in position. One swung aloft a heavy mellé time and again, on top of the post. Stripped to the waist, he drove it well into the ground. The inauguration was announced by Major Sakamoto with a tense expression. Silently we were aware that the railway construction had begun at last, and we renewed our resolve. Survey pennants showed the way forward. The sky above Nong Pladuk maintained its deep blue. A Japanese Army recce-plane's throbbing died out there in the hills towards the Thai-Burma frontier. The hum of voices of men working in the station compound could be heard, re-assuring like drum-beats that the railway had really started.

In February 1976 I revisited Nong Pladuk station. Thirty years had elapsed since the setting up of the 0-km guide-post. Here the Thai-Burma Railway had diverged (now the Namtok Line). The guide-post had disappeared, and there remained only the little station building. Of the many sidings, godowns, huts and so on not a trace remained. Some of the old pump-pedestals were there, buried in the soil. As I stood there in the middle of the railtracks where once the 0-km guide-post had been, those past times were recollected with deep emotion. Certainly nature and sentiment impelled one to echo Basshō's famous *haiku* ... 'the warriors are but traces of a dream'.

Chapter 12

PRISONERS-OF-WAR

In war, when enemy forces are in action, their troops who surrender and become captives in general gain by it. Among all countries in the world who approved it the later International Convention concerning Prisoners-of War was ratified in Geneva. Japan's position in regard to the Convention was that our military declined responsibility for prisoners-of-war, and when war broke out in 1941 Japan had not ratified or signed the Convention. However, in Japan's case in the past in the Sino-Japanese War and the Russo-Japanese War our troops had taken prisoners, and so it was expected by other countries that in this war, too, Allied Forces' troops would become captives in the same way.

Japan excepted, foreign countries' military in their organizational systems did not have many people who became volunteer soldiers and in battle could become prisoners-of-war properly so-called and they came under the provision of the International Prisoners-of War Convention as regards their treatment: captives themselves well knew about this Convention and under it would expect certain standards of treatment. They saw nothing dishonourable in this, and it was evident that they did their tasks faithfully. In England's case, it is the custom for the King to send repatriated prisoners-of-war a letter of appreciation individually, as former prisoners-of-war when I met them openly avowed.

By contrast, in our country's military systems set-up, soldiers were brought up in the spirit of public duty to die, and on the battlefield this rule of conduct was observed to the letter, embracing our country's demand to dedicate one's life to her, a command strictly enforced

... 'If captured one must not incur the shame of going on living.'
If soldiers by any chance unexpectedly became prisoners, they were dis-
graced for the rest of their lives. Because Japanese soldiers felt like this,
they could properly call into contempt enemy soldiers for not being
ashamed of cowardice. When foreign soldiers became prisoners-of-war
in battle and come under their enemy's protection, they know they can
take a rest from battle, but if the opportunity arises can escape. Also,
they trust their enemy will acknowledge liability to transmit their situation to their own people at home. In Japan's case, in the matter of this
Geneva Convention, because in her Army prisoners-of-war could not
exist, she did not ratify it, but the Allied Armies at the very outbreak
of war proposed that they ought to conform with it and that was their
agreed response.

The important relevant clauses in the Convention are as follows:

i The army status by rank of prisoners-of-war must be preserved.
ii The life of no prisoner-of-war may be taken by force without
    authority.
iii Prisoners-of-war are entitled to receive the rations appropriate to
    their rank in their own army.
iv Prisoners-of-war must be allowed to return to their normal way of
    living, and their sanitary conditions must be kept satisfactory.
v They shall not take part in any military operations.

In Japan's case, when hostilities ended in the southern war theatre,
immediately a large number of prisoners-of-war came under her
administration, and so the question is whether it is understood how
far the Geneva Convention is concerned with the organization of prisoner-of-war camps. An individual Japanese soldier could well enough
be vaguely aware of the importance of status to a prisoner-of-war, but I
feel he would be incapable of really comprehending it. From a Japanese
soldier's standpoint, seeing a prisoner-of-war usually aroused his contempt in point of fact. In the case of prisoners-of-war in general the
disparity in their manner of living does not make it hard, I think, to
comprehend the attitude of Japanese soldiers.

In Malaya more were killed in battle than had been expected but still
a very large number of prisoners-of-war had to be accommodated in

Changi for some time. Together with those accommodated temporarily from the Sumatra and Java war theatres, they made a total of about 100,000. In the camps prisoners had to live in temporary huts into which an inadequate supply of food and fodder created distress – such was the state of affairs. In the administration of the camps their accommodation, rations, sanitation and so on had to confirm to the stipulations of the Geneva Convention but I think there were violations arising from imperfections in procedure and misunderstandings.

In September 1942 in the camp at Changi, Singapore, prisoners who plotted to escape being liable to execution, there was an incident at Selerang barracks at which they were forced to sign a written pledge not to escape. That year in the autumn at Thā Makham prisoners caught attempting to escape were liable to be executed, so the same pretext was employed of forcing them to sign a written pledge. At Banpong the senior officer prisoner, ordered to punish men for escaping, said proudly, 'There is no precedent for British prisoners-of-war to be punished for escaping.' In either case, from the standpoint of prisoners taken in battle, I think that, given actual violations of the Geneva Convention, one must ask whether the Japanese Army may be judged to have been responsible.

The employment of prisoners-of-war as a labour-force on construction of the Thai-Burma Railway had been carefully thought out in the initial construction plan, but when Singapore fell their numbers had been far greater than anticipated. The Southern Region Army's administration had to supply rations for this large number and because the food situation in Singapore was critical it would inevitably cause distress. Consequently the location of railway construction-work favoured a policy of dispersal, a course quite properly approved. This unavoidable necessity in location of the railway's construction derived from a strategic angle and the question is whether employment of prisoners-of-war on it was a violation of the Geneva Convention. The build-up concurrently of the Great East Asia Co-prosperity Sphere, which was Japan's policy, linked up with the employment of prisoners and I don't know whether or not this became the issue.

In August 1942, Thailand prisoner-of-war camps were re-organized at Kanchanaburi and transferred from camps at Changi in Singapore to camps within the administration of the Army in Thailand. From

April 1942 to August 1943 a total of 47,629 were transferred from Singapore to Banpong and even as far as Rangoon. Specifically in the case of those employed on railway construction it is said that, in round figures, over 12,000 out of 59–60,000 died. On the Allied Forces' side, over five to one died in action, which seems a curious number even for a severe battle-action. That an almost similar number died from illnesses in Burma and Thailand seems extraordinary. The 'railroad of death' slur has little validity.

I met prisoners-of-war for the first time at Banpong in May 1942. They were unloading a freight-car – fair-haired, deep blue eyed giants, shabbily dressed, their torsos naked. I don't know whether they were British or Australian, but these were men who had surrendered in Malaya or Singapore. It was a pity, I thought, that when they became prisoners-of-war they had come up to Banpong without a trial. So, when they discovered they were to be employed as labourers on railway construction, what would be their reaction, forced to work with Japanese on an enemy operation! The Japanese on the construction, encountering prisoners-of-war for the first time, would probably find employment alongside them something unpleasant. Troops taught that in battle you must not be captured, but die, had nothing but contempt for men whose disgraceful cowardice allowed them to obey an order to become captives and still live. They felt superior, therefore, to their enemies, now their prisoners. And these were Europeans and Americans who normally feel superior to us, so still more did our men develop, I think, an attitude of superiority. Not being infantrymen in the conflict the railway engineers did not exchange gunfire directly with the enemy, so there was little feeling of positive enmity. On the contrary, they found when they encountered them that they were no less than ordinary human beings, but felt deep contempt for them. Because they didn't understand what they said and because their habits and way of life were different, our engineers behaved roughly towards them and annoyed them. However, our troops had commonsense and there were few prisoners, too, who failed to recognize that these were soldiers who had pledged with their life their loyalty to their fatherland. Our men were not really conscious of having ill-treated prisoners-of-war, but in my opinion there were in fact from time to time rough practices which amounted to many cases of ill-treatment. It is regrettable that men were made responsible, in the one-sided War Crimes Trials after the war at Singapore, for cruel acts committed unintentionally.

After the war when I was interned my guards were Gurkhas and from them I often received contemptuous treatment no different from what they had received themselves. In the prisoner-of-war camps in Thailand it was a question whether accommodation and rations conformed with the Geneva Convention's stipulations, and whether the Japanese Army over the total period were unable to devote enough care to their prisoners. The dietary habits of the prisoners of eating meat limited what could be provided and at times they complained about the Japanese rations being more than theirs. The truth is that in the rainy season transportation of food and fodder was difficult and the Japanese units' staple diet, rice, was also restricted.

Many of the prisoners' huts in the work sites were in jungly, mountainous country and first malarial fever, then various diseases, broke out. Particularly with cholera, determination in the use of preventative measures was essential, and of course use of un-boiled water from well or river was strictly banned. The Japanese had previously had anti-cholera and other injections strictly enforced, but for the prisoners no such direct, thorough action existed. Medicines and supply of medical officers were insufficient Particularly in the rainy season of 1943 when the finishing-date was brought forward accompanied by rush-construction and there was a sudden increase in the number of labourers, a situation was created in which not only medical supplies but also distribution of rations seemed something for which good intentions were lacking. Sickness among the prisoners increased, inadequate rations and dearth of protein led to under nourishment, and there were many outbreaks of malaria, dysentery and other diseases. Between May and August 1943 cholera flourished with an increasing number of victims. Compared with the Japanese Army, action to improve hygiene was imperfect but responsibility for overseeing prisoners was pursued. One should not forget that the Japanese Army units, too, were confronted with the dangers of the demon of disease.

About 11,000 Japanese, about 60,000 prisoners, and about 100,000 coolies were able to complete the railway construction in the short space of a year and a half. Prisoners and coolies in their tens of thousands were victims and their remains lay buried in the jungle, but there is no doubt that in fact the prisoners and coolies labour force made a great contribution to the railway completion. In 1944 Major-general Ishida Hideguma erected a memorial monument beside the Mae Khlaung bridge to enshrine the souls of the prisoners who fell victims during the construction.

Incidentally, a Buddhist bonze, [a priest who was] a former abbot, in recently years built a museum at Kanchanaburi for display of photographs and other memorabilia from the construction period, to commemorate the railway. He called it JEATH museum. He said JEATH, not DEATH, a revised 'death railroad', a name of ill-repute, and explained the word as 'J for Japan, E for England, A for Australia and America, T for Thailand, H for Holland, the six countries whose people built it, namely JEATH RAILWAY.' It seems a witty, amusing point of view. As one of the participants, I doubt if anyone can know whether it could have been opened to traffic if there had not been the workforce of coolies and prisoners working with us on its construction. Because of the spirit of the toil they experienced, one cannot suppress one's sympathy for them and give precedence to dedication of the deepest feelings to the souls of the great number of victims.

In October 1942 Lieutenant Adams, a British prisoner-of-war arrived at Banpong from Singapore. In the present context I quote part of his recollections:

We left Singapore station in a goods train, crossed the Causeway and went North in the Malay Peninsula. We were still alive but wondered whether we should ever be able to return to Singapore and we became rather depressed. In the freight-cars into which we were loaded, because they were 2.8 metres wide and 7 metres long, the thirty prisoners in each car were quite unable to squat: so many men at any one time could not stand up. The roofs and floors were of steel so the temperature inside was higher than outside, and as there was no through ventilation the foul atmosphere was intolerable. We heard that our destination was Banpong in Thailand, but no one knew where it was. When night fell air from the entrance on one side came in, a very pleasant cool breeze. We passed through stations with names we knew as places where there had been battles a year ago, Rengam, Kluang, Tampin, and in the evening pulled in at

Kuala Lumpur, capital of the Federated Malay States. Next day we continued our journey North, passed Slim River of the big battle, Kampar, on to Ipoh, thence crossing the Perak River into Taiping. That evening the train ran along the shore off Penang Island and at dawn on the second day came to Padang Bazaar, the station on the border.

Here we couldn't see any trace of the war, but as well as station staff there were two or three Japanese military policemen, *kempei*, standing there. On arrival we refilled our water-bottles. No meal was ready so, rather hungry, we travelled on. From Hat Yai we kept on going North into continuous South Thailand scenery. You could see a combination of coconut palms and cactus growing wild and rice-paddies under cultivation. On the right above the tops of the coconut palms at sea level the waters of the Gulf of Siam glittered and sparkled. When the train stopped at stations a crowd of peddlers came up, but we had no Thai money so there was nothing for us but to barter watches and fountain-pens for fruit and cigarettes. Day after day in the scorching sun we got sunburnt, sweaty and hungry, our guards checked and re-checked our numbers, and eventually we were pitched out into a temporary camp at Banpong. We heard that 'Thailand' meant 'Land of the Free', but we thought it doubtful.

Most Allied Forces personnel, at the time of capture, were able to stay with their units: thus because there was no break in the formation to which they were attached, many officers had thorough knowledge of the ORs and, together with their subordinates, got used to their way of life in the camps. There were not many who were separated from their comrades, the men they knew. These circumstances suited the prisoners, made them take heart. In the long hard toil of which a work-camp was full they kept their spirits up and were able to feel cheerful. When there was no change in the unit to which they were attached they endured their hardships well, and survived. In Changi even though they were not supervised by the Japanese they worked and in their own unit structure were looked after with their own senior officers taking the responsibility. Thus the officer-prisoners, who in general took no part in manual work, for such work left supervision and guidance to their NCOs.

But in Thailand and Burma when they were employed as labourers on railway construction work the supervision of prisoners was changed, the entire responsibility passing to the Japanese work unit. In camp, the supervision of their life was that the camp auxiliaries (the *heiho*, Koreans) received the daily request from the railway engineers for prisoners fit to work. The engineers' NCOs supervised them at work, and soldiers supervised the coolies in the same way as the prisoners. Numbers requested from the camps were needed for each day's work, but when the number of fit men fell short the engineers conferred in the camp and an adjustment was made. At the start of the rainy season in 1943, in order to speed up the work the numbers requested were increased. Very many prisoners, however, fell sick and could not work and the numbers fell off. The engineers then rounded up and sent to work sick men who should not have had to work, and also officers who were exempt from heavy manual work. As to who was fit to work and who was unfit, decision was left to the Japanese camp doctor and the prisoners' MO to decide: an external body-wound made a straightforward exemption, but decisions about men with fever or diarrhoea were perplexing to decide whether a man should go out to work or not.

Supervision by the engineers was based in getting maximum efficiency in what in fact was an emergency, so when the day's work stint was extended each day's norm was only achieved by coercion. Usually the prisoners did not have the services of an interpreter, their go-slow tactics often went too far and incurred severe scolding and harassment. Of course, the Japanese soldiers' natural instinct involved contempt for them and this affected their behaviour. The severe nature of the work and the demand for speedy finishing of tasks did, I think, destroy any chance of kindly treatment.

Prisoner-of-war camps in Thailand comprised six groups. Nong Pladuk was No. 1 Group, Thā Makham No. 2 Group, Wanyi No. 3 Group, Thā Khanun No. 4 Group, and Burma-side were two, No. 5 and No. 6. The Nikki camp and the neighbouring Songkurai camp were detached from Thai and put under Singapore administration. A detached camp was also set up at Tonchan.

A summary of the moves of prisoners-of-war from Singapore to the Thai-Burma Railway area is as follows:

In April 1942 Group A (to PoW always known as A Force) of 3,000 Australians were shipped to Burma and later entered Thanbyusayat. (Successive parties are described by Futamatsu from Japanese statistics. The true figures are given in Nelson: *The Story of Changi, Singapore*, Bureau of Records and Enquiry, Stamford College Press, Singapore, 1973). In June the Mainland Party, 3,000 all British, left Singapore station in five train-loads of which the first, B Battalion under Major R.S. Sykes, RASC, 600 men mainly 54 Infantry Brigade Group Company, RASC, 18 Division, left on 18 June, destined for Banpong. B Battalion started work at Nong Pladuk on 24 June as labourers clearing and building the base workshops and elaborate sidings for use by the Japanese 1 Railway Materials Workshop, Thai-side. In October large parties, all British, left from camps at Sime Road, Adam Park, Changi Village and Changi, totalling 14,260 and detraining at Banpong. In 1943 parties leaving for Banpong from January to mid-April were of mixed nationalities, British, Australian and Dutch, totally 17,760. As in 1942, these parties were transferred from Singapore administration to Thai/Burma administration. On 18 April the ill-starred F Force under Lt-col S.W. Harris, RA, began leaving Changi in thirteen train-loads destined for Banpong, 3,334 British and 3,666 Australians, and on 5 May H Force followed under Lt-col H.R. Humphries, RA, 1411 British, 670 Australians and 588 Dutch. Two further small medical parties of mixed nationalities left, K Force on 25 June and L Force on 24 August. F, H, K and L forces were never transferred to Thai-Burma Japanese administration.

From Singapore, when the railway had been completed, some prisoners-of-war were sent by sea in what they called 'hell-ships' whose accommodation for their full complement was insufficient and they were torpedoed by their friends in British or American submarines. These men were sent to Japan from the Thai-Burma region, from the Philippines and Taiwan. Off Taiwan the American navy and airforce attacked these ships, and added to the number of victims.[102]

On the railway construction a mixed group of British, Australian and Dutch officer-prisoner-of-war, to protect their ORs, took over the severe hard manual work and experienced extraordinary hardships.

In general, the supervision of the prisoners was said to be inadequate. In particular, in their needy circumstances, both medical supplies and number of medical officers were inadequate. Relief articles were sent from the International Red Cross Society, but in the Thai-Burma regions very little came to hand (Futamatsu was aware that very limited supplies were delivered to some camps, in some of which the Japanese soldiers stole them from the godowns [editor]).

In all these severe manual labour, the prisoners-of-war who survived did so because they benefitted from their individual spirit of endurance. Lieutenant Adams writes in his post-war reminiscences that, 'The British, whatever the hardship, bravely faced up to it with indomitable vigour, never failed to make jokes about it, and went out of their way to spend their everyday life cheerfully.'

Chapter 13

CONSTRUCTING THE RAILWAY

The railway construction was set up and operated by forced labour. For survey, air photographs were taken in advance and on a topographical map the selected route was pegged along the centre of the track. At the same time a detailed investigation was made of track, and gradients and curvatures were decided. On the basis of the route-chart, bridges and location of railtrack were decided, the construction-plan finalized, and putting this all together the volume of work was estimated. So, with this volume, the workforce needed was calculated.

Construction work accordingly got under way. To start with, ground-levelling for the roadbed, digging out and embanking was put in hand: bridges apart, this building work was carried out. When it was finished, the railtrack was laid on top of the roadbed, and the railway line completed.

On Thai-side, in July 1942 the Mōri Survey Unit pushed ahead from Nong Pladuk and set up the survey of the central line. From the Banpong area as far as Kanchanaburi there was a 50 km section of level track, and then the centre line was marked out, construction of the roadbed began immediately.

9 Railway Regiment, as construction unit on Thai-side, moved station to Banpong from the Burma front in June by way of Singapore and Bangkok. Regimental HQ at Banpong supervised supporting units as well as the Regiment itself. Colonel Imai was a soldier but he had studied civil engineering at Tokyo Imperial University and made an able commander of railway construction. In January of this year, at the

61

time when I was on bridge operations in Malaya on the River Krian, I had come to know him and so by an odd coincidence had the pleasure of meeting him again. 1 Battalion, having arrived earlier, took charge of survey arrangements. At Banpong 2 Battalion (Yoshida Unit) took charge of track laying, 3 Battalion (Inuyama Unit) and 4 Battalion (Yabe Unit) had the task of building the roadbed between Banpong and Kanchanaburi. Regimental Materials Workshop (Narihisa Unit) at Nong Pladuk and 1 Railway Materials Workshop (Hashimoto Unit) were together responsible for procuring and assembling materials and other resources.

In July, the Survey Unit moved on and building the roadbed began, with part of 3 Battalion pushing on to Thā Makham west of Kanchanaburi and starting to prepare the bridge over the River Kwae Yai (the Mae Khlaung) and part of 4 Battalion had the job of cutting through a rocky hill beyond Chungkai after first levelling the rice-paddy ridge along the River Kwae Noi. From Banpong as far as Kanchanaburi the ground was level, with a mixture of fields and rice-paddy with banana plantations, Japanese sugar-cane, and clumps of trees here and there. There were few houses along the highway, apart from the villages. Here and there were devilish bamboo-clumps which it was a terrible labour to cut through. By August the van of the survey advanced from Banpong alongside the River Kwae Noi about 80 km beyond Thā Kilen. The work of laying the railtrack also started. Laying it was pushed ahead by the railway regimental troops with text-book efficiency. Using 100-type railway tractors and 97-type flatcars, their method was to load sleepers and rails on a flatcar, push it in front of them, and lay track in sections by laying sleepers and rails on the roadbed, then joining each section up to the next.

On Burma-side, the construction unit was 5 Railway Regiment, with Colonel Sasaki in command, and in July they entered the small station of Thanbyusayat on the Ye Line. From there to Nikki in Thailand was about 115 km and 5 Railway Regiment had charge of this area, but the highway alongside the railtrack was unfinished. At Thanbyusayat were the regimental HQ and the Burma-side part of 1 Railway Materials Workshops and also 5 Railway Regiments' materials workshop who together had the task of stockpiling machine parts and other resources. 1 and 2 battalions were in charge of repairing the road to make it a trucking road for supplies, and of building the railway roadbed. 3 Battalion set up the survey of the centre line and from July Engineer Chiyō of the bridging unit was also sent there. The work got going with the advantage of cooperation by Engineer Chiyō.

In April from the main Southern Region Army came the official order to prepare construction of the Thai-Burma Railway and construction work was put in hand in earnest. When the monsoon ended in September the railtrack extended from Nong Pladuk for 50 km and had reached Kanchanaburi. C56-type pony engines exported from Japan ran the first 50 km of the Thai-Burma Railway, running on logs for fuel. The labour units respectively took up their locations in their advance, and regimental HQ was advanced from Banpong to Kanchanaburi.

The din of hammers in construction, from Banpong to Kanchanaburi, and across the River Mae Khlaung and upstream on the River Kwae Noi rang loudly and kept on reverberating.

With Sakamoto Unit I crossed the river and took up post at Wanyai, about 75 km upstream from Kanchanaburi.

Chapter 14

THAILAND

In those days in 1942 Thailand was a constitutionally-based monarchy with a king over the government. In ancient times this country was called Jamu and was a Burmese colony. In Japanese literature the character *tai* (Thai) was used but Thai in Siamese was a contraction of *Pratet Thai* which means 'Thai monarch'. At the start of the Second World War, Prime Minister Phibun's pro-British party held the reins of government. For strategic reasons Japan had to demand transit over Thai soil.[103] On the Cambodian border her Army watched its chance and made increasingly threatening demands for transit. Prime Minister Phibun quickly agreed to cooperate with the Japanese Army, and consequently with the start of hostilities a switch from the British to the Japanese side became urgent and advantageous to Thailand. However, this provided a superficial change and in 1945, with the war turning to Japan's disadvantage, she changed back in the end to a pro-British diplomatic stance. In South-East Asia at the time I think it would not have helped her to stay as she was, a nation which had yet to establish her standing in the world.

In the Spring of 1942, when the Thai-Burma Railway was begun, this country co-operated on the construction. The Japanese Army in its prosecution of the war found no obstacles in the way of its military transportation, co-operating with Thai National Railways. Between Banpong and Kanchanaburi the building of the roadbed, and between Kanchanaburi and Wanyai the re-modelling of the highway on Thai-side were planned to be apportioned out with the Thai, but the plan did

1

Yoshihiko Futamatsu (second from left), an engineering student at Kyoto University, photographed aged 24 in 1935. He is shown assisting in the construction of a bridge over the River Yodogana, near Osaka.

2

Yoshihiko Futamatsu in formal military uniform as an engineer on the Thai-Burma Railway in 1943.

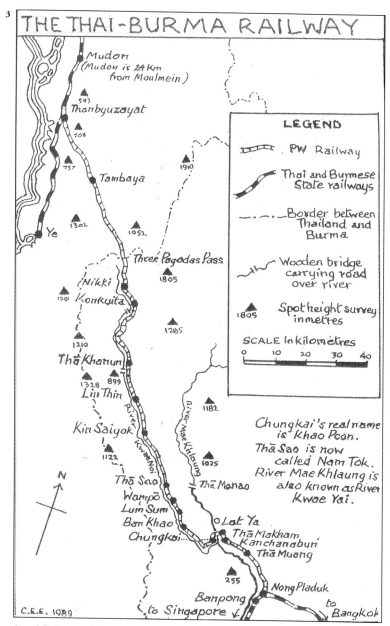

THE THAI-BURMA RAILWAY

3

Mudon
(Mudon is 24 Km
from Moulmein)

▲ 593
Thanbyuzayat

▲ 708

▲ 757
Tambaya

▲ 1910

Ye

▲ 1302

▲ 1052

Three Pagodas Pass

▲ 1805

Nikki

▲ 1291
Konkuita

▲ 1285

▲ 1210
Thā Khanun

▲ 1328   ▲ 899
Lin Thin

▲ 1182

Kin Saiyok
River Mae Khlaung
River Kwae Noi

▲ 1122

Thā Sao   ▲ 1025
Wampō   Thā Manao
Lum Sum
Ban Khao   ○ Lat Ya
Chungkai   Thā Makham
           Kanchanaburi
           Thā Muang

▲ 255
                      Nong Pladuk
Banpong   to
to Singapore   Bangkok

LEGEND

⬚⬚⬚ . PW Railway

〜 Thai and Burmese State railways

—··—··— Border between Thailand and Burma

〜⌒ Wooden bridge carrying road over river

▲ 1805 Spot height survey in metres

SCALE in kilometres
0   10   20   30   40

Chungkai's real name is Khao Poon.
Thā Sao is now called Nam Tok.
River Mae Khlaung is also known as River Kwae Yai.

C.E.E. 1989

Simplified map of the Thai-Burma Railway showing the Three Pagodas Pass.
Drawn by Ewart Escritt.

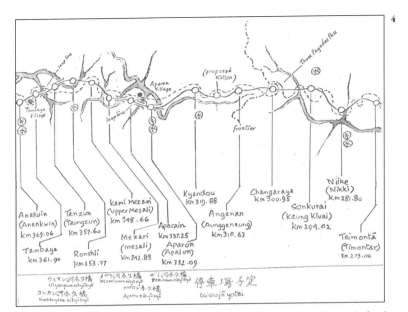

Part of the Engineers' Trace (Kōhei Plan) showing the Three Pagodas Pass made for the Transport Section of 5 Company of 3 Battalion of the 9th Railway Regiment (redrawn and translated by Ewart Escritt).

Original ink-wash drawing by POW William Wilder showing the building of the Wan Po viaduct, Thailand, dated 1943, and drawn during captivity.

6

7

Photographs of POWs building the Thai-Burma Railway taken by Japanese bridge engineer Yoshihiko Futamatsu.

A C56 pony tank engine crosses the 'Pack of Cards' bridge at Hin Tok, Thailand, at 4 mph. Drawing by Ewart Escritt from a photograph by engineer Sugano Renichi.

Japanese engineers survey the railway route ahead.

The steel bridge over the Kwai Yai after its reconstruction; photographed by Yoshihiko Futamatsu during a post-war visit.

Railway construction through varied terrain, phographed in 1943.

William Wilder ink-wash drawing of 'Hut interior at Nong Pladuk, Siam,
May 1944'.

Colonel Philip Toosey.

Ink-wash drawings by William Wilder showing (top) hut interior at Nong Pladuk, Thailand, May 1944, with POWs relaxing; (below) general camp scene at Nong Pladuk.

17

Ink-wash drawing by William Wilder showing 'Church at Bukit Timar' camp, 1942.

18

19

Drawing of the Three Pagodas Pass by Ewart Escritt at the time of the Pacific War from a photograph by an unknown photographer.

Post-war photograph of the 'three pagodas' by Yoshihiko Futamatsu.

Photographs of supporting structures showing the method of railway-line construction in different terrains.

The wooden bridge over the Kwai Yai under construction.

Photograph of the wooden bridge over the Kwai Yai with the bombed steel bridge in the background.

Drawing by Ewart Escritt from a (post-war) Ōigawa Line railway
ticket featuring POWs building a wooden bridge across a ravine.

25

Engineer Renichi Sugano on the C5631 in October
1943 – the first locomotive to run over the completed
Thai-Burma Railway

26

Locomotive C5631 at its modern-day site at the Yasukuni Shrine, Tokyo.

From left to right: Yoshihiko Futamatsu, Peter N. Davies, Renichi Sugano, Tokyo, 1990.

not work out. It seems that the prisoners-of-war received intelligence from England itself, and from the outside world they had reports from a pro-British organization's secret manoeuvres, and beginning in 1945 the targets for bombing in the Kanchanaburi area were indicated by partisans. It seemed evident that Japan had no friends.

The Thai usually brag about their country's superiority, their feelings run high, their manner is that of being sticklers for prestige. In weighing up the pros and cons of their behaviour one must record that the educational standards of some of their officials were high but the practice of bribery among them persisted. Because Buddhism is the State religion there are splendid temples within the Palace enclosure, and at national observances there is Buddhist ceremonial. For their year-names they use the Buddhist calendar. The people's enthusiasm for this creed runs deep and because they devote property to Buddha regardless of expense colourful and beautiful temples have been built even as far as remote centres of population in towns and cities. In consequence Buddhist bonzes from ordinary families are revered for discarding this mortal existence and are thought to be of higher status than ordinary mortals. In December 1942 the Banpong police-force and men of 9 Railway Regiments had a discordant incident in which it was alleged that a bonze had had a trivial clash with a soldier.

The Thai are customarily superstitious. They believe the Buddha guards children's heads so that if you touch a child's head with your hand they dislike it. As in Japan Buddhism makes one pray for comfort in a future life, and young people, too, take pleasure in visiting Buddhist temples, and like Japanese they press their palms together before memorial tablets in a Buddhist temple and in the same way have a feeling of being in a family.

Thailand is an agricultural country. A common scene is of neighbours helping to harvest each other's rice-fields which were transplants from communal paddy-fields. The four seasons are not clearly demarcated by climate but both fruits and rice-crops are abundant. Their peasants' life-cycle is meagre compared with that of Japanese farmers. They are sometimes slow in getting down to modern methods, and for ploughing they use water-buffaloes instead of horses or bullocks. Poor children are given to thieving. Propertied people must distribute their goods to the poor, even if poorer people have to steal when they

65

haven't even a single rice-cake they are considered to be no different from those who have given lavish presents. If a man who has stolen something returns it by the New Year the act is not regarded as a crime. They wash their bodies in cold water only. Men and women take cold baths together in ordinary clothes and ingenuously exchange their wet loincloths for dry ones, women exposing their breasts and hips to public gaze, which we found somewhat surprising.

It could be that the lumbering and clearing of trees and shrubs in railway construction land was deemed to be normal private use: accounting for procurement of some tens of thousands of rations, timber and materials for the large numbers of the Japanese construction force certainly had to be made with the main dealers around Banpong and Kanchanaburi. Thailand appeared to not be unwilling to co-operate but co-operation may have stemmed from self-interest in astute use of an unexpected profit.

To the world, Thailand means to the tourist Buddhism, elephants, and plenty of historical ruins. However, most Thai patriots think of the wild forests and mountainous terrain and the penetration, in the towns at least, of a civilized culture; but the inhabitants in the remote regions are not bathed in culture and go on living as they did in antiquity.

At the end of the war Thailand did not benefit as was said to have proposed to the Allies that she had been compelled to ally herself to Japan. But after the war her relations with Japan did not deteriorate and she remained rather friendly. Today, as far as the Burma-Thai Railway is concerned, Japan had left behind her a civilized heritage in Thailand.

Chapter 15

THE RIVER KWAE NOI

Running by the town of Banpong flows this country's second largest river, the Mae Khlaung. In the neighbourhood of the town it is over 100 metres wide. About 50 km upstream from Banpong is the town of Kanchanaburi. The prefectural office is here: in those days it was a small town with a population of 3,000. Near it the Mae Khlaung (also known as the Kwae Yai) has a confluence with another river. On the one hand, the River Kwae Yai flows down without a break from the mountains to the North, on the other, the River Kwae Noi has its source to the north-west in the neighbourhood of the Three Pagodas Pass on the Burmese frontier. The two run a distance of over 250 km and the river-basins' areas are calculated to be respectively 7,000 and 8,000 square km in extent. The river-basins are in mountainous jungle, it is a very rainy area and so in the rainy season there are many flash-floods and, the rivers being narrow upstream the water-level rises four to five metres a day, and at Kanchanaburi in the broad area of the confluence the volume of water rises in a short time, unbelievably, to 300 tons per second: the river widens and the overflow becomes like a gently flowing reservoir. Because the Thai-Burma Railway's route was aimed at the Three Pagodas Pass the River Mae Khlaung had to be crossed. Near the confluence, the river was some hundreds of metres wide at the time but although it was not deep the river-bed was silted up and a river-crossing there would not do, so the railway route planned to cross the Mae Khlaung about 2 km upstream of the Kwae Noi.

The route, having crossed the Kwae Yai, bent round to the left into the Khao Poon area on the bank opposite the confluence. The river then bent round right and the route ran back upstream on the north-west bank of the Kwae Noi. Transportation of commodities was carried out meanwhile by boat from a landing-stage in the river-bank down-stream from Kanchanaburi. The confluence site spread out wide before one's eyes. Reeds on the river-bank grew luxuriantly and the surface of the water spread out extensively like a big pond, and the far bank for some hundred metres faded out into the mist. Here and there dwellings were built out into the water. In the blue sky far above one saw low-lying hills which no doubt took you to the frontier.

On the topographical map from air photographs the Kwae Noi is downstream from the Three Pagodas Pass: it looks like white cloth spread out in the forest and the river twists, now narrow now wide. The reason for making the plan of the route run alongside the left bank of the Kwae Noi was not detailed but in May 1942 at the Bangkok HQ of 2 Railway Control I saw a map of the projected route already decided, together with aerial surveys made alongside the Kwae Noi. Aiming at the Three Pagodas Pass and to the north-west, they had naturally carried the route upstream alongside the Kwae Noi, but the flow of the river would make it difficult to utilize a highway in the rainy season, and so one would have to use small boats for transportation.

The true crossing-point on the Kwae Yai was at a place called Lat Ya on the opposite bank, a level way through forest. It took you to the Kwae Noi and if you continued west about 50 km upstream you came to Thā Sao (today's Namtok). After the war a former prisoner-of-war, Mr Escritt, told me in correspondence in 1977 that the problem is that the route as far as Thā Sao was chosen on the fixed assumption that it should run alongside the left bank of the Kwae Noi. In his opinion, if the route had taken you by the way of Lat Ya, very many prisoner-of-war victims would not have been needed for the Chungkai cutting and the plank-viaduct at Arrow Hill. As it happened, when I paid my first post-war visit to the Thai Burma Railway I went on a sightseeing tour by 'bus from Kanchanaburi to Namtok by way of Lat Ya. I could verify Mr Escritt's choice of route as being possible. However, in the area in those days lorries could barely get through on the highway. Mr Escritt's opinion is not mistaken but unfortunately at the time no

68

topographical map of this area had been drawn up, and both the means of making comparisons and also the time-margin were lacking. The distance would be comparatively curtailed but whether the difficulties of a route running alongside the river would be avoided I do not know, and transportation on the highway in the rainy season becomes difficult: the likelihood of the job being obstructed can be imagined.

The route was selected from the map, details of topography (level surfaces, differences in altitude) recorded, and line-curvatures and gradients planned. The factor of cost limits affecting radius of line-curvatures and gradients and the complex nature of the terrain made difficult any decision about the best plan and one needed to inspect personally the actual lie of the land before coming to a firm decision. This is why the CO of 9 Railway Regiment, Colonel Imai, personally led a recce party to investigate both the Kwae Noi and the route. It meant going upstream from Kanchanaburi by boat.

On 17 August 1942 his recce party, escorted by motorboats, indented for sampans, and set out from the landing-stage on the bank of the Mae Khlaung. I took part in this exercise. At the confluence early morning mists hung over the river-surface. Through the fresh morning breeze came the faint sound of pompom-engines and the small craft began to move against the gentle current. The rainy season was gradually coming to an end but the river-water still had the look of flooding, very muddy and a slimy grey colour. From the bank dwellings could be seen across a water-surface like a wide-spreading lake, and the willows on the banks were washed by the current. In the early morning our gummed-up eyes could dimly make out our mountainous destination. From a dull light purple the hills changed to green. Small craft, which could be seen left and right from both banks as the current accelerated, entered the centre stream of the Kwae Noi. We heard the pleasant sound of the pulsing of the small pompom-engines as they pushed ahead against the current.

The sky cleared well and the massed thickets on each bank showed green: the jungle was opening its stall and heat penetrated down to the surface of the water. Soon on the right bank appeared a rocky crag sticking out like a bone. It was the crag at Chungkai and the line of the railway curved round at the waterside at its foot. In the normal way one would have planned a tunnel at this point. The railway regiment's men had no tunnelling experience so I at once planned a cutting which in the event proved to be 100 metres long, maximum depth 40 metres, and about 10,000 cubic metres of rock had to be excavated. 8 Company of 4 Battalion of 9 Railway Regiment, Tarumoto Unit, were in charge and Australian prisoners of B Group, who had been sent up from Singapore in May 1942, were the labourers on this job. [Mistake by Futamatsu? These men were still in Burma.] The job involved blasting the face of the crag and was very dangerous, and there was no lack of victims, even sick men being forced to come out to work. In the cemetery at Chungkai they left behind some hundreds of crosses. At the Singapore War Crimes Trials after the war Captain Tarumoto Jugi, the Unit CO responsible for the labourers at the time, was unfortunately condemned to life imprisonment for ill-treatment of British, Australian and Dutch prisoners-of-war, an unexpected hardship to endure.

On both banks the jungle gradually grew denser, groups of tall trees towered loftily into the sky, devilishly thick bamboo clumps were entwined together, impossible to get through, and under it all vegetation grew beneath the trees, making a luxuriant growth of thickets. Here and there at the water's edge were sandbanks when there were beds in the river on the far shore. Things resembling human habitations were not actually houses but looked like houses even in this unexplored territory. Bends in the river were repeated so we could not tell were our boats were. The river's width was now broad, now narrow and the current at first gentle now became fast-flowing. From daybreak next day we went against a fast current for some time and consequently covered 30 km out in mid-stream. Out destination was Thā Khanun, over 200 km from Kanchanaburi and it was thought we should need another two or three days afloat.

The object of the recce party was to inspect the lie of the land along the projected railway route and the geological features of actual sites, and at the same time to check the conditions on the Kwae Noi as a means of river transport. We had queries about river-width, volume of water, speed of current, viability of landing-stages, temporary anchoring points, etc., and had also to decide what were the best places for billeting-quarters with queries about how best to assemble a labour unit, drinking water and so on. A labour unit needed to ensure a desirable choice of living conditions and hygiene. In addition to medical officers concerned with prevention of epidemics, engineer officers of the well-digging unit to supplement supplies of drinking water were needed.

The jungle continued on both banks, on and on, and inevitably the men became tired out in the monotony of the boats. The sun began to be submerged in the forest treetops. The boats lost way and neared the bank. This was an area full of clouds of mosquitoes in mid-river, an area in which men's thin blood became infected with malarial bacteria, and so the medical officers judged it safer to draw close in to the bank and make temporary anchorage. There was a beach with white sand where we tied up our boats and sampans. The men had been squatting all day on their haunches, they were tired and stretched themselves out in the boats off shore. At sunset the chill of the water-surface was tempered by the heat radiating from the jungle, and the men were wrapped in a refreshing coolness. The quiet night stole up to the riverside on a Kwae Noi itself wrapped in forest. Inside the mosquito-nets suspended on the boats the sound of wavelets lapping the gunwales was like a lullaby on the *samisen*, the three-stringed guitar, and we spent our first night's boating fast asleep.

At first light our mosquito-nets were very damp from a mist coming on over the river-surface so you could see nothing in the immediate neighbourhood. We washed our faces in river water, recalled urinating on the previous night in the river, realized the comforting thought that rivers went on flowing all night long, and had peace of mind. As the sun rose the mist cleared. From the reed-bed on the far bank a bird like a white heron (an egret) flew up. The river flowed gently, sunlight again appeared and began to sparkle in the green colours of the jungle along the banks. The boatmen warmed up their engines with blow-lamps, the sound of pompoms reverberated over the water and the boats pulled out from the bank.

Turning our bows upstream again we got beyond the forest up to the frontier on the mountain and could see the deep blue sky of the southern countries, cloudless and clear. The bows cut through the surface and with the splash sparkling in the sunlight out came a rainbow. The boatmen sounded the depth of the water whenever they approached the banks, explaining that rain upstream could cause flooding. Curious houses could be seen built out into the water.

The people who lived in them were fishermen who collected rain-water and never drank river-water. When we stopped we never drank river-water either, but made use of the Ishii type of water-pump. Water in an unglazed pottery cylinder was filtered out under high pressure and impurities including germs removed. The system was developed for military use in the field of battle. For drinking-water one then had to boil the filtered water. By loading large-size pumps on rolling-stock one could produce several tons of pure water in an hour. The water-pump was hand operated.

In the gentle flow the river's surface was as still as a mirror in which blue sky and white mist were reflected, but the river narrowed and a fast current swept by the cliffs lining the shore. The water came close up to a sandbar and hugged the edge of a rugged crag, with water-weed surrounding it luxuriantly in shallows lurking at the foot of a big bank, and again the river went on flowing into the far distance. Our boats wove their way as fast as they could upstream in rough water.

At noon that day we came to the place where the survey unit's pennant stood near the landing stage on the river bank. This was the Mōri Survey Unit. A sunburnt 2/Lt Mōri came down to greet us. All his men came from their tent nearby, and if you listened it was a visit long overdue. They took their midday meal with us, and 2/Lt Mōro told us how they lived in the jungle:

Deep in the jungle it is ferociously sultry. In dense thickets you feel as if you had shut the door in a small room. When you stay in the jungle too long you develop a headache. Drifts of fallen leaves make walking difficult, your head and arms keep getting caught in twisted branches, your cap keeps being caught in them, and one's skin gets scratched. We did not encounter any large wild animals but snakes and lizards abounded. We found peahen and pheasant eggs. We catch big embroidered snakes and iguanas and eat them. From time to time we see crocodiles in the river. Centipedes and scorpions abound; as well as these we catch big ants and brown frogs. It's hard to keep direction in this bad jungle terrain, hard to maintain the centre line of the route but each day we have been pushing ahead at a rate of about two or three kilometres.

Colonel Imai his commander was grateful for the work the Survey Unit had put in and encouraged them to take care in their work. Since leaving Kanchanaburi, in setting up the survey task they were in the first place creating a centre line for the railway track and pioneering the job: these men as a body had been getting more and more remote from civilization. With big snakes meandering about in the Kwae Noi it seemed wrong to have selected from a map a route for the railway to run parallel with such a river.

In the afternoon of the third day since leaving Kanchanaburi we approached a high cliff on the North bank. This was the point on the topographical map which was the debatable position described in Chapter 23, the '103 km' point. The lie of the land in this area included another big cliff-face which rose about 50 metres up from the water and continued along for about 200 metres, the wall-face rising perpendicularly, and on top there was a luxuriant growth of trees and shrubs. For a railway route there was no straight alignment which was passable at ground-level. Tunnelling was impossible so I had to plan a direct run half-way up the cliff by means of a plank viaduct. The geological structure of the rock mass would make it necessary to cut out the route, calling for much gunpowder. The Recce party tried to make as little volume of excavation work as possible in keeping the railtrack close to the river, but here there was no avoiding having to build this plank viaduct. In the event, 4 Battalion (Ifuka Unit) were responsible for the job. About 2,000 prisoners-of-war were the labourers on this very difficult task for the six-month period it required. The viaduct survives today, the Arrow-hill viaduct now called Tamakachya, and has been published on a picture-postcard as a souvenir of the Thai-Burma Railway at Namtok.

That evening we made an overnight stop at a very small hamlet called Wanyai and the following day went a little upstream of Wanyai to a point where the river narrowed sharply, flowing between rocky crags on both banks and there were waterfalls down into the river which created rapids. The boatmen uncoupled the sampans from the motor-boats and at full throttle just managed to climb the rapids, and the sampans were salvaged by men hauling on tow ropes from the rocks on the bank. When the river was low it was impossible, the boatmen said, to negotiate the rapids. Later, during the construction work the river could become a bottleneck and accidents occurred at places like this.

There supervened a complete change in the current which became calmer as the river widened out. On the North bank a cliff ran along for about ten metres, which made a splendid spectacle; it stimulated one's imagination in the way in which a marvellously painted forest in full colours does on a beautiful folding screen. Then several waterfalls came into view on the riverbank. The boatmen told us it was called Saiyok after the waterfalls. We made a temporary anchorage for the night at Kinsaiyok (New Saiyok) on a sandbar where the boatmen lengthened the anchor-hauser to reach a hut we had seen on the bank. The anchor-hauser was sunk below the surface, its lower half being invisible. We were surprised to find in the morning that the water-level had risen overnight by over six metres, but the boatmen had predicted floods from rainfalls upstream, took action in good time and were able to prevent damage to the boats.

That afternoon a thing like unbarked lumber passed near the gunwale. The boatmen told us it was a crocodile, was dangerous, and we ought to take care. Later we saw others and anyone who didn't know and went bathing in the river would have a shock. Crocodiles slept on the mud near the riverbank: if you saw a shape that might be one, you treated it with suspicion. Some large birds in the tops of tall trees flew across the river. They were peacocks and they flaunted their long tails as they flew over. They looked like the mythical phoenix-birds drawn in pictures. As our boats rounded a sandbar a peacock was displaying its tail in front of a devil-clump of bamboo on the bank, strutting calmly along accompanied by several short-tailed peahens.

On the fifth day we struggled to our destination, Thā Khanun. We had gone upstream some 200 km. To the river source near the Three Pagodas Pass was a further 100 km. Thā Khanun

was a small population centre of some dozen inhabitants. There was a tungsten mine under government management and some officials were in residence. Tungsten being a heavy ore, it was transported by elephants, two or three small sackfuls being loaded on their backs. The people here are subject to attacks of malaria and the children were pot-bellied from hypertrophy of the liver.

From Thā Khanun to Nikki, the terminus on Thai-side for which our Regiment had charge, was about 70 km. Here the jungle began again, virtually unexplored. The railway's arrival at Thā Khanun was estimated to take so and so many days and again the volume of work had to be forecast. It was expected to be a difficult, heavy task. Our return trip by river to Kanchanaburi took only two days. We were on the river, but the Thai-Burma Railways' construction had to be done on foot along the river-valley, confronting an interior amid forests: it was pressed steadily ahead.

Chapter 16

THE MAE KHLAUNG BRIDGE

The railway route in the Kanchancburi area ran from the crossing point over the River Mae Khlaung in the neighbourhood of Thā Makham near the tributary river, the Kwae Noi. The bridge at the present day on the Namtok Line is called the Kwae Noi bridge, but during the construction period it is correct that it achieved its fame as the 'Mae Khlaung steel bridge' (in Japanese it was called *mekurongawa eikyū kyō*, that is, 'the permanent bridge over the Mae Khlaung', to an engineer meaning a bridge with steel spans and concrete bridge-piers and bridge-abutments). As well as the steel bridge there was another, a wooden bridge, but that was prepared against flood times. The building of the steel bridge is now to be discussed (among prisoners-of-war it was called the Thā Makham bridge).

At the crossing at Thā Makham you had a river 300 metres wide with a water-surface of about 200 metres, and part of the crossing of the water-surface was the steel bridge with its steel trusses and concrete bridge-piers as a precaution against being flashed out by floods. The total length of the bridge was about 300 metres and over part of the water-course eleven spans of 20 metres each made the crossing. The wooden bridge was about 100 metres across with spans of five metres each. The big bridge was the only steel bridge on Thai-side and it was the longest bridge. In 1945 it was bombed and collapsed, but after the war it was repaired and is today's steel bridge on the Namtok Line.

After the war the film *Bridge on the River Kwai* (in Japan called 'The Bridge Built in the Battlefield') was based on the Frenchman Pierre

Boulle's novel and together with the tune of 'the River Kwai march' (actually the military band piece called Colonel Bogey) spread throughout the world the story of the building of the Thai-Burma Railway and of the prisoners-of-war who were the labourers on it. There are many fabrications in the story-line which forms the background of the film and it did not transmit the truth. The film was shot on a river in a forest in Sri Lanka and so it was not the Thai-Burma Railway. That it was re-planned by prisoners-of-war and that the camp commander was a historical person were among things in the film which were not true. We participated in its construction, but also, to a man, former British and American prisoners-of-war protested about the falsehoods in the film when they were given a preview. To cap it all, to say that the bridge was the same as the Thai one is absolute bunk. This is why we participants wish to settle clearly what really happened. Again, in the film is a fictitious report of an infiltrating officer whose job was to blow up the bridge, which is totally untrue of what actually happened on the real Thai-Burma Railway.[104]

In September 1942 the Mae Khlaung bridge was started by 5 Company of 3 Battalion, Fujii Unit, and concurrently 7 Company of 4 Battalion started building a temporary wooden bridge for light trains a hundred metres downstream of the steel bridge. The wooden bridge opened to traffic in January 1943 but the steel bridge, when the bridge-piers were completed, was handed over to Labour Unit (Konnō Unit) of 4 Special Bridging Unit, who carried out the job of setting up the girders. They finished it in April the same year. So, surviving floods in the river, and from time to time being bombed, until in February 1945 when the girders collapsed, the longest bridge stood up to the running of trains.[105]

The bridge construction was planned as a high-standard engineering job. To investigate the geological nature of the ground at the site where the bridge was to be built, a painstaking survey was made by a well-digging machine which 7 Well-digging Company (Yoshida Unit) mounted on a lorry, and with its fine skill completed an investigation of geological factors 20 metres underground in as short a time as one day. To excavate earth and sand from inside the well-cribs dredgers were necessary and Regimental HQ asked me to look for one.

In October 1942 Lieutenant Adams, who had been sent up from Singapore to Banpong, came into Thā Makham camp and was employed on the steel bridge. His memorandum on his job on bridge-girders ran as follows:

The Thā Makham camp on the east side of the river-bank of the Mae Khlaung was about two kilometres from its confluence with its tributary. Our job was to build the 220 metres of the wooden bridge. Our commanding officer in camp was Lt-col Toosey. To us prisoners he came to the camp as an old friend. A Japanese NCO said, 'Nine officers and fourteen ORs equal one elephant in work value', a strange computation in asking for men to work. In Changi officers had not done heavy work so they protested and did not comply. Our quarters were rectangular huts with *atap* thatch supported on thick bamboo poles. They were made with a central passage-way between split-bamboo sleeping places on either side, for each prisoner about two metres from head to foot and one metre wide. The attitude of the Japanese Army camp guards was troublesome and invariably it was the prisoners whom they beat. Outside the camp bamboo fence Thai women came to sell eggs and cakes and so on. Contacts between prisoners and Thai were forbidden and anyone caught doing so was beaten. The egg-selling women's mouths dripped with red betel-juice, but I cannot imagine their counterparts today are quite like that, they are charming and quite glamorous. Eggs were not allowed for prisoners officially but because of them it is a fact that many prisoners were saved from undernourishment.

This camp was reasonable as a place to live in but, to anyone who experienced them, the up-country camps were miserable places. For anyone attempting to escape, scanty rations, inadequate clothing, not knowing the language, and on top of that the different colour of skin ... and when you come to think of it conspicuous differences in shape, too, and also not being familiar with the topography of the several hundred miles to go in enemy territory, and the question of how many days on end one would have to travel after escape, all this made it an extremely difficult thing to contemplate.

Hardly had I arrived at this camp when one night six prisoners escaped from it. Four were recaptured next day and, having signed the written pledge at Singapore, were executed by shooting. Three weeks later the remaining two were taken by the Thai Army and brought back to camp. They were interrogated and, as accomplices of the four men who had been punished, they were bayoneted to death out in the jungle.

Each individual passed his daily chore doing various coolie jobs. From Changi they had transported the broken-down components of a radio set, reassembled it and secretly listened to broadcasts from New Delhi.

The work of driving-in the bridge-piers of the wooden bridge by means of a plum-bob was a primitive sort of engineering system. By man-power prisoners pulled up the heavy plumb-bob which they 'fished' for, then let drop. In what the Japanese called 'yo-heave-ho' work we heaved on the rope, obeying the call of the Japanese soldier in charge, *Ichi ni no san yo*, all pulling together in unison. For the first time I learned that Japanese pulled, not pushed, a saw. A Japanese soldier I talked to found it hard to believe that a butcher – not a very splendid trade in Japan – could be made a lieutenant.

By February 1943 the wooden bridge was finished and a light tractor-train crossed the Kwae Yai for the first time. Continuing, the job of laying the foundations of the bridge-piers of the Mae Khlaung steel bridge was begun, under Lieutenant Fujii, commander of 5 Company. To lay the foundations of the concrete well-cribs in mid-stream, small islands were made as a temporary footing and on top of these the well-crib cement was poured. We worked all day transporting sand, using pebbles with it to make cement. It was a dull job so we amused ourselves by mental arithmetic problems and spelling competitions, tried on jokes and developed arguments.

Each day the heat reached 30° in day-time. Rations were liable to be deficient, the physical strength of the prisoners was exhausted, and in rest-periods (*yasumi*) they lay down and slept. The Japanese soldiers were tougher physically than the prisoners and whether there is a difference in orientals' physical condition I do not know. We had a rest-day every nine days. We kept back and saved up a little of each day's ration and enjoyed our food on rest-days, but on full stomachs yearned for the opposite sex. Prisoners were afflicted by bed-bugs. The myriad weevils were mixed in with the cooked rice. Our medical officers joked that they were a source of protein. One day I was taken by a guard to Banpong and had the unusual experience of spending my rest-time in a coffee-booth. The patronne treated me to delicious fried rice and a yellow-robed bonze gave me a banana. The Banpong people were kind. A Japanese journalist came up to me and we talked about the real state of affairs in the life of the prisoners-of-war, but he said, 'All the same I can't report this' and that what I had said was 'a great pity'.

From the camp at Thā Makham, beyond the Kwae Noi, could be seen the hill-ranges at the Thai-Burma frontier over the far bank to the West above the jungle. The hills made us think of those in our own countries to which we hoped soon to return and trusted that would not be too far away. The way the war was then going was such that we could not be optimistic and we doubted whether countries we thought could be our allies would prove reliable.

In March we heard that the railway's completion was to be accelerated. To augment the workforce, prisoners were being sent up from Singapore, coolies from the southern region were assembled and successively moved into the outback. Each prisoner carried his own baggage on his shoulder. They tramped on in the rain without speaking a word.

A new company commander at Thā Makham took up his duties. The bridge-piers were completed and putting up the steel girders began. The new man had the look of a gangster and we nicknamed him Edward G and his serjeant, more genial, was Jack Oakie, but his corporal was an ill-tempered Black Demon.

In April 1943 the steel bridge was completed and the first train pulled by an engine crossed the Kwae Yai over it and on into the outback. Consequent on the completion of the bridge the railtrack got as far as Wanyai, and Thai-side construction soon achieved its first objective in reaching the Three Pagodas Pass, leaving 150 km still to do. From 1944 bridges were often bombed, and on 13 February 1945 USAAF Liberator B24s made a bombing attack which brought down into the river the three trusses of numbers 4, 5 and 6 spans, the bridge being rendered completely useless. After the war in 1947 and 1948 much of this collapse was repaired as reparations by our Yokogawa Bridge

Company, who made the two 30-metre-span trusses with which the repair was effected.

In February 1971 I had the opportunity of visiting the railway. It was already the dry season in Thailand and there was not much water in the Kwae Noi. I stood on the approach to the bridge and in the placid flow the deep green of the jungle was reflected on both banks, and over the far distant mountain-range at the frontier white clouds welled up. The shapes of what I had longed to see were there at this spot and the Mae Khlaung bridge could be imagined as it was during construction. With infinite deep emotion I recalled the day when I had stood together with my commander, Colonel Imai, on the waterfront. Both bridge-piers and girders seemed much the same as in those days but on the rails were machine-gun bullet-holes. At this moment a Namtok Line train, pulled by a diesel-engine, crossed the bridge. In my memory the sounds of rail traffic as of old were brought back to me after thirty-five years.

Chapter 17

KANCHANABURI

The route of the Thai-Burma Railway started from Nong Pladuk, a very small village, ran though the northern suburbs of Banpong, then along the highway to Kanchanaburi, reaching it by way of the villages of Lookgae, Thāruanoi, Thāmoan and others. Kanchanaburi is a town sited alongside the North bank of the river about 50 km upstream from Banpong. Its population was about 3,000. The prefectural office was in a row of houses along the North bank. West of the town the prefectural boundary followed the course of the Mae Khlaung and became mountainous forest. Today it is the key point for tourists at the confluence of the Kwae Yai and the Kwae Noi. In the 1940s it was especially important to the railway construction unit, 9 Railway Regiment, and together with Banpong became the pivotal point in the construction. On Thai-side Sakamoto Unit as advance party came into the town and in early August set up their HQ.

The town was a centre for collecting and distributing commodities and for timber and ores from the mountainous outback: it was also a collecting point for commodities from over the Burma border ... including smuggled goods. Because it relied on the Mae Khlaung for the transport of commodities the wharves on the river-front had become the centre of this small town. From antiquity Thailand had been prepared for invasion by the Burmese, and as a form of base defence work there was preserved a stone castle-gate in front of the prefectural office. The town was always called Kamburi for short by both

Japanese soldiers and prisoners-of-war, and they called the castle-gate the 'Gateway to Kamburi', and it became the point they looked for as a guide-post to the street. There was a paper-factory with bamboo as the raw material: it had a tall chimney. On the highway to Kamburi it made a good sighting-point from a distance.

On the North side of the broad highway in the town is a wide grassy meadow. The railway halt was planned at its northern edge. The quarters of the railway engineers had been built on it. The HQ of Sakamoto Unit, as they were the first to enter the town, was in requisitioned private houses along the western edge of the meadow. *Atap* was in abundant production near the houses, for the high floored Thai-style dwellings. Immediately after entering the town Sakamoto with his interpreter Chikawa called on the prefectural governor to greet him. Their relaxed ordinary turnout, for calling on a defence government office, was looked at askance, and a message came through that the governor was not at home and could not meet them. They changed into full dress, stuck their medals on, and called again. Thai-officials are particular about dignity and appearance. However, the governor was pleased with the visit and kindly invited the unit's officers to a meal. That day the officers put on their stiflingly-hot uniforms and proceeded to the governor's residence. The dinner-party took place in a lofty corridor in the front part of the residence and figured mats were spread on the floor. The officers squatted just as they were with their boots on. The prefectural officials wore their white summer uniforms and they, too, squatted on the mats. The cuisine gave out a strong aroma of spices and luscious meats and vegetables broiled in oil. We had no interpreters to sit individually with us, we just sat opposite our hosts and ate and drank. The officials' ladies in their best dresses familiarly received us with rice wine. They wore multi-coloured loincloths over their white tunics and were charming with their full busts and make-up: they were barefooted and quite wonderful.

From the wharf a row of shops in the market-place made it a lively, bustling scene. That the troops marched into town on foot was perhaps strange to the inhabitants but we had been welcomed in a friendly manner. On the meadow one after another *atap*-thatched huts were set up, the unit assembled and one saw Japanese soldiers all over the town.

The sudden increase in population livened up the town and it began to look more like a construction base. A Japanese military mess-room and common-room were put up. Sakamoto Unit's mess-room opened for business in a corner of the meadow. There was a pretty girl in the canteen who was popular with the younger soldiers. In the canteen the soldiers enjoyed the tastes of their homeland in rice-cakes broiled with vegetables and in soups. The sun set behind the mountains in the West and a cool breeze would sweep across the meadow. Squatting on the grass we sat up late in the evening talking about home and this and that; these times made for us congenial interludes, forgetting we had ever come to war. The constellation of the Big Dipper was high above us, then the Southern Cross began to rise above the horizon. Southern nights then grew cool, and we went to sleep to the cries of the tokay (a large gecko found in the area), to generate energy for tomorrow's wartime activities. Soon the troops would have to endure the rain as well as the heat of this mountainous region, and to experience the hard labour of railway construction work and master it as best they could – no one imagined that a year later this town would be in the front-line with enemy air-raids.

In September the railway was opened to traffic and with it came the sound of engines' steam-whistles in the town.

In 1977 when thirty-odd years had elapsed after the war, I revisited the town's streets. The paper-factory chimney which one could see from afar had disappeared and the rows of houses along the roads seemed completely changed. Of the unit's HQ and living quarters on the meadow there was no trace but there were crowded shops and houses. Along the south side of the highroad, Kamburi had become the final resting-place of the Allied campaigners who were buried there, several thousand gravestones being set in orderly rows in the grass. The old railtrack was there as before but a small station-building had been put up. The prefectural and municipal officers were in new premises but the Gateway to Kanchanaburi was still there. From the wharf the paddy-ridges along the river were unchanged, the mountains upstream were in a purple haze and the river flowed quietly on as it did in those wartime days. I closed my eyes and a scene swam into view of the pennants I remembered fluttering in the breeze, the pennants at the mast-heads of the fleet of little boats we had assembled, and I could hear the reverberation of the pompom-engined craft. In the silence of the wharf there came into view ghosts of men I remembered, and two or three little boats slowly made their way upstream. People who knew the town in construction days would know what I mean. It was as if time had stood still.

Chapter 18

THE JUNGLE

Upcountry from Kamburi the same highway ran from Thā Makham for seven or eight kilometres, crossing the river West of the town. It was a narrow road with an uneven surface, and in heavy rain one got muddy and vehicles had difficulty in passing each other. The engineers repaired it as best they could because it was the overland route for lorry transport. Local inhabitants drove narrow-axled bullock-carts with wheels of large diameter, and these could move in the mud on the road surface. When the road was repaired the engineers commandeered a number of bullock-carts to transport rations and materials. A single bullock-cart load was not much, and the cart being slow it took a week for a load of rice to arrive at its destination: and because the herdsman carried a load of rice as fodder for the bullock, people said the rice delivered was half what it should have been. The way over the unfinished bridge was made of heavy slats made of bamboo. When the river was in flood they sank below the surface so that often in the rainy season there was no transit. In fact, movement of goods by road ceased and in the strong current of the Kwae Noi transport by small boats was the only way, and in September, when trains first ran as far as Kamburi, transport of materials and rations was achieved by loading them into sampans hauled by pompom-powered motorboats.

In the jungle forest the engineers' and the prisoners' quarters were tents from which the prisoners marched out daily to the work sites. We selected for these quarters well-drained spots, felled trees and shrubs, made clearings, and in no time at all tents became our mode of living.

In the undergrowth of dense forest we survived in the jungle, for cover collecting branches from the tall trees and it all made a strange sight. We mowed down the undergrowth and within a day or so weeds of which I didn't know the names lay buried in the ground.

A day in the jungle: first the rays of the morning sun began to sparkle and dazzle on the leaves of the trees and shrubs. Cicadas sang with their customary vigour. With the heat the damp ground grew hotter, the fragrance of the grass was stifling and even if you didn't move sweat poured out. The temperature soon rose to over 30° and every movement tormented you. In the jungle snakes and scorpions kept frightening you, tiny insects flew around, big ants kept nipping you, and we found it distressing. There was no protection for the prisoners from mosquito-bites and they were always faced by the risk of infection. On the ground leaf-mould collected and it was surprising how quickly, in vegetable gardens which the men made, small seedlings grew, to grace our dining-tables. The engineers caught many fish in the Kwae Noi, which gave us an additional source of protein. Roast peacock flesh and parakeet mixed with rice, pumpkins and so on made the engineers' meals quite rich. We gradually became accustomed to life in the midst of the resources of this dense forest. It was a remarkable experience and was evidence that man can adapt to such circumstances.

On Thai-side, 9 Railway Regiment's 1 Battalion led off the survey, 3 Battalion handled labour on the Mae Khlaung, 4 Battalion were busy excavating the Chungkai cutting and began the roadbed for the plank viaducts at 103 and 109 km, and regimental HQ was advanced to Kamburi. On Burma-side, too, from the end of June 5 railway Regiment inaugurated their survey of the route, and both 1 Battalion and 2 battalion, from their base at Thanbyusayat moved ahead on roadbed construction.

In October, on Thai-side, Sakamoto Unit advanced their HQ 125 km from Banpong to Wanyai and the survey unit meanwhile pushed on further westward from Wanyai. Prisoner-of-war camps in Thailand were now established at Wanyai as a branch of the administration to control them. 42 Supply Unit set up a supply base there and, until the line was opened to traffic, supported an infantry unit facing a potential battle-line on into Burma across the Three Pagodas Pass. In November, Main Southern Army officially announced the Thai-Burma Rail Link

Line, and in Bangkok 2 Railway Control became the HQ of Thai-Burma railway construction. Major-general Shimoda Senriki took up post as C-in-C, and arranged for the directional command of the construction.

In the midst of deep jungle the powerful din of railway construction echoed day and night.

Chapter 19

FROM BANGKOK TO SINGAPORE

On 1 October 1942 work started on the Mae Khlaung steel bridge. The foundations of the bridge-piers were laid as concreted well-cribs, and for excavating the hard, tough river-bottom apparatus was needed, apparatus called a Gatmel dredger. Under water on the river-bottom the sharp edges of its blades bored into and pulled up the foundation, the edges of the bades closed up, bored into the earth and sand, gripped the load and carried it up: such was its mechanism. But at the time a Gatmel could not be found in Thailand. On 1 November I was specially assigned by 9 Railway Regiment HQ to search for one. The official order ran, 'Railway Official Futamatsu to go on a business trip to Malaya and Singapore to collect under-water dredging apparatus. Sjt Nagata and Superior Private Yasawa to be attached to him.' That term 'to be attached' meant that regular soldiers must cooperate with a *gunzoku* without supervision. 'Attached' to me were Sjt Nagata in charge of machine parts and Superior Private Yasawa as orderly. Out party left for Malaya, leaving Sakamoto Unit at Wanyai.

When we got to Banpong we found the Southern Thai National Line was impassable to the East of Nakhon Chaisiri on account of flooding of the River Menam. We stood by waiting for two or three days until a steamer became available for Bangkok from Nakhon Chaisiri, so we got to Bangkok despite being unable to go by train directly to it. All you could see was what looked like a lake and of course the railway line was under water. In the South Thailand plain here and there you could see coconut palms and the roofs of houses apparently floating on the water. The wide surface of the muddy water at the peak of these hot days glittered in the sunlight, and ripples gathered over the railway line embankment. At a wharf near the station a small roofed steamer was waiting for people arriving by train. Women farm-workers carrying vegetables, business-like Chinese, yellow-robed bonzes and so on, a miscellany of common people crowded onto the upper deck of the ship which quivered and shook as it moved away from the wharf. The sound of the ship's siren carried over the surface of the water, the branches of the willows at the water's edge were dimly reflected in the muddy water. Ducks swam across the bows of the ship. I could not tell where the waterway was but the ship's captain skilfully took the helm looking for it. The Menam flooded the plain for two hours and our ship set out in a strong current. When we had passed beyond the railway bridges a large Buddhist pagoda could be seen ahead. As we approached the main stream of the Menam the colour of the water changed. In Thai, *menam* means 'Mother of the Waters' and the annual flood onto the plain naturally puts new soil onto the fields and makes them fertile. Going down on the main river, when we had gone under the Rama VI bridge in Bangkok, we encountered successively some barges, a motorboat, a freight-carrier, even a fishing-boat with sails, and then a sampan which went past a ferry, packed with people, which wove its way through the many little craft while our own boat meanwhile hove to at a wharf on the bank opposite Thonburi. The Traveller's Tree in the forecourt of the Oriental Hotel, which is near the wharf, shook its broad leaves in the breeze, and one could see resident visitors sitting on the benches on the lawn. There was a kind of stillness here floating on the water, a stillness giving no indication at all that there was a war on. As we landed, town noises floated up and to us who had just come from the dense forest at Wanyai the smells of the town had lapped the shore as we drew near it. We rode in *samlor* (three-wheeled tricycle cabs) which accosted us at the foot of a supply-inn on the darkened street.

We had to wait for a ship out of Bangkok due for Malaya and so spent several days in the city. When we had entered it the water in the Menam still bore traces of what looked like flooding. To let lighters pass the bridges there was a canal entered through a bridge high enough for minor craft to pass. Over some gate-posts on top of the bridge it was beautiful because there were Bougainvillaea flowers blooming. There were green lawns in the forecourts and the buildings had been plastered a cool white. In the streets were lovely rows of trees. The residence steps upstream in Bangkok were clean and tidy but over on the opposite bank were squalid, dirty backstreets. It was a town with extremes of poverty and wealth. The temples and pagodas with which the royal palace is surrounded, the magnificent royal palace itself, one of dream-like beauty, and the many-windowed big dome of the central railway station, architecturally, make this country's history and Buddhist tradition both modern and civilized, a unique scene of towns and cities revealing a mixture of the ancient and the new.

Within the city were markets of diverse price-ranges. In them, vegetables, meats, various groceries and miscellaneous goods were on sale. There were many sorts of vegetables and one could find almost any sort one finds in Japan. There were bean-curd and even devil's tongue starch paste. Of fruit, the main things were bananas and papayas and, from January onwards, juicy water-melons, were on sale. In season, durians, mangoes, mangosteens, rambutans and so on with their brilliant tints, greens, reds and yellows, stimulated the appetite. There were many miscellaneous goods and daily necessities made in Japan. In those days, Thai goods could be bought at the exchange rate of one *baht* (we used the colloquial *tical*) to one Japanese yen. As examples of prices, 10 cigarettes cost 5 *sen* (100th of a *baht*), a cake of soap 10 *sen*, a cup of coffee 10 *sen*, 100 kg uncooked rice 20 *baht*. And the country's speciality, ivory pipes, could be bought for 10 *baht* each. The sound of steam-whistles of ships plying on the Menam could be heard from the markets, floating faintly on the evening breeze, the reflection of the Temple of Dawn on the far bank shone on the river surface and evening tints came to a sky dyed red over Bangkok.

On 28 November I embarked at Bangkok on the *Balaya*, a Norwegian steamer bound for Malaya. It was a year and a half after my home unit, the bridging unit, had been stationed in Malaya. The ship steamed South to the Gulf of Siam, the weather turned nasty, and with her long 1000-tonne hull she kept on rocking. However, with the night-wind cool on the upper deck we were in the mood to enjoy the voyage thoroughly. On the evening of the second day came a sudden order to heave to, and the ship stopped. An enemy submarine had been sighted, the ship was in an uproar, but we were relieved when the crew were ordered back to normal stations. In the afternoon of the third day we dropped anchor off Singora in Thailand. This was the site of the battle when our Army had landed in the face of the enemy the previous December. Facing us could be seen white-capped waves breaking on a shore backed by coconut palms about a kilometre away. In a lighter moving towards the shore, with a sand-bar and a gale blowing against us carrying the spindrift of the breakers, one realized how difficult it must have been to effect a landing in the face of the enemy. There were the white-cap waves on the shore, the blinding sunlight shone down, the tops of the coconut palms shook in the wind.

We travelled on a Malayan Railways Line train by way of Hat Yai, and the following day arrived at the HQ of Narisawa Unit, the bridging unit, at Ipoh. It was 1 December. We did not have to change trains here and I got together with old friends I had not seen for some time and we exchanged much talk about things forgotten. The Unit had been restoring railway bridges in various parts of Malaya. The same day I was back on the train for Singapore. At Kuala Lumpur the Chief Civil Commissioner, Kasai, got into our carriage. Alas, on 30 December he was killed in an aircrash at Kallang airfield when setting out for Sumatra, where Sumatran Railways were being constructed.

On arrival at Singapore I presented myself at 7 District Army HQ. In the staff officers' room, which had a sweeping view over the former Singapore Fortress, Fort Caning, now the civilian administration centre for Singapore Harbour, I met the Staff Officer i/c railways. He kindly showed me a Gatmel dredger on a dredger-ship in the bay. On a quick inspection it proved unsuitable, because excavating well-crib foundations needed a larger size of dredger. At the time Kasaya, a civilian administrator who held office in 25 Army Military government, helped me and daily we hunted inside and outside the city for a suitable machine.

A year after the occupation of Singapore the disruption caused by it seemed to have been overcome. The Ford Factory which had been the meeting-place for the parley between General Yamashita and General Percival was preserved in commemoration, commemorated also was our troops' stern battle, in the Shōnan Shrine, erected as a monument to the dead. The manager of Raffles Hotel had been unearthed. There it still stood with its green arbour in the town, rescued from the havoc of war. A reminder of the British colony which had been developed by the East India Company, it now became the official central supply unit. There, too, were those visible signs of former British control: St Andrew's Cathedral, Orchard Road, Connaught Drive, Raffles Place. They formed a spectacle which was in character with the town. The British had been proud of the dignified look of the towns and cities, the main thing remembered in the southern countries. From Swiss Bridge built in the archipelago in the West in the heart of the commercial centre lived the overseas Chinese merchants. Singapore Station near the old Keppel Harbour was re-named Shōnan Halt, and every day tourist trains came and went. Keppel Harbour became Shōnan Harbour and many transports, naval craft and warships called in every day. The barracks of the former British garrison at Changi became the camp for the numerous prisoners-of-war taken at Singapore.

I looked for Gatmels as far as a tin-mine near Kuala Lumpur but up to the end of December all that Civil Commissioner Kasaya and Serjeant Osada found were unsuitable. Then I received a telegram, 'Gatmel in Bangkok come', a very surprising telegram. We had been unable to find one in Bangkok, I had been ordered to look for one elsewhere, months in Bangkok, months in Malaya and Singapore on my vain trip to find one, to me the telegram came as a blessing, a very popular piece of news and an unexpected opportunity.

On 31 December I came back to Kamburi after a sixty-day absence. The Southern Cross could be seen in the evening sky in the southern countries and I recollected in my mind my own homeland. Together with Lieutenant Hijikata, paymaster of Sakamoto Unit, I rang out the Old Year, in my war travels greeting a New Year for the second time.

Chapter 20

RUSH-CONSTRUCTION

On 1 January 1943, at Sakamoto Unit HQ at Wanyai we decorated our billets with the *shichi-go-san* (7–5-3, lucky numbers) ornaments, but in bamboo only, for New Year's Pine & Bamboo, and on a Thai-Burma site celebrated the New Year with *mochi* (rice balls) made with Thai rice. In the midst of the jungle with the heat making one sweat, a hot New Year, no one was able to feel quite the full New Year spirit. We prayed for our homeland's prosperity and when we had completed the formal ceremony of bowing from afar to the Imperial Palace, many of the troops took a siesta and listened to the shrilling of the cicadas. Officers and men wondered for how many months they would be living the jungle life, bathing every day in the Kwae Noi, and bit-by-bit becoming used to enduring the heat, the dangers, the coarse food and clothing ... all this was what their sense of duty led them to accept in this job.

After the previous November when the order to construct this railway was formally promulgated, the Construction Unit HQ also inaugurated it, and the GOC, Shimoda, also held an inspection of the current circumstances. Already from September the previous year trains had been running between Nong Pladuk and Kamburi, but the roadbed West of the Mae Khlaung bridge, together with work on the Chungkai cutting and the plank viaduct at points 103 and 109 km, and also the building of the bridge over the Mae Khlaung not having been completed, the situation was that the temporary wooden bridge was said to be nearing completion. The van of the Thai-side's Survey

Unit was nearing Thā Khanun, but the embankment for the centre-line had not as yet reached Kinsaiyok. On the other side, the survey in Burma had got as far as Nikki in November, but the roadbed had only reached Thanbyusayat. Engineering had been planned to take one or two months until the end of the year, but the volume of work on Thai-side which remained to be done, together with that on Burma-side, added up to over two-thirds of the total volume of work. In the circumstances there was some progress: how far a forecast could be made of its completion seemed impossible to conjecture, and at Construction Unit HQ, too, they were worried and impatient.

At both the Nong Pladuk and the Thanbyusayat bases rails and other materials were steadily being stockpiled. On both Malayan Railways and Burma Railways the work of removing rails accelerated and these two lines co-operated in stockpiling rails for our railway. Sleepers and girders were stockpiled and lumbering of timber, etc. went on vigorously, and gravel for roadbed use and logs for firewood as fuel were also gradually stockpiled in preparation.

In December of the previous year, after we had begun to use the underwater excavator when building the Mae Khlaung bridge, the work went ahead at a normal pace. The task of constructing this railway depended entirely on the conditions of the terrain on the spot, terrain not adaptable to the use of machinery. Our Army made no preparations for using earth-working machinery, and in building the roadbed we depended entirely on a labour force and so calculations of work-volume were wholly based on that and the period needed in turn was also so based. Nucleus of personnel were the military, and a large number of prisoners-of-war became the labour force: from such calculations it was clear that the work volume could not be squeezed into one year. Both HQ and the two regiments recognized how difficult it was to forecast the time-limit for completion of the job, and they began to feel anxious and uneasy.

At the very time when such a crisis existed, an order reached us *gunzoku* to be reinstated in our home bridging unit. It was believed to be for repatriation to Japan. We were happy to be scheduled for repatriation, but in our confused mental attitudes we felt loath to part, as engineers, from our railway engineering job. However, on 4 January our attachment to Sakamoto Unit came through at Wanyai. From the wharf there our small craft set out in midstream with their engines reverberating across the easy-flowing current of the Kwae Noi. Of the many recollections of my familiarity with the river, from the opposite bank amid the reeds a white egret flew up. In my mind's eye, setting out from the jetty by the wharf, come the forms of officers and men of Sakamoto Unit ...then they fade away. The January sky cleared up on both banks of the jungle: I recall regretting I had to be separated from it all, and in my mind's eye my little boat when downriver, going on and on indefinitely. I prayed we might finish the railway one day soon. In the end it took a further three months but I had not imagined even in a dream that I should twice have to endure having to live in this jungle.

Although we greeted the New Year in the second year of the Great East Asia War, there was no sign of any favourable turn in the war situation right into mid-January. Brilliant victories at the outset of hostilities made our people happy but these victories were accompanied by a widening battle-front, by lines of communication stretching far behind the front line, and it became more difficult to keep up our strategic success. Besides, the Allied Forces' counter-offensive campaign was beginning to become more effective, their recovery of command of sea and air covered the areas of resources we had occupied, and in the campaign area it became difficult to transport resources.

Burma had also been under the former oppression of British control. Our Burma Expeditionary Force planned their attack on India but its success depended on a seaborne supply-line by way of the Andaman Sea. But now our fleet's naval strength in the Pacific had no reserve force to ward off attacks by the British Eastern Fleet from bases in India and Ceylon, and the seaborne route to Burma looked like receiving attacks by enemy submarines. The British-Indian Allied Forces planned to re-capture Burma, pushed on from Calcutta as far as Imphal, and in their support USAAF bombers penetrated into Thailand as far as Bangkok. Our Burma Expeditionary Force's overland supply-route came under air observation during the railway's construction in Thailand.

In mid-January 1943, the railway staff officer of 7 Region Army who had been posted to the South was unexpectedly summoned by *Dai-honéi* (IJA GHQ in Tokyo) and ordered to describe the present state of affairs of railway construction. IJA GHQ heard also a sitrep report from the chief staff officer, Eastern Affairs, and ordered the railway to be completed in May of the current year. The railway staff officer was appalled at this reckless command and explained what at the time was the volume of work still to be done, and he stressed its difficult nature and a three-month postponement, which meant in the end an order for completion at the end of August, was accepted. At the time in January one doubted whether one could possibly conjecture that the volume of work could be digested in a year, and people thought it impossible to achieve in about eight months. IJA GHQ's requirement depended on their investigation in depth in 1939 that 'this can be done in one year by two railway regiments', on the face of it an authoritative judgement, but in reality an unreasonable one. So far as battle-action is concerned, when enemy forces attack with superior power, even if we Japanese are numerically inferior the impossible becomes possible depending on strength of mental spirit. However, in the actual struggle of railway construction, to digest the planned work-volume there was no way for 'the possible' to be achieved. In a matter like this, detailed attention to technicalities and calculations is necessary. The result of our struggle to achieve the unreasonable actualities of IJA GHQ's strategical needs was to cause many victims, and we ended up with an imperfectly-constructed railway with no prospect of maintaining transportation viability. On top of that, too, it got its bad name as 'the railroad of death', with the many victims at the War Crimes Trials.

Main Southern Army accepted this demand for rush-construction as an Imperial command and so Major-General Shimoda, C-in-C of the Thai-Burma Railway construction units, immediately passed on the order to his subordinates, Colonel Sasaki, commanding 5 Railway Regiment, and Colonel Imai, commanding 9 Railway Regiment. When they heard the order their subordinate officers were astonished at such a reckless command and one after another stressed how impossible it was. The two regimental commanders now had to plan completion by August, relying on Southern Army's support. Augmenting the labour force and supplying the requisite materials, etc. were immediately fixed up. The Southern Army commander especially urged on the two regimental commanders, and both men, in their heavy and tragic responsibility, hardened their determination on receiving their orders from HQ in Singapore.

The two commanders, having been ordered to complete the railway in a hurry pitched into the arrangements necessary for *kyūsoku kensetsu*, (rush-construction). On Thai-side, 4 Special Railway Unit, who had been stationed in Malaya, were brought in to help, and on Burma-side 5 railway Regiment's 4 Battalion, who had been stationed further East, were brought in. An extra engineer unit, a signals unit, a service unit, etc. came in and a supply unit and a field hospital had to be added. At the same time the working boundaries between the Thailand 9 Regiment and the Burma 5 Regiment were reapportioned to a point 250 km from Nong Pladuk, which meant that on Thai-side the stint was increased by 30 km. To augment the labour force another batch of prisoners was sent up from Singapore, about 10,000 being drafted into Thailand. Coolies were also recruited, mainly Malayan and Burmese, with the co-operation of the two military governments, and so were semi-compulsorily conscripted. 2 Railway Control, HQ of the construction units, moved their HQ up to Kamburi. At the same time, 9 Railway Regiment's HQ was fixed at Wanyai and 5 Railway Regiment's HQ advanced to Thāzun.

By the end of January the various arrangements for rush-construction were in hand and some idea of the speed this kind of work required had begun to make headway. At this moment on Burma-side the C-in-C, Major-General Shimoda Senriki, on a recce to inspect conditions in a medium-sized bomber-plane, encountered some obstacle in the mountains in jungle south-west of the Three Pagodas Pass and his plane crashed.[106] The C-in-C was accompanied by Staff Officer Major Irie. Together they died on duty, a noble human sacrifice of rush-construction. Major-General Takasaki, at the time in Manchuria, was officially announced as Shimoda's successor.

In mid-February, Colonel Imai paid an unexpected visit to the bridging unit HQ at Ipoh in Malaya. The unit had had their repatriation withdrawn when the order came that they were to take part in the Thai-Burma Railway construction. They had completed their job of restoring bridges on Malayan Railways at the close of the previous year. The bridge over the River Krian was virtually finished, and shortly afterwards they were attached to 7 District Army and had been standing by waiting for repatriation. When the rumour spread round the unit that repatriation apparently would have to be withdrawn they were amazed and disappointed. Not only that but they learned their new job would entail entering the Thai-Burma jungle. In their inmost hearts they could not conceal their displeasure and anxiety, could not settle down, were confused. I, too, had previously had to dismiss hopes of repatriation with not a little dissatisfaction. However, after my experiences of upwards of a year since the war began, I had come to recognize that a military man could not protest in the face of an order, and had abandoned any idea of refusal.

Through his second-in-command, Colonel Narisawa, Colonel Imai explained the setup of the construction and the unit was told about the considerable complications created by recent acceptance of IJA GHQ's order for rush-construction. The bridge-building techniques of the unit were highly valued and he asked for their co-operation. Colonel Imai had said. 'I received from HE Count Terauchi Hisaichi, the C-in-C, in Singapore, his quietly worded order ... 'Be so good as to accept my request'.' Colonel Narisawa said that Colonel Imai expected his Regiment to help the C-in-C's determination to build up the rush-construction spirit. The bridging unit had already given up hopes of repatriation, he told them, and had not opposed this second return to the battle-field, and the *gunzoku* sent by Railway Control had renewed their patriotic determination. We agreed that the Colonel genuinely understood our distress and that in the end we had to accept a heartless order. We *gunzoku* had no doubt it was our duty to co-operate with the Regiment.

The bridging unit were now separated from their commander, Colonel Narisawa and a new *gunzoku* formation was set up under command of Major Murahashi, under command of Colonel Imai. I was allotted to take the duty of personal adviser to Colonel Imai. In March 1943 my old friends from Malaya, the former Murahashi Unit, had arrived at Wanyai HQ by way of Banpong and Kamburi. It was 10 March.

Chapter 21

THE BASE AT WANYAI

It was not until March that the rainy season began to end. Daily squalls became shorter and because there was no heavy rain it was low water in the River Kwae Noi. Even the water running down from small mountain streams dried up. The temperature fell morning and evening, and at night before dawn the warmth of a blazing bonfire felt good to us. It felt like Autumn in Japan. However, as the sun climbed so did the temperature, and the atmosphere grew dry as in a hot midsummer with us. As the day proceeded the cold and the night-dew ceased, but our 'bedroom', the mosquito-net, got damper and damper before dawn. The changes from Autumn to Summer and from Summer to Autumn were like daily seasonal changes and we had difficulty in getting used to them. From the year before the Japanese unit billets had become extensive and presented a lively scene. On Thai-side the jungle was cut back and cleared for 9 Regiment's HQ and a level clearing created, the buildings being mainly of timber and appropriately thatched with *atap*.

Okamoto Unit had a change of command, becoming Imanaka Unit. Under Lt-Col. Imanaka the Unit advanced to Thā Khanun. At Wanyai, the base for rush-construction was consolidated bit-by-bit: for this central HQ each unit had been building numerous billets and godowns for storing machine parts and provisions. Meanwhile the new earth works, on which the line had opened to traffic in the previous Autumn, were completed and the highway from Kamburi took one-way traffic. Lorries loaded with food and fodder for the engineers, coolies and prisoners came up and down the road, and cars loaded with supplies and machinery came and went one after another. Everyone's work in the jungle depths grew busily active and overflowed with live-liness. Thus there was a deep Spring flavour, it seemed, about rush-construction in the jungle. On a newly-erected gatepost a sign-board was hung out, written in *sumi* with bold brush strokes, saying, 'Imai Unit HQ', and within the gate a guardroom was proudly set up. Out-side the gate could be seen prisoner-of-war huts of the Wanyai Group, *atap*-thatched and surrounded by trees and shrubs, and prisoners could be seen going about their work. The *atap*-thatched huts had open walls with big openings. Luxurious jungle growth kept pushing nearer in, and a kind of vine, of what sort I do not know, twined round in snake-like coils, making tree-trunks lumpy and dark, its leaves deep green. Trees and a broad-leaved shrub like cactus made a strange enclosure in jungle surroundings on which strong sun beat down. It was a hot, stag-nant, gloomy atmosphere. When rain fell, green jungle looked brilliant and lively, but wet rain make one rush indoors, ending up by making clothes and matting damp. At night, it was cold, and with the cold came mosquitoes which breed in the jungle, and they got inside our huts. Wherever you were you could hear the humming of insects. In such a setting our life at Wanyai persisted day-in-day-out.

In March 1943 a 'sitrep' of Thai-Burma Railway construction showed an advance of 20%. On Thai-side trains were already running on the section of track as far as Kamburi, 50 km from the starting-point at Nong Pladuk. West of Kamburi there were the Mae Khlaung steel bridge, the cutting-through of track at Chungkai, and the punish-ing work of the plank viaduct and other work in the 103 km area, but laying the railtrack itself had not got as far as Wanyai. Thus the section of track to Kinsaiyok and beyond for about 100 km remained to be completed.

4 Special Installation Railway Unit, the one which became the reinforcement on the order for rush-construction, had left behind the personnel needed for service on Malayan Railways, took with them all those who had been due for repatriation, and were diverted to the Thai-Burma Railway construction as leading bridging unit, with an engineering unit, construction unit, and transport unit, on Thai-side working with 9 Railway Regiment. Successively these new units got through to the site. Imperial Guards' engineering regiment also

helped on building the lorry highway. The rear supply train moved into position, also a sanitation unit, and these units went into the outback. 9 Railway Regiment, main construction unit on Thai-side, set up their HQ at Wanyai, fixed each battalion's section of track for which they were responsible as far as the Tamuron Part area, which became the boundary point, shortening the job by about 35 km, and thus coped with rush construction work.

Bit by bit the van of 1 Battalion of 9 Railway Regiment was already nearing the Nikki area. The Regiment's main effort was building the roadbed on the section of track at Tamuron Part West of Thā Khanun. 2 Battalion concentrated on preparing the continuation of the rail-track as far as Wanyai and they gradually took charge of running trains. 3 Battalion, transferred from work on the Mae Khlaung bridge, put all their efforts into building the roadbed between Thā Khanun and Kinsaiyok and beyond. 4 Battalion, developing the section between Kamburi and Kinsaiyok, were busy on part of the cutting at Chungkai and on constructing the plank viaduct in the 103 km area, and were in charge of roadbed construction, concentrating their main efforts on Wanyai and beyond. The regimental workshops at Nong Pladuk and at Kamburi were responsible for supply of construction materials for each unit, supporting the battalions on Thai-side.

On Burma-side, 1 Battalion of 5 Railway Regiment were responsible for extending the railtrack which 2 Battalion and 3 Battalion continued as far as the Three Pagodas Pass, giving priority to work on the three steel bridges over the Zami, Mezali and Apalon rivers. In general these battalions led the advance of the work.

HQ of 2 Railway Control moved up to Kamburi, was collectively in control of supporting units such as Southern Army workshops, prisoner-of-war camps, supply train and field hospital. Major-General Simoda had died at his post in January and he was succeeded soon by Major-General Takasaki. The two railway regiments urged all units on in their rush-construction work, all aiming to complete by August in their fight to defy the natural obstacles of the jungle.

The local bridging unit who came up via Banpong set up their HQ at Thā Makham in mid-March, and 3 Labour Unit (Konno Unit) succeeded 9 Railway Regiment's 3 Battalion's work, responsible for building the Mae Khlaung steel bridge. 1 Labour Unit co-operated in various ways in the bridge-building work of 3 Battalion in the neighbourhood of Kinsaiyok. In mid-November the previous year, to help build a temporary bridge over the River Sittang, 2 Labour Units, detached in Burma, had come under control of 5 Railway Regiment and they gradually grappled with the difficult work on the rice-paddy ridges of that river.

At Banpong more prisoners-of-war were drafted up to augment the labour force and coolies were recruited in each country from Malaya, Sumatra, etc., arriving at Banpong by train and pitched into the work, going on foot to the work-sites. This sudden increase in numbers in the Thai-Burma region inspired the chant 'Assault on Rush-Construction' (*kyūsoku kensetsu no shingeki fu*) and it began to be sung loudly every day.

On a day in mid-March in the council room at 9 Railway Regiment's HQ in Wanyai each battalion commander, the Materials Workshops commander and principal officers of subordinate rank were assembled. Captain Kuwabara (not the man who had originated a plan in 1939 at IJA GHQ), attached to regimental HQ, explained the main points in the orders for the Regiment's campaign based on a plan for rush-construction, answered two or three questions, and the CO, Colonel Imai, his manner stern, made his own comments:

I think my campaign order based on the present plan of work for rush-construction of this railway, is something we just have to accept. The period of time expected for completion runs to August or upwards of five months, and this is carrying to extremes the great volume of work to be done, and it is obvious that it is not easy to adjust to this timing. None-the-less, pushing aside innumerable difficulties our main pre-occupation must be tough determination to complete the railway by August. Each officer must renew his resolve and severally expend every effort to achieve his duty. The lie of the land in fixing work boundaries is complicated and because we enter the climatic conditions of the rainy season it is estimated that our task will become still more difficult. Further, it will be impossible to guarantee adequate replenishment of food, fodder and materials. It depends simply on the men demonstrating their spiritual power in earnest work: nothing but their spontaneity will win through in the end. Particularly in hygiene scrupulous care must not be neglected. Carelessness in prisoners-of-war and coolies will also cause victims. Each Japanese officer will opt to make strenuous efforts.

Officers below the rank of battalion commanders pledged in spirit that the CO's determined statement made them, too, determined to complete the railway within the time-limit laid down. I had only just arrived at my post but was also summoned to attend the conference and heard the instructions but, thinking about the volume of work and the time-limit, I remember my feeling of unease that the plan was barely possible to succeed. Later on I questioned the Colonel about this problem. He replied, 'As a soldier I must obey the Emperor's commands. Even complying with unreasonable commands a soldier must exert himself even if this means inevitable death, so there is no excuse for dwelling on the hardships of subordinates.' He spoke with a sad look clouding his face. He had studied engineering at Tokyo University and took his degree in that subject, but he was a soldier as well as an engineer. It was his fate to be a man who carried misfortune on his back.

In the interval between April and August we had to crowd in a volume of work calculated at upwards of 20,000 cubic metres of earth a day and 10 metres a day of bridge-building. One could do it depending on a sufficient increase in the number of labourers on earthworks. But bridge-building required engineers and the number of engineers available for it was limited. Thus what arose from the order for rush-construction built up to a busy task and the coolies' job greatly exceeded the original forecast. However their work potential was low so there could be no let-up, their daily stint was increased and this compulsory labour was cruel. The prisoners and coolies on the job were rather negligent: the Japanese engineers could not permit negligence and constantly scolded them, shouting, 'Supeedo' and 'Hurry uppu' to them. The prisoners-of-war thought this was callous cruelty.

To prevent delay in building the Mae Khlaung steel bridge the time-limit was extended. As far as Wanyai and West of Kinsaiyok a roadbed extension was planned which took you to within hailing distance and at Kinsaiyok a double-track extension was set up at this base. Regimental workshops and 2 Battalion started sending in advance rails and materials, using boats on the river. With the approaching rainy season the volume of water rose, and engine-powered sampans went upstream to Kinsaiyok loaded with rails and sleepers. The number of boats which plied up and down the river increased, and on the highway into the jungle lorries intermittently kept going to and fro. The sound of logging in the jungle reverberated and reverberated and you could hear the roar of rock being blasted. So with Wanyai base at the centre of rush-construction it was all becoming something of a breath-taking experience.

Chapter 22

THE LABOUR FORCE

In an investigation pre-war at IJA GHQ it had been estimated that two railway regiments could build a railway linking Thailand to Burma in one year, but careful thought was not given to what mechanical gear might be needed. Accordingly, in practice, labour for roadbed construction was assumed to depend on human effort. In March 1942, under Southern Army's 2 Railway Control, from the start it was assumed that a human labour force would do it. From topographical maps the earth-work of roadbed construction on which the railtrack could be laid was estimated to total at least 15 million cubic metres of earthwork, and bridge-building a distance of upwards of 30 km. The period of construction was estimated as two years and the number of labourers needed was assessed as over 25,000 each day. On the fall of Singapore, in the Malayan battle-area and the successful occupation of Java and Sumatra, the prisoners-of-war of British, Dutch and Australian nationality were numbered in March 1942 as around 100,000, and they were mostly in prison-camps at Changi on Singapore Island. For the Japanese Southern Army it was in the natural order of events that, as these men were still alive, that they were seen as the labour force for constructing the railway. However, one does not know whether it was an infringement of the Geneva Convention International Pact on Treatment of Prisoners-of-War because Japan did not ratify it. The British and American Governments started the war so whether their action was against the Japanese Government's diplomatic stance and whether Southern Army really understood the situation and were well-informed or not one does not know. However that may be, in Southern Army's plan it was stated that prisoners-of-war and locally conscripted coolies would be used as the labour force.

As a result of the survey mentioned in Chapter 9 it was forecast that the volume of work required was greater than had been forecast in 1939, but by January 1943 it became strategically essential to demand that the time-scale should be shortened, to be effected by rush-construction, and that work force had to be augmented. Most of the prisoners employed as labourers were sent up from camps at Changi on Singapore Island, and they totalled about 60,000 men. Apart from A Group (to prisoners known as A Force) who went to Burma by sea in May 1942, prisoners from Changi were sent up by rail to Banpong in Thailand and marched to their work sites from that town. The last was H Force, the eighth and last group. (Futamatsu apparently had incomplete access to the statistics. H Force came up in May 1943, and two more groups followed them in June and August, namely K Force and L Force.) In August 1942, the camps in Thailand were reorganized separately for administration and six groups were set up by place of work. In February 1943 these Thailand camps came under control of Thai-Burma Railway Construction Units HQ, who now became responsible for control of prisoners employed as labourers.

The camps themselves were responsible for the prisoners' affairs, their movement, accommodation, rations, health, sanitation, etc. The system was that, apart from the Japanese camp commandant, executive officers and NCOs, the guards were auxiliaries, *heiho* (not normally of Japanese nationality) who hailed from the Korea of those days. These guards assembled the number of prisoners required that day by the engineers, marched them to the work site and handed them over to the engineer work commander. When the job was done the guards marched them back to camp. These auxiliaries acting as camp guards thought themselves superior to the prisoners, and the lower-ranking Japanese troops had the same attitude in relation to the prisoners, and if the latter did not comply with what they thought they should do they resorted to violent practices, beating and kicking them. In the Japanese Army there is absolute compliance with orders given by those of higher rank and it is the custom to levy corporal punishment on the spot to men of lower rank. The soldiers and auxiliaries practised the same principles on the prisoners on the job and one can imagine that corporal punishment was added, directly in person, when a prisoner did not comply with orders and commands.

When prisoners first received this barbaric corporal punishment they were naturally astonished and taken aback. They were not to know that the soldiers and guards inflicted corporal punishment among themselves, soldiers who were also taught that they should consider it shameful to be captured in battle. It followed that it was true that prisoners received what to them was ill-treatment: one has to admit that there is no doubt that Japanese troops added this barbaric cruelty to their treatment of prisoners-of-war. In such treatment, consequentially on cruelty, it was also the case that the job itself taxed the labourers' strength beyond its limits, they were punished for going sick, and this was associated with the risk of deaths. Medical treatment came within the scope of the camp's administration but it is certainly true that because of lack of facilities, shortage of medical officers, scant medical supplies and so on, it was impossible to achieve a satisfactory state of affairs. For the prisoners generally, our inability to move them, our inability to take action about preventive inoculations against tropical epidemic and contagious diseases, our inability to take the sick along with us when we had to move, the dearth of medicaments, the shortage of doctors ... all these factors made impossible the treatment of sickness one would have hoped for, and these factors in the end created many victims. Particularly in the rainy season of 1943 at Songkurai, Kinsaiyok and elsewhere it was the wretched case that one could not trust to one's ideal of medical treatment for victims of cholera.

At the end of February 1943 the time-limit for completion had to be curtailed, and to meet the demands of rush-construction the daily volume of work was increased and so was the labour force. Accordingly the number of prisoners actually at work demanded from the camps by the engineers greatly increased. The task itself in theory could be done but in the circumstances the volume of work done decreased, sick men could not do it, and between prisoners' senior officers, medical officers and Japanese commandants frequent arguments arose. Because it was sick men being forced out to work, the volume of work decreased, but also the numbers of sick rose, so the increase of the labour force varied inversely with its efficiency.

The engineers depended on arranging for prisoners to do rush-construction work from March to October which averaged over 30,000 men at work on any one day, and the total labour force within this period probably reached ten million. [Not clear – see below estimate of one million?] The engineers themselves on the job totalled about 10,000, which in terms of efficiency doubled the prisoners to about 20,000. When one considers this fact, one realizes that it is no exaggeration to say that the railway's construction depended on the work of prisoners-of-war.

On the labour force, as well as the prisoners, there were coolies conscripted from the area. From March 1943, with the backing of each of the southern military governments, recruitment of coolies began. It was claimed that food was abundant in the area and wages high, and many coolies were enlisted and rushed from Banpong to the work sites. In Burma, too, following a military government's HQ directive, which was sent to village headmen of each locality, conscription took place semi-compulsorily, and the coolies penetrated into the interior from Thanbyusayat. They were said to total 30,000 men. There is no detailed record but the total of coolies on Thai-side together with those on Burma-side was probably about 100,000. On any single day it was estimated that the maximum number of coolies at work was about 10,000 and in the period March to October all told an estimated of up to a *million* is not excessive.

The coolies, naturally, were employed under the direct control of the engineers, who had to deal with their accommodation, rations, sanitation and so on. The coolies were Hindus, Indonesians, Malays, Burmese and so on, of various nationalities mixed together and their customs and habits differed. Because of their different foods, and disparities in their way of life and habits and their different religions, one was forced to divide them within their huts; at times it was no different from driving them into their graves. With the onset of the rainy season there were epidemics of cholera, typhoid and other contagious diseases, and the combination of malarial fever and of the wrong foods resulted in many skeletons being buried in the jungle. The root cause was partly, it was thought, due to the coolies' own inability to conceive what impurities were inherent in their environmental way of life.

In the rainy season the supply of rations was very bad and for the hundred thousand men of the labour force (prisoners and coolies) in the end proper quantities could not be supplied and there was also a loss in quality. The huts, too, at the work-sites were roofless on jerry-built superstructures. Particularly was it impossible to supply clothing and medical supplies.

Even despite such conditions the railway was finally completed by the prisoners-of-war and coolies working with us. It is certain that this railway could not have been finished without their help. They defied the demon of ill-health and finished the job, and lamented the souls of the many victims whose bones lay in the jungle. It was probably the result of the indomitable spirit with which the survivors worked, even when it looked as if they were zealously labouring even in an enemy's strategic railway. In any case, 'we and they together' were able to build up a monumental achievement.

On the approach to the Mae Khlaung bridge at Thā Makham and on a hill at Thanbyusayat stone monuments were put up to the souls of the victims of the Thai-Burma Railway, perhaps a unique mark of atonement by a Japanese Army for their victims.

Chapter 23

SURVEY UNIT

Wanyai was 125 km from the starting-point at Nong Pladuk. The route skirted a high precipitous cliff on the river bank, then moved on to a hilly zone. Then for roughly 25 km it carried on to the north-west and reached a grassy plain surrounded by thick jungle. There were no trees or shrubs on it and a marvellous hot spring made it swampy. The plain was about 100 metres up from the river level, and a station was being planned here, at Tampii. From the site of the proposed station down to the riverbank the section of track was on a down gradient and had to cross a ravine 30 metres deep.

When I returned to Wanyai in March the CO asked for a study of the route alongside the river. I investigated the point I have just described and worked out that a bridge would have to be 100 metres across, maximum of bridge-piers over 30 metres with 4-metre spans on a wooden bridge, clearly an unstable construction which would oscillate under the weight of a train. I explained to the CO how dangerous this type of bridge design would be and ventured to suggest to him a modification of the route.

One day in late March *Daihonéi* sent a staff officer to the base at Wanyai to see how the construction was going on. The CO mentioned to him the problem of the bridge and next day we took him as far as the point where the problem lay. Down from the cliff-top the river surface could be seen glittering like silver. In the vicinity dazzling sunlight poured down, the greens of the trees and shrubs took one's breath away, and from the jungle at one's feet the heat seemed to be boiling up.

Mōri, the Survey Unit commander, came out to meet us, pointed out the bridge-building site and explained the problem. It was a precipitous place and both on the map and on the ground a difficult spot to build a bridge. The staff officer was appalled at this topography and turned to Colonel Imai, saying, 'Regimental commander, why not try a switch-back?'* A switch-back is a method in which, when there is a rising slope, a sort of ladder or staircase is made in the form of a route folding up on itself. On this precipice no margin was allowed so it was impossible terrain for a switch-back. I was amazed, and said, 'On a cliff like this it's impossible.' It was an occasion for spelling out what one meant, but the CO said, 'I think we go along with what the Honourable Staff Officer was pleased to imply,' glaring at me as he spoke.

Colonel Imai's special skill was in engineering, and I was astonished that he appeared to approve the staff officer's unreasonable idea and did not question it. The Survey Unit commander had lent me his verbal support, doubting whether the staff officer's idea was feasible. I said, 'The success or failure of the Thai-Burma Railway hangs on the success or failure of the route chosen. Please listen to my appeal!'

Second-lieutenant Mōri stood stiffly at attention in front of Colonel Katō, the staff officer, and responded rather shakily, 'I certainly approve. I will do the best I can manage.' I saw with blank amazement this unexpected turn of events. When I came back after the midday meal the Colonel whispered in my ear, 'Just now you were discourteous. You behaved badly to your CO and Mr Staff Officer, but please hunt for a route which in one way or another is sound. I appeal to you!' Before my eyes here was an example of how military ethics could make a soldier accept an illogical order, and could understand, too, the complications which arose from the recent rush-construction order.

---

* Switch-backs are a standard method of avoiding lengthy high-gradient hauls on mountain railways. In the plan O = points:

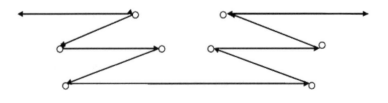

That afternoon 2/Lt Mōri and I had a good look at the survey map in his tent, and examined a possible bridging location upstream where the ravine wasn't so deep, planning a detour which meant setting up a route which was feasible for a bridge. The volume of work to be done before and beyond it would increase but the safety of the bridge would be secured. The facts about this modification to the route were found on this occasion to be known at the time to the British Army. After the war a former prisoner-of-war, Mr Escritt, gave an account of it in a letter to me in March 1983. He wrote, ' The Japanese Army corrected an error in their survey,' The planning of such a railway had to be secret, but employing prisoners-of-war presented a hazard and it may be that there is evidence here of counter-intelligence.[107]

Towards the end of August it proved in the long run to be impossible, in the time allowed, to assimilate such a volume of work. 'Supeedo', 'hurree uppu', 'getto bizee' the engineers shouted encouragement at the top of their voices and all got down to work in earnest, engineers, prisoners, coolies alike. I myself as an engineer in any case wanted to complete the railway and I burned with enthusiasm, here at Wanyai working in the jungle.

Near a mountain stream in the jungle two or three kilometres west of Tampii the Mōri Unit's barracks were erected. We called it 'The Malayan Settlement' because the buildings looked like Malay dwellings. It was set up alongside the river and became the sole workroom for the two or three unit members who, shadows of their former selves, on a crude desk drafted a map of the modified route, enthusiastically carrying out their survey. Wooden posts for marking out the new centre-line, together with sextants, ranging-rods, plane-tables and so on were piled up. Unit HQ and link-line-to-be were connected by a temporary telephone line on which sounds came through indistinctly.

2/Lt Mōri, his badges of rank covered by a threadbare cloak to keep the heat down, put on his gumboots and went for a quick run out, his vigorous figure boiling hot, to inaugurate the laying down of the centre-line of the survey. It was already six months since setting out from Banpong in July when the Survey Unit in the van, 30 km West of Kinsaiyok, had decided on this spot as their main work-centre. The job was to set up on the ground the route chosen from the map. They were making a roadbed from a blueprint on a map so the speed of construction varied from time to time. It was a grave responsibility. In the tortuous nature of the ground the work was particularly difficult and the toil they were put to was abnormal. The commander's youthful looks did not match his blotchy, unshaven face as he told the tale of the hardships of life in the jungle, but he said confidently that he was not worrying. 'People often become virtually immune, do they not,' he said, 'to malarial fever and in any case quinine is an effective alleviating drug, is it not!' he said brusquely and laughed at the idea. With one exception his men had caught malarial fever so they took quinine daily. The healthy young men had few attacks and went out to work, but they expressed their concern about whether their food supply was adequate.

When they went out to work they had to endure the heated atmosphere of the jungle. From poisonous leaves oppressive heat sprang up like an exhalation, so one breathed with difficulty and had headaches. The heaps of fallen leaves were soft to the touch but ice-cold shivers ran evilly down their backs. Centipedes, flies and scorpions were frightening and one encountered snakes of unusual shape. Soldier ants kept falling onto the back of the neck, and little flies tormented one, flying into the eyes. There was no relief for sense of either sight or hearing. In the depth of deep forest in the undergrowth under the trees there was an inches-deep thick layer of fallen leaves and the light of the sun was obstructed so it was dim even in daytime. Visibility being limited one had to call out one's position to the next man to confirm it, and they often lost their way. Certainly it was daytime when the sun was out, but one lost the ability to define the period of daylight.

Squalls broke out suddenly. From between the leaves big drops began to fall. Instantly the rain reached the bamboo-grass. It splashed up like driven arrows, hitting everything, and everywhere was misty and dim. The rain stopped at one metre, did not evaporate, visibility was nil. Under one's feet leaves began to pile up and straightaway there was stagnant water. Suddenly, with one's whole body crying out for cover, the rain penetrated to one's underwear and uncomfortable shivers ran down one's spine. At times like this one was made acutely aware of the powerlessness of man made sport of by the violence of nature.

When squalls went over, the rain clouds were blown away by the wind, and you could see the blue sky which made one forget all about the rain. The sun broke out and shone on the tree tops and things began to dry up, but discomfort caused by the temperature supervened on heated, drenched bodies. In such circumstances it became in the end impossible to carry on working. When night fell, the temperature all round the camp fell rapidly. Mosquitoes emerged and inside the mosquito-nets their 'night shift' began at the oil lamps. To guard against attack by wild animals they kept a bonfire going all night. When the moon came out over the jungle and the Southern Cross climbed the sky, then all in the unit fell asleep.

In circumstances like these Mōri Survey Unit kept up their usual endeavours in a spirit of grin-and-bear it. Even on the job they came out to bow to the Imperial Tomb, out in the jungle with the full azure sky extending above them. Cool breezes flowed in from somewhere and they could hear the shrilling of cicadas, and from the trees birds' cries rang clearly in the heated atmosphere. Here and there in the woods the reverberation of logging axes could be heard. From the hillside they could see over the tops of the trees and shrubs the sparkling white wavelets of the river and on and on before their eyes flowed a sea of foliage on the steep slopes. On bodies dripping with sweat cool breezes gave them a pleasing sensation and enabled them to forget for a brief moment the heat of the southern countries. In the middle of the forest the centre-line of the railtrack was cleared and the survey-flags showed up vividly on it. They could see in the misty mountains the route through to the Thai-Burma frontier.

The youthful Survey Unit commander squared his chest and looked out across the jungle-forest. As leading soldier on the construction of the railway the heavy responsibility he shouldered floated uppermost in his heart, whether he had his eyes fixed on the sky over the Three Pagodas Pass or perhaps the sky above his beloved homeland.

Even today in my memory the Thai-Burma construction goes on playing in *allegro* an attack-note of loyalty to the Throne.

Chapter 24

TEST RUN

By July the previous year about a year had elapsed since construction had started. The efficacy of the rush-construction ordered in March this year became manifest as the news came through that the excavation of the rocky hill on the Chungkai section of the track was within a few days of completion, as also was work on the plank viaducts at 103 km and 109 km. The completion of construction of the Mae Khlaung steel bridge together with the planned opening to traffic of the railtrack extension was under control of the engineers' railtrack extension unit, 2 Battalion, who had previously been waiting at Kamburi station, eager to become wholly involved in the further extension of the railtrack.

On Burma-side, 5 Railway Regiment at the close of the previous year had completed the lorry highway as far as Nikki. They now wrestled in earnest with making the roadbed, pushed on the railhead to a point about 30 km East of Thanbyusayat, set up their regimental HQ at Taungzun and, when their 1 Battalion had completed the temporary bridge over River Sittang, drove ahead with roadbed work, helped by 4 Battalion, who came from the East to reinforce them. They hurried on with the job, too, not being sure, with the rainy season coming on, how far they would get.

On Thai-side, too, in addition to the important section between Wanyai and Tamuron Part, each unit daily risked death in their endeavours to keep up with the volume of work, and there was still a little on the section uncompleted. From June a second railhead extension on from Kinsaiyok was nearly finished. At the time 9 Railway Regiment believed the railtrack could be completed by the end of August, Construction HQ inclining towards that bare possibility.

Reinforcements arrived at each site and prisoners and coolies were successively introduced into the outback. The year before, an engineering unit and a service unit had taken part in constructing the highway leading to the Wanyai and Kinsaiyok bases and they had opened to daily traffic with lorries, an infantry unit, reluctant prisoners and coolies all mixed up together., In the rainy weather wheeled traffic got through with difficulty on the muddy road-surfaces. As far as Wanyai commodities were being taken up in small boats, but West of Wanyai supply was expected to create problems. However, the railtrack was expected to reach Wanyai very soon. The opening to traffic of the entire railway was imminent.

Thai prisoner-of-war camps came under command of General Shimoda's successor as C-in-C, Major-General Takasaki. His HQ set up a water sanitation unit and field hospitals supported by 42 Regional Supply Unit. These units took up their duties in the outback at this critical juncture, at Wanyai, Kinsaiyok, Thā Khanun and Nikki, besides on Burma-side at Thanbyusayat, Apalon, Kyandaw etc.

It was within the secret limits of Thailand and Burma, over which the rainy season was about to break, that what one may call the inevitable struggle was beginning to become a decisive battle. On a day in mid-May 1943 a telegram was dispatched from GHQ to the C-in-C: 'On Thai-side on the Thai-Burma Rail Link, with effect from today, the railhead from the Nong Pladuk terminus reached the 124 km mark at Wanyai.' The Mae Khlaung steel bridge had opened to traffic so the track-extension could go ahead from Kamburi westwards.

That day the sky over Wanyai was clearing up. Forests had been cut through so that a second iron road could go on its way towards Wanyai station, making a grand, reassuring demonstration of the glorious way in which men had played out the battle-with-nature game under the powerful sun of the southern countries. Straightaway one could hear powerful sirens echoing through the trees. On the far side of the railroad came black smoke, and gradually the shape of an engine loomed up. The distinctive sound of a C56-type engine was heard as it set out to do its test run. The day before, at last, 2 Battalion's railroad-laying had reached the Wanyai station compound, all 74 km of track between

Kamburi and Wanyai had been completed, and this was the day when the test run was to be undertaken.

The test run was made in the presence of Colonel Iwasawa, Chief Staff Officer, Construction HQ, and of Colonel Imai, commander of Thai-side construction, and behind them were the railway engineers, all straining attentively to watch the engine as it moved forward. It met the points at the station compound, its speed dropped, and then it moved on into the station compound ... one could sense underfoot, from the creaking sound of its wheels, its movements over the ground. It moved! The railway was viable so far ... With the men's admiration wrapped in it, the engine, its wheels creaking, stopped. Safe conclusion to the test run! Everybody's shout of *banzai* echoed through jungle forest: the station staff's joy overflowed. In charge of the operation alighting from the engine was Major Yoshida, commander of 2 Battalion. He advanced in front of Colonel Imai, gave the courtesy salute, and reported: 'Between Kanchanaburi and Wanyai the test run had now been brought to a safe conclusion.' Commander Imai had begun to receive the report with a tense expression on his face, but in a twinkling of an eye let his relief flow to the surface. He expressed his formal thanks, his 'Thanks for your trouble', to Major Yoshida and wrung his hand with joy on his face, his sense of pride could be seen. He had been waiting a long time for that train to come to Wanyai, and his joy and deep emotion were now complete. It was no more than a hundred days before planned completion in August.

Everyone had had to persist in a battle with natural forces, cutting through the tops of hills, burying the spoil, crossing mountain streams in their advance. It was a desperate struggle day and night to achieve completion by rush-construction which the labour units had made, and despite the imminence of the rainy season the engineers kept up their high spirits.

Chapter 25

BRIDGE-BUILDING AND
SHIFTING EARTH

Building a roadbed meant both building bridges and shifting earth. A roadbed to carry a railtrack had to be designed with gradients and line-curvatures, but when one looked at it on the ground it became essentially a matter of high ground being cut through and levelled off and of low places being plugged up to bring them to ground level. This is how the roadbed was formed. Mountain streams had to be crossed by building bridges and this meant unavoidable extra labour.

The total length of the railway was 415 km and there were over 300 bridges, apart from the culverts, but few of them were over 100 metres across. On Thai-side there were the Mae Khlaung steel bridge and the double plank viaduct at Arrow Hill at 103 km; on Burma-side there were the three steel bridges with their wooden by-passes over the Zami, Apalon and Mezali rivers. For small spans of 10 metres and larger spans of 70 to 90 metres the railway engineers used standard 'text book' bridge-building methods. Bridges occurred about one in every kilometre. For girders on the wooden bridges they used 30-cm squared timbers, one per rail. On top of the foundations made by pile-driving the bridge-abutments and bridge-piers, the framework was made in the form of gate-styled columns one against another. It being entirely a temporary method, clamps were used to bolt up the timbers. It was enough to carry the weight of a train on the bridge but not enough for oscillations on impact. Location and extent were decided, and when the height of the bridge-piers was fixed it became a viable job because the construction was simple. This type of construction was not for permanence so the weak places needed strengthening against flood-times and heavy rains, the safety-factor of the foundations being low. After the railway was opened to traffic the enemy's bombing inter- rupted movement of traffic, the bridges being the constant target, and the construction being simple they collapsed, but again because of their simple construction they could be repaired.

The area included many jungle mountain streams which had to be bridged, and so a lorry thoroughfare was really necessary. In the bridge location a survey had to be carried out and assessment of necessary materials and of the volume of work to be done was needed, after which the materials squad got ready bridging machine-parts, together with the necessary pile-driving tools, girder-timbers and other tools and car- ried them in together with labourers, the prisoners-of-war and coolies; and when girder-construction was completed the railtrack squad with sleepers and rails laid the railtrack on the bridges. Using these meth- ods the bridge-building job averaged out at over 10 metres a day, the distance asked of the work units. Because it was rush-construction, the work went on day and night, rain or shine indifferently, and apart from the engineering skill needed to do it, the locations of the work created limitations and so, in the period needed for it at the time, the progress of roadbed construction was hampered.

Constructing the roadbed was mostly shifting earth. It was ground- levelling on planned modifications and became literally a fight against nature. There was no plan to use mechanical power because that was unsuitable in jungle conditions, so we had to use manpower. To level and raise ground-levels in ravines the labourers had to hump earth and sand. To break through rocky crags bit-by-bit blasting was used with its accompanying danger to men at work. The norm of a Japanese soldier's ability in levelling was four cubic metres a day, but work needing blast- ing made a norm of only one cubic metre, and it was hard work, too. The engineers could not expect prisoners and coolies to achieve even a third of a Japanese soldier's norm, hence the great volume of work expected of them.

Building the roadbed was done by 'human wave' tactics. The total volume of earth shifting, levelling and raising ground-levels was put at about 15 million cubic metres plus, and the total number of working days being 500, it averaged out at over 30,000 cubic metres a day. Each day the men worked on the job shifting earth totalled over 20,000.

Between Wanyai and Kinsaiyok a subsidence occurred just when the railtrack was scheduled to reach Kinsaiyok. The engineer unit commander directing the job took a ride with me on a tractor to a point opposite the work on the site at Kinsaiyok. That evening when the moon set there was a quiet starry sky over the jungle. The air felt cold after midnight. With gradual ending of the rainy season the scattered squally showers had ceased. When rail-tractors went out you could hear faintly the sound of their engines somewhere in the distance. The commander ordered our tractor to stop and sure enough there was the sound of an aeroplane and in the distance a red and blue light could be seen moving in the sky. In a flash we left our tractor and lay flat on our faces in the grass. The sounds of explosions came near us. Perhaps the railtrack, on which light shone only faintly in the starlight could not easily be made out from the air. In the uncertain silence to the roar of the explosions was added the humming of insects in the grass. Previously, recce aircraft had been coming over to reconnoitre the railway, and there had been air-raids on Moulmein and on Thanbyusayat. Air-raid precautions were necessary and AA-guns had been sited at Thanbyusayat and at the Mae Khlaung bridges. Air-raids on track under construction also had to be prepared for. This time the sound of bombs was more distant and the day's tension was over, when just as we turned back to camp came news of an accident. Several flatcars loaded with rails were being driven by a rail-tractor when it met a freak down-gradient, the flatcars were derailed and fell off the bridge. For accidents and damage to rolling-stock the workshops at Nong Planuk were responsible, and those at Kamburi helped. In an emergency machine-parts, etc. were sent promptly by aeroplane from a base which had the tools and bolts needed for the job in stock, some being of Japanese make.

'Human wave' tactics in rush-construction were at the limits of man's strength and in the end surpassed it. Even if one thought it was not impossible to finish by the end of August, in the circumstances one could hardly be optimistic about the future ahead.

Chapter 26

THE RAINY SEASON:
THE MONSOON

In Thailand, Malaya and other countries in the South-East-Asia region, a round of sudden squalls of rain falls every day. Out of a clear sky it suddenly becomes misty, one expects big drops of rain to fall, it becomes a cloudburst. It sweeps everything away in its fall, but after some ten minutes it stops. The clouds clear off and with sunlight filling the neighbourhood the temperature rises, pools on the ground soon dry up before one's very eyes. Such squalls become frequent, intervals between them brief, it seems to go on pouring in a series of rainstorms. Such is the rainy season.

The rainy season in the Thailand-Burma regions usually lasts from May until the end of August, In Japan it lasts a long time so the volume of rain there is large. Particularly in the Three Pagodas Pass region the rainfall in this Tenanasserim belt approaches the world's heaviest rainfall of over 200 ml a day, with occasional rare cloudbursts with 100 ml falling within an hour. In some months a total of 2,000 ml is reached; in Japan this equals a year's average rainfall. In the dry season there were no cloudy skies and the way it cleared up was a marvel. The rainy season was also called the period of monsoons.

When the rainy season opened the surface-drainage of the roads became bad, rainwater accumulated, it got very muddy. Cars had their wheels trapped in quagmires, unable to move. Automobile accidents often piled up and in the end it became extremely difficult to get through at all. Over the deep ruts even bullock-carts with their wide diameter wheels could barely get through. The engineers could move on foot only. Prisoners-of-war and coolies moved blindly on from Kamburi to Wanyai and from Wanyai to Kinsaiyok carrying their heavy baggage, trudging on, soaked by the rain. In single file they stumbled on all mixed together, engineers, prisoners, coolies, Japanese troops aiming at the frontier. These troops carried stripped-down mountain-guns and heavy machine-guns on their shoulders, trudging on in silence carrying equipment-parts on their backs. Mud-smeared, drenched with rain and sweat, these troops moved on into the jungle, each man hoping fervently for what surely must happen one day, the completion of the railway. The engineers thought that our allies, the Thai, should have helped to reduce their labours. They learned bit-by-bit, too, that the war situation on the Burma battle-front was unfavourable. Officers must not, of course, vainly discard their orders on a battlefield in sympathy with the feelings of the troops but they certainly felt it would be a good thing if the war came to an early conclusion.

Hardly had they plunged into rush-construction when along came the rainy season some two months afterwards. Progress gradually declined. The railtrack had barely got as far as Wanyai when the rainy season prevented roadbed construction from keeping up with what had been planned. There was also an incident in which embankments and bridges were flashed away by a heavy rainstorm: but still, day after day, some work kept on being done in the midst of the rain.

On any morning when the rain kept pouring down one did not think unusual a daily total volume of rain of over 200 ml: every day it fell in sudden violent downpours and both day and night it felt chilly as if it were the onset of winter. Surrounding the huts devilish bamboo splinters were poisonous and the clumps were soaked, from the verge of *atap* eaves raindrops fell all the time and the deep tranches round the huts constantly overflowed onto the muddy paths. When evening came the dampness of the rain together with the chilly air supervened. Smoke from camp kitchens trailed low down in the rain and the rain put out fires. The telephone was affected and kept on making low cheeping sounds.

With raindrops dripping from the hood of his raincoat a military runner came rushing up from HQ and the loud voice of an official officer was heard: 'What's this? Has Hin Dat been flooded? What have you done about it? Summon up 3 Battalion HQ!!' An officer's voice came through on the telephone: 'Yes, with the embankment washed away will the bridges go too? ... Ask for a detailed report and find out whether the work units have suffered damage!' The HQ runner took off his headphone and said to himself, 'How feeble you've been indeed. Have you now held the work up?' With these words he went into the unit commander's office. After an inspection the day before there had been heavy rain in the Lintin area with maximum rainfall of 100 ml an hour, and the river was flooded. From water running down from the mountainside the embankment had been submerged and in the end swept away, ending up with about 2,000 metres of the roadbed being washed away. There had been a cloudburst which in an hour plunged everything into a curtain of water as far as the eye could reach, it was as if 'the bottom of the sky had fallen out'. No special protection could be taken in such a cloudburst, embankment and bridges were under water and collapsed as a result.

When the Kwae Noi was in flood there were regular floods in Tenasserim, too, two or three metres deep. Normally-narrow rivers widened in a day by six or seven metres. The rivers were ripe for floods and even the bridge over the Mae Khlaung with its permanent steel structure was in a sea of running water: on one occasion on the route upstream I found the actual confluence of the Mae Khlaung and the Kwae Noi couldn't be seen. At a point near the outflow of the River Onoi embankment and bridges were washed away and remained at risk. The road over the bridge there was expected to be washed away and its framework truncated. Because of drift-wood and big bamboos being carried down from upstream, the temporary bridge over the Mae Khlaung collapsed several times. From Kamburi as far as Wanyai vehicles could not easily get through and it was of small advantage that some materials had to depend on boats to carry them. This was done by powered sampans which carried full loads of provisions and materials from Kamburi to Wanyai, thence to Kinsaiyok and on again to Thā Khanun, taking from three to seven days going upstream. Each day over 200 boats went upstream. But even at the start of the rainy season trains had been running as far as Wanyai, continuing daily to run over the Mae Khlaung steel bridge, as might have expected of railway transport.

With the approach of the rainy season there was no question of rest-days. In the Thai-Burma region the labourers employed on the job, prisoners and coolies, totalled over 100,000 men and supply of rations became a serious problem; transport after it started became even more difficult. The hardships suffered by the supply-trains were terrible, with their job of transporting provisions and fodder and also rations for the troops passing through. By June, transport of the staple food, rice, could not be maintained and the staple foods of the labourers had to be reduced by half. Some supply-trains, when their own off-the land resources were inadequate for themselves, necessarily relied on receiving supplies from other sources. Of course, the prisoners-of-war and coolies had their staple foods reduced by half, the effect of which was to reduce their efficiency at work. There was also the problem of keeping up their health, health affected by lack of adequate nutrition. Boat transport on the river carried so and so many tons of rice but it had to be unloaded on the river-bank into bullock-carts. The loads of rice, carried *en route* 100 kg, had to carry fodder also for the bullocks, and halving the rations made the supply-train clerks' job difficult. There were also the supplementary foods, vegetables and meat, all in short supply. As a result, the number of prisoners and coolies who became victims of inadequate nourishment increased. In barracks vegetables could be grown in self-support and at camps near work-sites wild herbs and banana-stems were used as food. Fish were angled for from the river and in the hills snakes and lizards were eaten. A few wild boar, pheasants and wild fowl were caught, but the available means of subsistence for food for the labourers came close to that of primitive man. Meat is a source of protein, but to supply it to men of different nationalities, particularly to prisoners-of-war, proved almost impossible in practice.

Wood is a natural food for insects and we got used to seeing birds flying furiously after them in the jungle. We became well-used to primitive man's way of life, well-used therefore to understand his ineptitude. At the Wanyai base meat and eggs were scarce and rationed and, if somewhat stale, an egg was truly a feast. Even damp and mouldy cigarettes were valuables and to the engineers made best gifts.

For the coolies and prisoners-of-war the lack of foodstuffs resulted in a decline in efficiently and in the long run under-nourishment led to an increase in the number of sick. Men in the Japanese Army were affected in the same way and this hindered progress in the work. By June, on Burma-side, because of the shortage of food work finally came to a halt, and later it came to such a pass that some of the labourers were evacuated. That the rainy season would obstruct the work was fully anticipated and it was expected that the labourers would have a hard time, but with such rain, with the lack of food so long endured, they could not put a further foot forward and had to give up.

By July the railtrack reached Kinsaiyok, and reverberation of rail tractors could be heard there. Still the rain went on falling.

Chapter 27

KINSAIYOK

Kinsaiyok was about 50 km, more or less, from Wanyai upstream on the river Kwae Noi. On the railtrack it was 172 km from Nong Pladuk and 120 km from Kamburi. There were narrow mountain streams which fed into the river and few plots of level ground on the banks. In the neighbourhood the riverbank became a cliff and near Saiyok (in Thai this means waterfall) a mountain stream became a waterfall which fell into the river from the top of a cliff, a beautiful sight. Kinsaiyok means New Saiyok, i.e. set up by the Japanese engineers, not a Thai place-name.

This was the point the labourers had reached in April 1943 and, in May, 3 Battalion of Railway Regiment embarked on construction of roadbed west of Kinsaiyok, which became the next construction base with radio hook-up for the engineers and a branch office for prisoners-of-war and coolies, No. 3 Group. There were also the branch office of 42 Supply Unit and the Japanese field hospital.

Hardly had roadbed work west of Kinsaiyok begun than the rainy season started. The route ran along the high ground on the north bank and there were many small bridges to build over the small streams rushing down into the river. This in turn complicated the roadbed work. At Lintin, west of Kinsaiyok, an incident occurred when the embankment was washed away and at Kui Ye there was a good deal of earth shifting for the prisoners and coolies to do. At Hin Dat, over 200 km from Nong Pladuk, a hot spring gushed out, the well-known Hin Dat Hot Springs, and when the railway opened to traffic the Japanese set up a field hospital recuperation centre. (Futamatsu refrains from mentioning the 'comfort station' for 'comfort' girls set up here for Japanese soldiers and Korean *heiho*.[108]) Brankashii, at 208 km, was the halfway point on the total 415 km length of the railway. Here was being planned a base for engine-sheds and installations for water and fuel supply. About 10 km to the west was Thā Khanun where 1 Battalion were to be stationed.

In March that year when the order for rush-construction was promulgated, on both Thai-side and Burma-side the demarcation-point was set near Tamuron Part at 245 km, but progress after the order made it possible to demarcate at Konkuita, at 262 km. Initially 9 Railway Regiment's responsibility was the section from Nong Pladuk to a point near Nikki at 294 km. This was now shortened by 32 km, and 5 Railway Regiment's responsibility from Thanbyusayat to Nikki was extended to 153 km. In mid-April their 4 Battalion came back from the East and joined in the work on the railway.

9 Railway Regiment's main task lay between Wanyai and Hin Tok, their 4 Battalion taking on this section, 3 Battalion doing the section between Hin Tok and Thā Khanun, and 1 Battalion the roadbed construction west of Thā Khanun. The rainy season dampened the spirits of these three battalions but the work went on night and day.

On Burma-side, 5 Railway Regiment's HQ moved up to Taungzun and their 4 Battalion, their temporary bridge over the River Sittong being completed, joined up with 1 Battalion. Thus the Regiment could now deploy their entire force on the whole section of track between Thanbyusayat and Konkuita and, despite being hampered by the rainy season, pressed on at full capacity. The section between Ronshii and Kyandau on the slope of the mountain west of the Three Pagodas Pass added an extra dimension to the severity of the work with the three steel bridges, with their temporary by-pass wooden bridges, over the Mezali, Apalon and Zami rivers.

If the rain cleared up it was hot, as usual, and on the tracks in the jungle leaves fell and scattered sporadically and it seemed as if one's whole body was dyed a deep jungle green. The regimental commander set out with me to inspect the work near Hin Tok. When we were going up a gentle slope, right by the roadside there were prisoners-of-war lying down on their midday rest period, eating their lunch.

They were surprisingly at ease and looked cheerful. Although these men had given up fighting in action and as captives were under our jurisdiction, yet they were, it seemed, not being bothered about being prisoners-of-war who thought that as survivors they should be repatriated. They went on chatting, looking at us. They did not expect their clothing to be renewed and because of the intense hear they had thrown off their clothes and were naked from the waist up. From backs to chests their white skins were burnt, regrettably, deep red. To Japanese soldiers they looked like red devils clad in wrestlers' loincloths. Their boots lacked soles but they wore them just the same.

Colonel Imai looked into the contents of one of the prisoner's mess tins. With a smile the man held it out for the Colonel to see. In it was nothing but boiled rice, no side-dish. Thinking there must be a misunderstanding the commander addressed him in English: 'Apart from rice isn't there anything else to eat?' The prisoner laughed and said, 'Only rice', and another man lying next to him said, 'Burnt rice is nicer' ... this was their ironic humour.[109] It was a mild protest. The commander's face clouded over and he turned to me and said, 'It's too bad, isn't it, to give them no adjunct to their cooked rice.' On return to Wanyai he immediately contacted the prisoners' camp and requested them to improve the prisoners' rations.

Colonel Imai was an engineer supervising earth-shifting, but essentially he was a soldier. He well knew the technical difficulties incurred by rush-construction but as a soldier he could not go against a superior order. As commander he had to carry the unreasonable to its conclusion and being a conscientious man it was a torment. He always thought of his subordinates, and they like him had the humanity not to disregard the services of the prisoners-of-war and the coolies.

He told me the following anecdote about prisoners drilling the rock-face at the 103 km point. On the day in question, in the scorching heat footholds on the rock formation became hotter and hotter. A couple of prisoners were working together hanging by a thread, it seemed, half-way up the precipice, drilling into the rock with hammer and cold chisel. As he went up to look one of them was pouring water into the drill-hole from a bamboo pipe at his hip substituting for a water bottle. The commander asked why he was pouring his own drinking-water into the drill-hole. The prisoner replied that it cooled the chisel.

The Colonel asked how, being permanently on jobs on an enemy's strategic railway, he could put such zeal into this drilling-job. The prisoner calmly replied, 'The drilling is my job'.* This reply, commented the Colonel, demonstrated the prisoner's will-power in such adverse circumstances to consider he must do his job zealously. The Colonel was struck with admiration for his attitude, a magnificent thing. Although the man was an enemy he thought it splendid. These prisoners, when the railway got over the Pass into Burma said jokingly, 'We'll ride home to London on it. England is bound to win.' They said this with complete confidence and I thought they had a taut self-control of their mental attitude with its unquestioned confidence in victory out of their adversity, and two years later, when their indomitable self-confidence proved justified, one saw it was the spirit of these Englishmen which underlay their real temper.

After the war in 1981 a former prisoner-of-war, Mr Adams, came to Japan and called on me. He said, in this context, 'We were able to survive by enduring adversity and by persisting in our endurance of it by mutually encouraging one another', and in his book he also admired the indomitable strength of spirit which surfaced everywhere ... and I, too, well understood what he meant. They actually had fun in what was a jungle way of life. They kept their musical instruments and loved singing, and on occasion produced plays and revues, and by such devices preserved some sensitivity and sensibility in an otherwise drab life. In the way they lived they extracted something intellectual and they invented better substitutes for daily necessities. They kept alive on quite inadequate rations, and in spite of all hardships their labour in contributing to the completion of the railway was not to be diverted. Large numbers of them gave up their lives and fell as sacrificial victims in the depths of the jungle. In a corner of the prisoners' camp at Kinsaiyok was a cemetery. Surrounded by a fence were a great many

---

* In his text Futamatsu adds in brackets ('This is my task'). What the prisoner certainly must have said was 'job' not 'task'. Futamatsu's text says 'This is my duty'. On the word *shigoto* see the translator's note to p. 4 of his translation of Chapter 15 of Futamatsu's *tainmentetsudo kensetsu ki*. See also his note to p. 12 of Chapter 24 (in the Department of Documents, Imperial War Museum, London).

crudely-made wooden crosses, painted white, in orderly rows. It made a quiet spot in the midst of the jungle. At each fresh grave-marker the prisoners bowed their heads and made some sort of prayer. They were the comrades-in-arms of the men who had died and were buried in a foreign soil far from their fatherland. With the breezes blowing through the trees, leaves scattered round the grave-markers and buried them. As the hot sun rose high the air was filled with the incessant cries of cicadas.

In November 1943, four or five months after the railway opened to traffic, I was put in charge of conservation of railtrack at Kinsaiyok. My unit's quarters were quite close to the prisoner-of-war camp. In April 1943, about the time when the rainy season broke out, Lieutenant Adams was moved from Thā Makham to Kinsaiyok. In this book he recollects Kinsaiyok as he saw it in those days:

I had lived for some time in Thā Makham when I was moved to Kinsiyok. For the transfer I had to walk along the railtrack, crossing over the temporary wooden by-pass bridge stepping from sleeper to sleeper, and passing through Wanlain, Bankhao, Thā Kilen, but compared with Thā Makham these places were foul with many sick men in them. On the way at the Chungkai cutting and the plank viaduct at Arrow Hill it was evident to my party that these places had been tough to work in. The railtrack had not been completed so we walked alsong the roadbed, passed Wampō, and halted for the night at Thā Sao (today's Nam Tok) where we bathed in the river. The depths of the trees and shrubs in the deep jungle growth seemed to overwhelm us, mere mortals. To judge by the vital strength of the vegetation one felt how feeble is the strength of man. The camps up-country became progressively worse. The *heiho* guards treated the prisoners brutally.

After three days' march we arrived at our objective, the 170 km point near Lintin, where the camp was near the riverbank. Our quarters were dilapidated huts which were awash with the rainwater. Our predecessors had been prisoners sent down from upcountry camps and they had had to leave a very weak and sick officer, Trader Horne (Captain L.E. Horne, RASC) who welcomed our arrival from the bottom of his heart. He was put into the sick bay in the hospital hut but alas he died. He was a splendid fellow, well thought of in our Group, an unforgettable man. Our quarters were on swampy ground with clouds of mosquitoes so there were many victims of malaria. Amoebic dysentery and tropical ulcers were also not infrequent. The dead from previous occupants were buried in a cemetery nearby. Compared with the camp at Thā Makham it was not a likeable place, one could not feel at home in it. The camp office-head was Lieutenant Suzuki. Our liaison-officer, Captain Morris Janis, RASC, protested that sick men were being forced to do hard manual labour by him, to make up the numbers demanded by the engineers, but Suzuki would not listen. The work daily became more severe. The work-period was extended and when it became dark kerosene lamps gave light to work which was too much for our eyes to cope with. The heat was oppressive, it rained day after day, we became sluggish and our resistance slumped. All of us prisoners were thoroughly tired out, often working ten hours a day.

With June came outbreaks of cholera in the coolies' camps upriver, the cholera germs were carried by the current along the river and in the end they invaded Kinsaiyok. The Japanese Army tried to eliminate cholera and the deaths it involved. The prime precaution was to boil all drinking-water. The corpses of victims had to be incinerated. Bathing in the river was prohibited. Yet despite these precautions there was a sudden increase in the number of deaths. The hospital huts were full, no bed-spaces left. With the rain the ground round the camps never dried. One could not rest a moment. Ditches overflowed and the stench of the filth assailed our nostrils to a degree hard to bear. We were worried about the swarms of flies scattering germs. Medical officers trying to stem the disease were themselves infected by it and some died.

News of the outside world circulated throughout the camp. To us, this was our only reassurance. Just at that time the American Navy's brilliant actions in the Aleutian Archipelago and on Attu Island, turning the Allied Forces to the attack, were disseminated. Our secret hand-made radio set (we called it 'the canary') from time to time caught broadcasts from New Delhi and was a great solace.

On the work-sites birds and animals were scared off, but the wild flowering plants of the jungle bloomed in profusion and their abundant colours and marvellous shapes increasingly charmed our senses.

It was now that wonderful news came from home. My parents over a year earlier had received by mail news that my 18 Division unit had announced formally on the radio news that I was missing after the fall of Singapore, confirmed by letter. 'He is alive', the message said, but nothing else. I had waited so long for news from home with a heart full of nostalgia, full of memories.

Chapter 28

DISEASES AND EPIDEMICS

With the advent of the rainy season the hardships on the construction-sites were caused not only by the rain but also by fierce and terrifying air-raids by the enemy. There were, too, disease epidemics. In the River Kwae Noi area along which the route ran, in the river-basin people did not live right in the jungle, but some contracted malarial fevers and were subject to outbreaks of various other infections. The demon of ill-health represented a fact of life which had to be expected, threatening their lives. When outbreaks of fiercely contagious diseases occurred such as dysentery, cholera, bubonic plague and so on, they spread widely in a flash along the waters of the river. To the Thai, this was nothing new. When the Japanese Army were planning the railway construction, counter-measures against epidemics were considered in real earnest and so, after the first step of investigating a route for the railtrack itself, the question of prevention against epidemics in the water-supply was also considered. To make the interior of the jungle fit to live in one had to be prepared to investigate assured supplies of drinking water and so on. Precautionary measures were taken by the engineers against epidemics of infectious diseases and vaccination and immunization of Japanese troops were enforced. In the rainy season of 1942 few of the engineer units and a minority of prisoner-of-war labourers were affected by such conditions so it was possible to go a long way towards defence against invasion by this demon of disease. In 1943, the year in which in March, in the rainy season, the order for rush-construction was being enforced, river-flooding at the work-sites was widespread. Concurrently, numbers of prisoners and coolies were precipitately increased. The number of labourers reached a total of some 100,000 men. As you may well imagine, for such vast numbers, to take foolproof measures of protection was impossibly difficult to achieve. On top of that problem, it became difficult to transport food and fodder and the shortage of supplies for the entire workforce caused standards of nourishment to decline. A slump in general health continued, rehabilitation from fatigue was hampered, and few escaped illness of some sort or other. At times like these when attacked by viruses a patient's condition was likely to stop improving. It seemed impossible to provide medical treatment for the sick and, as people became radically infected by viruses, carriers appeared. Thus sickness became widespread. Especially were the men worried about violent outbreaks of infectious strength.

In the rainy seasons, hordes of mosquitoes came out and there was a sudden increase in the numbers of victims of malarial fever. We well knew it was *anopheles* mosquitoes which sucked the blood of their victims and carried and propagated the germs. On the under-nourished there were many onsets of malarial fever. The fevers were virulent and there were many cases of mistaken diagnoses and death. The decline in nourishment caused by lack of food was the ultimate cause of ill-health and caused chronic diarrhoea and dysentery, and for lack of vitamin B men contracted wet beriberi. Further, wild animals' droppings defiled the soil in the deep forests, got into men's wounds and they developed tropical ulcers.

At the start of the summer of 1942, when construction work began, efforts were made on camp sites to maintain sound practices in the use of drinking water and sanitation, and anti-infectious disease standards were strictly enforced. For protection against malarial fevers it was standard practice to take quinine. But with the advent of summer in 1943, because of the sudden increase in the numbers of prisoners and coolies on the work-sites, it became very difficult to maintain standards. Before the railway construction began, it was rare to find anyone living in the jungle and there used to be few cases of viruses attacking human beings, but with this sudden increase viruses came with them. It was remarkable how many men became carriers of malarial virus.

Initially all was not well with sanitation and viruses and, to cap it all, coolies had a very poor sense of responsibility about sanitation. In the long run the prisoner-of-war camps were plagued by lack of medical facilities and of medicines. It began with attacks of dysentery. Then with the rainy season there came in the end an onrush of cholera. It broke out to start with in the neighbourhood of the frontier, and was propagated by the downstream current of the Kwae Noi, spreading in a flash like primordial fire. The Japanese Army's preventative water supply unit and their field hospital sanitation squad put out their best efforts, but cholera broke out among the coolies, from them to the prisoners-of-war and from them finally to the Japanese soldiers. In the illness with which this precipitous pathological change was associated, cholera treatment came too late and deaths occurred. For this disease, neglecting to boil drinking water and mis-use of river water spread contagion and it was necessary also deal with the excrement of sufferers properly and to incinerate the corpses of the dead. Cholera victims were isolated as far as possible but because the disease was so precipitate the hospital huts could take no more patients. Since they had then to stay in their quarters the risk of infection increased. In one camp the increase in the number of deaths was such that the collection of firewood for incineration could not keep pace.

By July, cholera had penetrated as far as the base at Wanyai, 170 km downstream from the Three Pagodas Pass, the river flowing alongside the work-sites and proliferating widely. One saw the same thing happening on Burma-side, too, along rivers as it did on the Kwae Noi and quite as fast as on Thai-side.

The rate of infection from cholera was high and so was the death-rate for those who caught it. If carriers, prisoners and coolies were isolated this caused a marked decline in the rate of infection. All this affected the progress of the work and the health of the labourers declined with it.

The circumstances that inoculations of prisoners and coolies did not prevent attacks of cholera showed that there was no single cause of infection, but many, and lack of medicaments led to a high death-rate. The coolies went on drinking unboiled water. The prisoners' staple diet was boiled rice and so with lack of nourishment in emaciated bodies they, too, readily contracted the disease. This was the root cause of the increased number of sufferers. In the end, with the rainy season continuing from June into July, a hundred labourers died from cholera every day. There had been no reason to suppose that there would be epidemics of such ferocity; such violence was beyond anticipation, but it is true that the Japanese Army did not take sufficient countermeasures in time. There were too many victims and the Army, I think, did not do enough and deserves criticism.

On construction work the number of victims included not only those who died of cholera but also those who contracted malarial fevers, and under-nourishment and loss of blood from tropical ulcers also contributed. From serious epidemics on railway construction the authenticated number of victims was over 10,000, or calculated as a death for every ten metres of the entire length of the railway.

It is obvious that the stigma, 'Railroad of Death', originated in the main as a result of the order for rush-construction in February 1943. The battle against epidemics petered out with the end of the rainy season which naturally extinguished the virus bit-by-bit.

We had to endure torrential rain in the rainy season and fight against violent epidemics, but somehow the job continued to make progress.

Chapter 29

CATTLE DRIVE

A British prisoner-of-war, Lieutenant Adams, was in Kinsaiyok camp for several months but in mid-June the prisoners, who were under Lieutenant Suzuki, the camp commandant at Kinsaiyok, were moved up-country to Konkuita. It happened that Kinsaiyok camp had bought a hundred head of cattle for their meat to take with them when they moved. Lieutenant Adams, as 'cattle officer', culled and took them out as beef cattle on the hoof into the depths of the jungle. From his interesting book comes the quotation from his chapter called 'Cattle Drive', an account of their journey on foot:

> It was the dead of night. A guard woke me up and told me to go to Lieutenant Suzuki. I didn't like being called out like this. Had I breached a camp regulation or was he investigating an incident at Changi? I had no idea, knocked anxiously on the commandant's, door, went in and there by Suzuki was Service Corps Captain Morris Janis who greeted me with a simulated smile. He told me that on our move to the new camp the 100 head of cattle would be accepted there, but someone was needed to supervise the move and had to be selected ... I was ordered to do it. My recent anxiety fell away and I felt quite relieved, but this responsibility did not sound like a very pleasant job. It was, I understood, about 100 km to Konkuita. Janis explained that to take cattle on the hoof there would take perhaps ten days and in his opinion it would be a risky operation. He looked earnestly at my expression as he said, 'You're a butcher by trade,

my friend, so you'll have to get used to becoming a 'cowboy', won't you.' He well knew my trade and recalled why I had become a Service Corps lieutenant. I undertook to do what he wanted but my feelings had flopped at the realization of what I was being expected to do.

I had to depart that very morning and Captain Janis told me to select 19 ORs whom I thought competent, to let him have a nominal roll, to give men their instructions, and that a Korean *heiho* must go with us. Apart from myself, I could not be sure the nineteen men could do this kind of job, so from the start could not know whether or not it would be a worthwhile exercise. I hurried to my quarters and woke up the men I wanted to take with me, and explained what the job was to be. To a man they agreed to go with me. They all had enough energy to walk and to care for the herd, and on balance that they thought they might perhaps do it. They were glad to travel together so there was my list of nineteen completed. I had my own doubts but it was the stimulus of the new responsibility that made me unable to sleep. It was, of course, already in the small hours before dawn. I could not help remembering my home in Worcestershire now at its seasonal best ... here the rain persisted and in the gloom columns of mosquitoes could be seen flying at the edges of the eaves.

The senior men in my 'cattle-driving squad' were serjeants Robinson, Lawrence, and North, and privates Tyler and Turnbull. Escorting us was *heiho* Takeda and he was formally the soldier in charge. I had the new special title of 'Cattle Officer' written on my armband. *Heiho* Takeda's rifle was the sole armoury. As soon as it was light I went with him to inspect our hundred head of cattle. They had been sorted out into a special corral and there was also the important question of fodder. They were mostly worn-out beasts too old to be useful, there were a couple of bullocks, a couple of cows with calves at foot and a few young bulls. When I returned to camp I found the main body had already left. They had loaded up their baggage on a sampan and set out from the waterfront. Like them our cattle squad had breakfast of boiled rice and 'banjofish', our nickname for dried codfish. With us we carried ten days' supply of food and fodder, sacks and ropes, each man setting out with his personal effects slung on his shoulder, and for butchering, I carried a broad-bladed woodman's hatchet, a parang.

We brought our cattle from the corral and with *heiho* Takeda in front set off on foot into the thick of the jungle aiming at Konkuita. I had our food and personal effects put on the humps of the ox-cart oxen. Ten minutes later, as we were walking through a grove of bamboos, without warning at a work-site where the roadbed was being built the noise of a rock-blasting charge roared out. The terrified cattle ran off into the jungle. Confusedly we searched for and rounded them up but there were four we couldn't find. Of the four, two were yoke-oxen on whose humps I had put our personal effects. I was depressed. It was my first big failure as 'Cattle Officer' but, learning by it, I assigned each member of the squad to his particular duty. In the van two men acted as guides with another to act as runner if they encountered anything out of the ordinary. In the rear were men looking after cattle which did not keep up with the herd. Of the remainder I put two to walk on each flank of the herd to keep them together on the move. In addition were men to carry cooking pots and to collect firewood. I myself reverted from the van to the tail-end of the squad to maintain control of the cattle on the move. Each member of the squad carried a stick to keep up the cattle-drive.

Heiho Takeda walked alongside me. I found he was becoming even more unlikeable. He despised me, it seemed, and because of his pompous attitude I deliberately ingratiated myself like a servant to him. Up to the day before Kinsaiyok was for me no place at which to feel at home and so the further we were able to get from the place the more able were we to enjoy some feelings of ease. Whether there would be any opportunity of escaping from whatever life there was for prisoners-of-war or not we did not know. For this squad of twenty men there was only one guard. There were also rations and the fodder for 100 head of cattle. If we killed Takeda we had no notion where we might escape to freedom. In a short rest-period we discussed escape, one of my NCOs saying such an opportunity would not occur a second time. However, when our comrades had failed in their attempt to escape at Thā Makham and had been recaptured I knew their fate had been death. I also remembered we were conducting 100 head of cattle as provisions for my fellow-prisoners and judged the cattle-driving squad was a serious responsibility not to be abandoned. I rejected the NCOs idea and gave up thoughts of escape.

I was accompanying cattle and so went at a snail's pace, making slow progress on our march. We approached a Japanese Army unit's barracks and asked for supplies to replace those lost with the yoke-oxen. They shouted, '*baka yaro*! (idiots!)', and chased us out. By sundown our boots and clothes were mud-soiled, flies and bugs buzzed round the cattle and tormented them. They were exhausted. I myself was barely able to keep walking. The calves were too tired to be able to keep up with their mothers. They were in a pitiable state, one of them died and the mother would not leave it, a loss of a couple more. As darkness fell we groped our way to a prisoner-of-war camp called Quema. We borrowed from them an old tent, and bivouacked together with the cattle which we rounded up into a circle, put on a picket to keep watch, and went to sleep. In the middle of the night a dizzy old bullock put his muzzle on my shoulder and went to sleep. Next morning, miraculously, the sun rose in the sky. At our feet lovely orchids bloomed in profusion. The cattle woke up, trampled on them, ate them like weeds for breakfast.

This day's route lay up a hill some distance from the river. *Heiho* Takeda had no duties except to walk. He disliked all officers, he said, who made him walk. He got tired and made a prisoner carry his rifle. He fell behind the squad, fell completely out of sight but we had to go looking for him, of course. When we had asked for food and shelter from a Japanese Army barracks he was our interpreter and also evidence of our 'respectability', in both respects a man we could not do without. From this period his attitude began to change a little, good news for us. Perhaps he had overheard our discussion the day before about escaping, or perhaps he was simply afraid, as a single Japanese surrounded by a posse of twenty Englishmen. We went on up this hill, a steep path to the top of a cliff. Below us trees and shrubs were spread out like a wide green carpet and the river below them all was invisible. Bad footholds forced us down into a valley, at the bottom of which was a pretty wide mountain stream. We made a simple raft and put Takeda, a non-swimmer, on it with his rifle and got him across. Then we put our own non-swimmers on the raft and got them over, and the cattle crossed over in the water.

The slope on the far side was slippery, the water swept a couple away and they drowned. This made a total of eight we had lost. The cattle's fodder had to be weeds under the trees as there was no time to search for the grass they liked, so none of them had enough to eat. They were a pitiable sight.

Early on the third day our route crossed over a place where work on the roadbed was going on, so I asked permission from the Japanese NCO in charge to cross. Meanwhile a bullock planted itself down on the comparatively cool roadbed embankment. Desperately I gave his tail a good twist but he gave no sign of moving. The corporal rushed up and shouted at Takeda who indicated that I was the officer responsible for the cattle. Without warning the corporal hit me hard. I apologized with, 'Honourable Corporal, I beg your pardon', and got away fast. Afterwards Takeda sympathized with me and gave me a cigarette saying, 'That corporal is a short-tempered bastard.' It was a pity I could not speak very good Japanese. Both the *heiho* and the corporal did not understand my apology so the corporal hit me. It was a rule with us to keep at arm's length of the Japanese you were speaking to, he might or he might not bash you.

Kinsaiyok had finally been degraded by infamous cholera, and there was a strict ban on drinking unboiled water. The ban was issued on the morning of the day we set out. Sjt North, who had previously violated the embargo, began to show cholera symptoms so he was left behind in the hospital hut at Kinsaiyok. Sjt Lawrence's tropical ulcers got worse, he could no longer walk, so we had to leave him at the first camp we came to. There was another camp we did not like the look of, thinking they might rustle some of our cattle, so we passed by without stopping. The same day we came to a camp where we found some prisoners in pretty poor shape. We listened to their story: for lack of protein many of them had died and they really were in great distress. Some of our friends were there and as an act of mercy we left them a bullock. With its loss we were now down to ninety-one head. With our remaining herd we had great difficulty in climbing up a steep, slippery hill walking in water in which corduroy logs which had been laid down had floated up in two feet of water (corduroy logging is a means of 'stepping-stones' to provide footholds on steep hills). The cattle, rain-soaked, trudged on with saliva dripping from their mouths. When we rested, unable to put a step further, we tried not to get soaked, lying down painfully. Towards evening we saw smoke ahead of us. Men's voices could be heard, those of men we knew – it was our own main party. They showed no sympathy with us cattle-squad men, were not interested. I was exhausted and wanted to find someone to relieve me as cattle-officer. We had groped our way bit-by-bit to Brankassii camp and expected to find arrangements for a meal. Luckily there was also an Australian camp here who were good enough to show us into their bivouac. In barely three days we had walked over 20 kilometres. It rained all night but next morning they looked after us, giving us a midday meal and filling our water-bottles again the torrid sun. We were sent on our way by these kind Australians for another day's journey with the cattle.

The rain cleared up, hot sun blazed down on us, our wet clothes dried and we got some warmth into our bodies. We walked for a long time enjoying the sunshine. At the next camp Colonel A.A. Johnson of the Suffolk Regiment in my own 18 Division was in charge, and he asked our guard if we could stay overnight there and take a day's rest. *Heiho* Takeda appreciated the Colonel's kindness but would not accept his offer, so we kept on walking.

We had to climb a rocky hill which confronted us. The track up the hill was narrow, four or five feet wide, and on the left-hand side was a dangerous precipice. When we had climbed a little way up a Rising Sun flag came into view hoisted on a hut-like building. We made the cattle go up one at a time, but the last ones made a dash for it, clearly an accident impended. There was no room for cattle in a row abreast and when those in the lead got to the point at which there was a deep ravine they stopped. The others shoved them from behind, they gathered in a cluster, the road shoulder crumbled under their weight and in a flash four beasts trampled on each other legs and rolled over down the slope into the ravine. I rushed up the slope to count the cattle. There were eighty-seven head left.

With Takeda I approached the *atap*-thatched building on which flew the Rising Sun flag. I bowed courteously to the sentry and to the flag and requested an interview with the senior NCO. It was the quarters of a Japanese Army supply unit, and by chance the troops were not in camp, so my squad were given permission to stay the night in camp. I explained about the accident of the cattle falling into the ravine. If we could be allowed time to look for them I proposed to offer the NCO some beef. Returning to the scene of the accident I found that one bullock had been caught up in the top of a tree projecting up out of the undergrowth of shrubs. It was dead. At risk of my life I was dropped on top of the tree by a rope tied to my waist, butchered the bullock and had the haunches hauled up the precipice. We bathed in a pool of cold water on top of the precipice and gave ourselves a thorough wash. The sun had set and the evening moon was rising over the hill-top. When we got back to camp our comrades had got ready the meal and were waiting for us. The supply unit men, in return for our marvellous beef, gave us an allowance of black tea with sugar and cigarettes. We took a long time over our luxurious meal, all we needed for complete extravagance was rice-wine and women. That night with my appetite quite satiated I could not sleep for the flood of memories of my parents and friends of my youth, There followed our day of rest and we stored up energy. The place, near Thā Khanun, was on a plateau 270 metres above sea-level. I was particularly glad we had no high hills into which (as at Chungkai) we would have to tunnel.

When we parted from the kind supply unit soldiers we checked the herd total and during our rest-day some cattle had run off somewhere or had been rustled. With seventy-three in sight we were short by twenty-seven head. We were responsible for seeing 100 head to our destination and both *heiho* Takeda and I were seriously alarmed.

That day we came across groups of wild monkeys. They made a great clatter, climbing and jumping across from tree to tree. I was walking in front and suddenly an iguana five-feet long sprang up and confronted me. Someone jokingly said, 'Lieutenant, Sir, please jump on its back and strangle it!' In this area where few men had ever trodden beautiful flowers bloomed in the middle of deep forest, flowers whose names were unknown to me. Clouds rolled up, rain fell again, our spirits fell, our sense of feeling good dried up.

From the front a runner came back to me to report that there was a herd of cattle grazing without any herdsmen in sight. I reconnoitred and it looked as if there must be a Japanese unit somewhere near.

By rustling some I thought I could probably make up the number of which I was short. In the event of our rustling being found out whatever punishment I received I admitted would be fearful but I was determined to carry the thing out. I cut thirty head of healthy beasts and they were lost amid our own herd. *Heiho* Takeda controlled his alarm of being met by someone; after all, he was an accomplice. But both of us had been worried about our default in numbers and, given a successful operation, I could trust him to keep quiet. Our herd was now back at a hundred plus, and so with the surplus we could weed out weak beasts. We were delighted with the success of our rustling effort. All the same we got away fast and put as many miles as we could from the scene and from our jungle bivouac.

It was the ninth day since we had left Kinsaiyok. We kept to an old road which I thought led to the Three Pagodas Pass, and by the roadside we saw a native squatting on a tree-root. He was a cholera victim in the article of death, begging for water. The stench was terrible and at his feet ants had collected. Flies buzzed incessantly around his eyes and mouth. He was near death: I thought, do I kill him or did I pity him too much to do it? I gave him a cigarette, the best I could do, abandoned him and we went on our way. It was a shaming thing. His beseeching look as I left him will stick in my memory as long as I live.

A report came from the van that there was what looked [like] a cemetery with corpses visible. I went to look and there were derelict broken-down huts thatched with *atap*, absolutely no sign of life, the huts surrounded by corpses in wild confusion. In this coolie camp cholera must have raged fiercely and fatally attacked them down to the last man, and the camp abandoned, over a hundred corpses lying there, truly a frightful spectacle of the horrors of war. On the corpses were ants and clouds of flies accompanied by the stench of dead bodies. A kind of atmospheric disaster filled the air, I couldn't stay a moment longer. It was as if as a boy, alone, I had seen an apparition staggering towards me and I had to run away.

On the evening of that day, at the foot of a steep hill, a stream ran under a narrow bridge which led across to a rice-paddy ridge. On it there was a Japanese sentry. The stream was deep and the current fast, men could not cross in the water but we were able to shove the cattle, at least, out into the middle of the stream. With the sentry's permission but on condition that no cattle could use the bridge we ourselves crossed on the bridge. The cattle were driven down into the stream, but one crafty beast came running up onto the bridge. I brandished my stick at him but lost my foothold and ended up by falling down into the current. It had been raining day after day, the stream was very full, my clothes got soaked and heavy, I thought I was drowning and let out a yell. They threw a rope, I caught hold of it, and barely got up onto the bank, but the onlookers thought it funny and let out peals of laughter!

That day we followed a track which took us to Kreung Krai. Here they were in the middle of building a wooden plank bridge over a creek on a sharp bend of the river. There was no room for a prisoner-of-war camp so Kreung Krai was just a bivouac. Our old 18 Division friends got a meal ready for us. We dried our clothes by the camp fire. I was fully conscious how much a prisoner-of-war's life contrasted for the better with the coolie's misery I had seen that day, and naturally felt some small consolation at the thought.

Next day hardly any rain fell. We pressed on driving the cattle. At about three o'clock there appeared the queer figure of a prisoner wearing ragged trousers and a worn-out shirt, with a Trilby hat festooned with leaves and feathers. He saluted me and said in his husky voice, 'Lieutenant Adams, Sir, you are welcome to Konkuita!' He and I had served together in the Suffolks' regimental office. We had made it to Konkuita. At last we had driven our cattle here on the hoof. In ten days we had walked over 90 km from Kinsaiyok. The men had made the passage, crossing ravines in the jungle, crossing water-courses, enduring the rain and the heat, conducting with them one hundred head of cattle. I myself was glad and greatly relieved to have carried out my responsible job. I had persisted well with my cattle-driving squad and greatly appreciated the men's tough work. The cattle, too, gave a credible performance on the hoof. They were our loveable slaves. I dragged my exhausted frame along to meet Suzuki and Captain Janis and received their greetings on completion of my task.

Chapter 30

LIVING IN THE JUNGLE

WATER

In the hot season you welcome cool water. Throughout the year there is
no clear distinction between the four seasons in the various countries in
the South but it is always hot and for various reasons water is important
and precious. There are many encumbrances in the way, both physical and psychological, to prevent one getting used to heat. Cold water
goes a long way to alleviate discomfort and drinking, bathing, rinsing
clothes are several ways of using it. On occasions when one finds there
is little or no water it is a serious matter. Men can't live without it, and
life in the jungle without the blessing of water is incredibly difficult. In
our life within the secluded boundaries of Thailand and Burma there
was so much rain and abundant water-courses but the water did not
always serve a useful purpose. The brimming waters of the River Kwae
Noi were fearfully muddy at times and could not be used for various
purposes. Water-courses in the jungle were dirtied by rotted vegetation,
animal excrement and so on and could not, therefore, be drunk. It was
impossible to dig wells to get at underground water. In particular there
were times when bacteria abounded in water causing terrible contagious diseases, and it was, therefore, essential to keep water clean and
sterilized.

People who had to live for some reason in the jungle invariably
collected rainwater and used that. Even rainwater could become bacterial but they used their wits and kept it pure. In the earthen pots in

which they collected rainwater there were mosquito-larvae but these local inhabitants drank water unconcernedly with the mosquito-larvae in it. That larvae bred in it showed it was pure. When offered water with no larvae in it we were quite apprehensive and did not feel like drinking it.

Into the Kwae Noi fed mountain streams and along them any people living there soiled the water with their sewage. This did not prevent them from using it for bathing and washing clothes but it was quite unsuitable for drinking. The upcountry people's life-style and that of our boatmen was to drink rainwater and they were invariably equipped with earthen pots to collect it. They did not drink river water.

The railway construction units used stills to purify water and decrease bacterial risk. These were small-pattern jobs, hand-operated, which definitely boiled up water and in principle killed bacteria. To drink water unboiled in a cholera area was strictly prohibited and there was also an embargo on bathing in the river. Work unit barracks were sited in places where there was water to prevent inconvenience in bathing, etc. During persistent rain the flow of water was muddied and could not be used but during squalls we bathed in the rain as it fell from the sloping roofs of the huts, washed ourselves and did our laundry. We cooled our sweaty, dusty bodies in cool showers of rain and anyone who has experienced the bliss of cool, refreshing rain-drops is unlikely to forget it. On the line of march and during rest-periods the water in our water-bottles relieved fatigue. Water was the specific remedy and at the time one thought of it as the cord on which life hung. However, when the sun rose high in the sky and the heat gradually closed in on one, to have water in one's water-bottle helped, figuratively, to dispel the depression of loneliness. In the tropical South water is precious and nothing can replace it.

THE TOKAY

You were woken by the shrilling of cicadas and if you looked up from your mosquito-net there on a thick beam in the *atap*-thatched roof you might discern a dusty-grey animal about ten centimetres long which behaved as if it owned the place. It had a fat but short tail. When it saw you it would move slightly, raise its throat and jerk out a snoring sound. Then suddenly it would cry loudly, 'tok-tok-tok'. It was the first time I had seen a live tokay (a large gecko). It is an oddly-shaped animal and when we heard in the stillness of the night a cry from what sounded like somewhere in the past, we felt indeed that we had come to a foreign country. Tokays are peculiar to the southern countries of Thailand, Burma and Malaya. They often go on calling between three toks to five toks in a low tone, then stop. The first time I heard its cry I couldn't see 'the master of the house' and so I felt uneasy, but it became part of the intimate scenery of the southern countries to the extent that at night one waited for the tokay's cry. When the native people heard it cry seven toks they believed it meant that they were blessed with good luck, but it very seldom made seven. In the stillness of the night when one heard the tokay's cry the lonesomeness of one's journey was emphasized and one could not sleep for the homesickness which I thought would never end.

CHAMELEONS

We often saw in the jungle an extraordinary animal, the chameleon. They are twenty centimetres long with long tapering tails and large triangular eyes. On their back is a frilly mane like that on some species of lizard. With an extending tongue they skilfully catch their prey, small insects. Their body-colour can change from ashy brown to brilliant cobalt blue. You catch then and their body-colour changes in a flash. They can change at will from protective coloration imitating their surroundings to a conspicuous warning colour in emergencies. As a man often changes his opinions, chameleons by comparison can change instinctively. These animals change their body-colour depending on the circumstances, now revealing themselves as they normally are, now concealing themselves, a wonderful thing to see. They are no use as food if you catch them. We learned from the local natives that iguanas, which are bigger than chameleons, can be used as food. They taste like chicken with a delicious flavour of persimmons dried on a skewer. Iguanas are caught in clever snares. The natives select a bamboo node of diameter through which an iguana can pass, keep by them a five-centimetre-long section of bamboo-pipe of the same shape, make a thin, narrow pointed end and construct a bamboo spring. They fix a cord to the pointed end of the spring, put a tip on the cord-trap and adjust it to the inside of the bamboo-pipe. They bend round the tip of the spring and fasten it in the mouth of the bamboo-pipe and when this restraining tool pushes from the middle of the pipe it makes a device for springing the trap. Iguanas dig holes and live underground and so men set the traps at the entrance to the holes. This is an interesting method of catching them.

FOREST FIRES

One day I took a lift in a work-unit lorry bound for the HQ of construction unit at Wanyai. The sun set and twilight came floating in amongst the trees in the deep forest. The driver was in a hurry and accelerated on the uneven highway so the lorry ran bumpily up-down, side-to-side. He was a bit off-course and as it grew dark he switched on his headlights. Bang in the headlights a devilish bamboo clump came into view. I thought I could see flames and there was a crackling noise, but there were no signs of men about. I looked closely and a blaze could be seen among the weeds under the trees in the jungle and evil-smelling smoke came drifting along. I thought it might be a forest fire and became apprehensive. The speed with which flames spread in a forest fire is unbelievable, but when what lies in front in the dense forest has burnt out the chance of it going further is dissipated. When trees and shrubs in the dry season are dried out, and a breeze sets up, it is thought that chafing among the trees is quite likely to ignite them. When forest fires break out, it is very difficult to put them out and it is not surprising that they spread a kilometre in each direction. Only the tree-trunks remain unburnt, they stay erect, and the area becomes a burnt wilderness.

Our lorry regained its speed although the smoke ahead obscured our field of vision, and we extricated ourselves from the danger-zone. To cultivate new land in the deep forest it even needed a man-made fire to burn down trees and shrubs. The remains of the fire in the soil makes good compost for raising crops. In a forest fire tall teak and rowan trees get burnt, a great loss, but I think a country enviable which has such abundant forest resources that to lose some trees was no great problem.

Forest fires can leave dangerous traces. When we went down on the highway in the growing gloom the barracks at the base of Wanyai could be seen in headlamps between the trees.

ELEPHANTS

Elephants helped in the construction of the railway. In this country, when heavy rocks and timber have to be moved, they use elephants. In ancients times it was elephants which moved into action as the war potential in fights with neighbouring countries. They also take part, gorgeously apparelled, in ceremonials. An elephant's power derives from its large girth and body-weight, and it has been estimated that its strength is ten times that of a man. For work in deep forests they are chiefly used for moving heavy things like rocks and timber. They are worked by mahouts with whose commands they conform.

They were scheduled to be used on the railway construction. Both on Thai-side and Burma-side in the main timber-producing areas from South to North elephants moved into the jungle with their mahouts. In the best working season in June 1943 there were about 200 elephants in use over the entire area.

Elephants are often raised and trained by Mahouts. The mahout straddles the elephant's neck, its long trunk sways from side to side, it walks with a shambling gait. For such a big animal its eyes are small, its big ears flap as it moves, it takes long strides as it goes. Other than its trunk this ash-grey animal has no other grasping limbs. It is intelligent and normally docile.

Acting in accordance with its mahout's commands in its ear elephants perform various jobs. They roll up heavy objects with their trunks to carry them. To knock things down they move them by pushing with their forelegs. They pulled things with chains suspended from their forequarters. They cleverly use their trunks like hands positioning beams and squared timber, adjusting the load to fine tolerances. They roll up small objects in their trunks when shifting heavy rocks. They push things over with their big forelegs, but it the object is very heavy their action is to lift it up with their trunk, prop it up with their forelegs and push it with their heads. It is well known that their body-weight is heavy and the weight is supported to some extent by the forelegs which is confirmed by the way they let down their limbs cautiously. Because of their weight they do not go across small bridges but wade on the river bottom, and as they move ahead they raise their trunks above water to breathe. On occasion, they lift up their mahouts in their trunks and give them a swim.

Their fodder was not specially provided. At night their forelegs were shackled so they could not walk far, but they were not tethered. In the jungle they ate bamboo leaves, tree-buds, bamboo-shoots, and in the morning returned back to their mahouts. When they went into the jungle, if they were to carry people, howdahs were put on their backs. Elephants are hindered in their advance by branches in the undergrowth and by creeper-vines which they seize by their trunks, pull them down, and then trample them underfoot. Men riding carelessly in a howdah kept getting caught by branches in the undergrowth and being hit by branches of trees.

Elephants dislike and are apprehensive of man-made tracks. When one suddenly meets them on the way they brandish their trunks and bellow. They are frightened to go down a track. When we came to a mountain pass, there was a notice-board which said, 'Elephants at work', a warning not to go down a track. If you do meet one on a track the mahout will turn the elephants' head to face you and then back away into the jungle. If even so the elephant will not calm down the mahout pounds on its forehead with his long-handled *ankh*. What look like tears appear in its little eyes from its pain and accordingly it retreats. In a way it's a pathetic, humorous spectacle.

From time to time there were elephant escapades. One morning some elephants thrust their trunks into some grain-sacks in the provisions and fodder godown. The soldier i/c cookhouse noticed the large bulk of the elephants full of contraband from the godown, and lined up the mahouts and complained, 'You were given a full hundred kilograms!' There is a risk of elephants running amok. On one occasion an elephant went berserk and chased the prisoners-of-war. One prisoner was coiled up in the elephant's trunk, his sinews and bones were crushed and he died instantly. Another was thrown into a nearby furrough to be trampled on. The breadth of the elephant's foot was greater than the width of furrough and the man had a narrow escape from death by being crushed underfoot. It sounds like a fabrication but it is a true story. Despite such accidents, elephants were star actors in helping the construction work.

LIVING IN THE JUNGLE

When a man spends a long time living in the jungle he realizes his way of life is to keep alive. Various devices made life liveable and men ingeniously made tools to that end. Out of bamboo they made chessmen and mahjong tiles. Out of paper they made complete packs of floral playing cards. In bamboo baskets each man made for himself chopsticks, a spoon, a fork and so on. The curfew orderly made them forget the toils of work as they talked together about their homeland, visualizing it while writing their letters home. Flowers bloomed in their talk of home: they forgot the toil in their gambling games. When night fell, everyone felt homesick and yearned for his homeland, its fields and mountains floated under their eyelids and in dreams they saw the dream-faces of their family friends: these men in the battlefield had no choice but to become sentimental. On the map it seemed a short step, really many thousands of kilometres away, this separation from home. Outside, the jungle was simply solid green all day and every day. Those bamboo posts had supported the *atap* roof for over a year; men longed for the feeling of *tatami* (floor matting) and the loved *fusuma* (opaque sliding doors) and *shōji* (translucent paper sliding doors) and being Japanese wanted the common things of life, wishing they could put on *kimono* (Japanese clothes). On sleepless nights when, carried away by intolerable homesickness, a man went outside, there above the rows and rows of treetops the Southern Cross twinkled in the night sky. The surroundings were spread out in a hushed silence like that on the ocean floor. The railway construction work still went on and on, but what would the future outlook for the war be, what hope of repatriation.

Such were the worries this wearisome life did not halt. The tokay's cry rang out. Next day, too, on and on until the railway was open to traffic ...

Chapter 31

SOON TO THE THREE PAGODAS PASS

It was at the end of August that we drew near the Pass. Since our advance from Kinsaiyok in June the second extension of railtrack-head, accompanied in its progress by roadbed construction, gradually approached Thā Khanun. The railtrack-head on Burma-side, too, was nearing the frontier and all the roadbed in the Nikki area was in mid-construction. At this juncture the section of railtrack to be completed was about 100 km plus, and the situation was that the railway could not be completed by the scheduled end of August. Five months after rush-construction had been pushed ahead in earnest, that five months had proved insufficient. The whole railtrack made a railwayline about 300 km long, and a third more work on construction was calculated to be needed. Once the line was open to traffic a base was needed for complete equipment for rolling stock in the running of trains, with necessary equipment for security, for engine-shed equipment, for water-supply equipment and so on. Firewood, too, for engines had to be stockpiled. To complete what was left there were 100 km of railtrack to be finished within about a couple of months.

In mid-August Major-General Takasaki was completely confined to his sickbed (with malarial fever) and had to hand over command. His successor, Major-General Ishida Hideguma, took up his post as GOC, Thai-Burma Railway Construction. From his HQ at Kamburi he reported to his superior at Southern Army HQ his determination to complete the railway in a planned period of about two months. The connecting-up point for the Thai-side and the Burma-side regiments was definitely laid down as to be Konkuita at 262 km, and the regiments were instructed to push the work ahead.

On Thai-side the CO of 9 Railway Regiment advanced his effective command to Tamuron Part, and the regiment disposed their entire force on the gap up to Konkuita, putting their maximum effort on hastening the work on the remaining roadbed construction. On Burma-side, 5 Railway Regiments established their HQ at Kyandaw, and from the Three Pagodas Pass at the frontier there was a section of track of about 40 km into which they threw the total strength of the Regiment and hurried on the work. From August, because of the complexity of the section, their efforts included excavating rocky hills, with not a little work on bridge-building. Installing railway stations at Nikki, Tamuron Part, Konkuita, etc., putting in equipment for water-supply, for inter-communication, for fuel supply and internal fixtures, all these remained to be done. Extending over the entire line appropriate action was inaugurated for collecting branches for fire-wood, gravel for use in roadbed flooring, and collecting the stockpiling rubble. Previously from June air-raids had begun on the Thanbyusayat and Nong Pladuk bases. On the Mae Khlaung bridges camouflage netting was spread and an AA-gun team placed in position.

In this way the final chase came for both sides for the joining-up point at Konkuita. The jungle shook with their efforts.

At the end of August the long rainfall ceased and we entered on the dry season. Transport reverted to normal and the shortages of food and fodder ended. The violent assaults of cholera died down and the work in the jungle took a favourable turn, but the labourers, without distinction of day or night, were plunged into continuous labour without sleep or rest. On the highway lorries ran continuously, loaded with supplies, food and fodder. On the river, too, transport by boat went on, loaded sampans went up-river against the current, and the noise of logging sounded in the jungle: all these activities were conquering nature in advancing the construction work, and they reverberated loudly. In a day we crossed one valley, took the top off a hill in the evening, the next day we pulverized solid rock and plugged up a deep ravine, each day extending the railroad towards the joining-up point.

Our target was the Three Pagodas Pass across the Thai-Burma frontier 300 km from Nong Pladuk, 116 km from Thanbyusayat. The site

155

was in a hilly zone 275 metres above sea level where, buried in fallen leaves, three small Buddhist pagodas stood. The base of the central pagoda indicated the frontier, left and right being on the east Thailand and on the west Burma territory. When the railway was planned, the aim was to go over the Three Pagodas Pass.

The day was soon approaching when Thai-Burma Railway trains would go over the Three Pagodas Pass. We went on praying for the achievement of our mission to secure our lines of communication to which our allies, [not sure to whom this refers – Editor] in a hard-fought fight on the battlefields in Burma, gave their support. Even today we keep recalling over and over again that work in the hidden Thai-Burma frontier in the jungle.

Chapter 32

TOWARDS THE SETTING SUN

In July, when the rainy season was due to start, in the construction work at Songkurai no distinction was made between day and night on rush-construction work. For the railway engineers, prisoners-of-war and coolies alike, shouts of 'Speedo!' chased everybody up and the work went on without a break.

It was around that time when an incident occurred in which a British prisoner-of-war in the camp at Songkurai broke out and escaped. He was Lieutenant James Bradley, RE, who was blessed with good luck and after the war was repatriated. In 1982 he wrote an account of his escape, published under the title *Towards the Setting Sun*. I was given a copy by the author and was able to get his permission to quote parts of it, an account of the Thai-Burma Railway as seen by a prisoner-of-war.

Lieutenant Bradley hailed from Cheshire in England. On 13 January 1942 in the transport *Duchess of Atholl* (Futamatsu wrote *Richmond* in error), in company with part of the British 18 Division, he had entered Keppel Harbour, the port of Singapore. England had already declared war on Japan and they arrived as reinforcements for the defending army in Malaya. Bradley was an officer in 18 Division's 53 Brigade Group's engineering company: they moved into a front-line position at Ayer Hitam in Johore, but almost at once the British defence gave way to the Japanese offensive and by the end of January, inevitably, they had withdrawn into Singapore Island. On 15 February the commander of the defending army, Lt-General A.E. Percival, as the resources of war were dwindling and sources of water supply were drying up, ordered his total forces to stop fighting, and surrendered to the Japanese Army.[110]

Barely a month after Lieutenant Bradley had landed in Singapore the surrender took place. He became a captive, and ended up by being imprisoned in Changi prisoner-of-war camp. Since the Spring of 1942 several tens of thousands of prisoners-of-war were accommodated at Changi, and around that time there was set up a labour force for the Thai-Burma Railway construction which was being started, and prisoners were moved in successive batches to the Thai-Burma area.

In May that year 3,000 Australian prisoners-of-war in a body which prisoners called A Force were moved to Burma and from then up to April 1943 a total of about 40,000 prisoners, British, Australian and Dutch, were moved into Thailand and Burma. On 18 April 1943 Lieutenant Bradley was drafted to F Force and moved to Banpong in Thailand. F Force was a mixture of 3,334 British and 3,666 Australians, but half of them were unfit. Next in May H Force departed, a mixture of 2,669 prisoners, British, Australian and Dutch, and after them on 25 June K Force, a medical group, and lastly L Force, a mixed group, set out from Singapore. All these groups or forces of prisoners-of-war were estimated to total over 58,000 men [the total, in fact, was 61,106 – Editor].

At the time F Force set out, the gist of the clauses of the order issued by Major-general Arimura, commanding prisoner-of-war camps on Singapore Island ran something like this:

'This move is to an area where the food situation is good and there will be no heavy work. The move will be by train and from the station of arrival to the camp is a short distance and there will be no marching to it. In the group will be 350 medical personnel travelling with you' ... but in actual fact the reality was nothing like this.

What follows is quoted from Lieutenant Bradley's account:

On 24 April 1943 for over a year I had been exiled in Changi. Before leaving I had judged there was no means of escape open to me from this labouring job, but after all if an opportunity presented itself I determined secretly to abscond. Against that moment I thought I would take a compass along with me, so I had one fitted into the bottom of my water-bottle and carried it with me.

The Japanese Army became obsessive about prisoners-of-war escaping. In September 1942 Major-General Fukunaga Kyōhei, then commanding prisoner-of-war camps on the Island, had forcibly confined a number of prisoners in Selerang Barracks. It was a warning example that prisoners attempting to escape would be shot.

After travelling for three days and nights in a freight-car, hot and hungry, we arrived at Banpong. From the following day our sections of 500 were divided up and in succession were marched on foot to our work-site. On the march we avoided the heat of the sun and marched at night. There was also a steel bridge under construction in mid-river. We walked the 50 km to Kanchanaburi and went on West of it to Thā Makham and crossed the river by a wooden bridge which had been built. Work went on at night on a cutting at Chungkai and a large number of prisoners were toiling at a plank viaduct at Arrow Hill which we passed. On the sixth evening we reached Wanyai camp in a hilly region of jungle and on the left bank of the river. Some thirty-odd sick men were unable to walk any further.

It was a tolerable camp but we were not allowed inside the fence. F Force took their sick along with them, and the local camp guards were probably afraid of infection from them. Those sick men who could no longer walk were left behind in camps, were not likely to recover and probably died. On the march men mutually helped one another, carrying a man's baggage or lending a shoulder as they walked. Our MOs helped those who fell out from weakness, sent them to the rear of the column and toiled marvellously on their behalf.

We started to walk at seven in the evening, rested at seven the following morning, slept, and averaged about 25 km a day on the march. By the morning of the eighth day we had walked about 170 km and entered Kinsaiyok, but no one knew we still had another 130 km to walk. There was a contagious disease there and we were unable to go inside the camp. When we left Kinsaiyok, over the river the full moon was rising: it was a still night.

Work on railway construction was heavy toil. The engineers were in a hurry to complete the railway. In the password 'Speedo' lay the cruelty of the work. F Force had been thrown in to make up the inadequacy of the labour force. The Japanese infantry, too, who were hurrying to the front in Burma, carried on their shoulders the guns to break down their enemy's resistance. That most of these reinforcements, a year afterwards, would no longer be alive no one would be likely to guess. On and on, they crossed over steep hilly country, crossed deep ravines, persisting in their forward advance. On the morning of the tenth successive day after leaving Banpong we had struggled along 262 km to Konkuita. From there we walked for several nights, just walking, no one had the energy to talk and we helped each other in silence as we went on. We were thoroughly tired out: since setting out we had gone on walking for about 300 km in the space of twenty days and had at last reached our goal, Songkurai. We came under control of a prisoner-of-war camp at Nikki commanded by Lt-col Banno. There were not a few victims of this march and it was called 'the three hundred kilometre death march'. Since we left Singapore not a single word of what Arimura's order said was matched in the performance.

Songkurai, near the Three Pagodas Pass on the Thai-Burma frontier, was the most westerly part of Thai territory. F Force were employed on building the embankment on the section of track about 37 km southeast of the Three Pagodas Pass.

Lieutenant Bradley's account goes on:

Songkurai camp was in a logged and cleared level space with simple huts as quarters, huts with bamboo supports and atap-thatched. In May in this rainy season zone the rain persisted every day and inside the huts was a sea of mud. The latrine-pits were inundated and on the passage-ways sewage was floating, hygienically an evil carried to extremes. The prisoners, and even the sick for whom heavy work was impossible, were put to heavy work. To make up the numbers needed on the job one had to decide strictly who was incapable of heavy work, and the sick had to do light work. The number of heavy workers was that demanded by the engineers and it was as if they disregarded men's real ability to work. Both officers and men without distinction took part in heavy work and were under fire with boos and jeers of '*kora*' ('Here you') and '*baka jaro!*' ('Fool!') and the engineers hit and kicked us. In the blazing heat of the sun and in freezing rain we had to work until we almost collapsed. Our staple food was boiled rice with little to go with it. Food was provided for those on heavy work but not for the many sick who could not work, an evil distinction. At the Nikki camp, when the dreaded demands of the work unit were made for prisoners to do heavy work, all the men at Songkurai were sick. In the event, of 5,000 prisoners-of-war a bare 700 were able to do heavy work.

Many men went down with malarial fever. A few had dysentery, too, and there were victims of tropical ulcers. Our rations were short and an unbalanced diet supervened, and because medical supplies were few the sick did not get enough medical treatment. In June on Burma-side there was an outbreak of cholera which came over the frontier and invaded Songkurai. Here it became necessary to have an isolation hut. A Japanese sanitation squad checked prisoners' stools. Every day some died of cholera.

On the sanitation squad's check-list I was the only officer entered and was at once confined to the isolation hut. I had diarrhoea at the time and because that was nothing unusual to bother about, when I was isolated I was only nervous, surprised and anxious. I was moved into the isolation hut in a violent downpour of rain which made the earth a germ-carrier, and I can't remember how many sleepless nights I had. The hut was full of sick men. As a protection against infection victims' corpses were incinerated and in the end I became the man in charge of incineration. I shall never forget, ever, that disagreeable job. Corpses which remained about the area unburnt were frightful. There were many dead and there was never enough firewood. Finding substitutes for firewood became my main job and every day I had to hurry. Men who had been helping me the day before, next day became corpses and they, too, had to be cremated. Sick men's rations were deliberately withheld by the Japanese and were divided out of the heavy workers' rations by the prisoners themselves. Men said it was better to die than not to work.

Prisoners were often missing, thinking that in the circumstances of illness of cruel work, and of no hope of freedom they despaired and wanted to die. The rainy season's weather, with rain falling every day, was thoroughly damp and gloomy. The prevalence of cholera increased the risk of illness, every day we were just tired out by the cruel work. How many prisoners secretly in their misery thought it not unreasonable to run away from the environment and escape?

Lieutenant Bradley finally determined to escape.

My colleague Lt-Col. Wilkinson came to see me at night. The guards were afraid of cholera and did not come near the isolation hut. He had made a plan of escape and invited me to go with him. The Colonel thought that people in the world outside should be told of the miserable conditions in the Thai-Burma area. I had already decided to escape if an opportunity arose and the plan the Colonel described that night made one with which I complied. We knew the plan had its difficulties but some chance of success, and we knew that to go on living at Songkurai was even more difficult. Someone might wonder what incentive there was for the plan but any plan depended for success on its leadership and Colonel Wilkinson was a man we trusted implicitly. If successful, I should meet my loved household again, and had no doubts about my trust in the Colonel.

There was no special fence at the camp so escape was not difficult. However, it was surrounded by jungle not easy to get through and also, if we chanced to be seen, our skin colour, different from that of both Japanese and Thai, would give us away. There being a reward for catching escapers the risk was further increased. Accordingly, after breaking out, we would have to avoid meeting people outside. We could not use a route along the river-bank. From Songkurai it was about 80 km West to a coastal town called Ye and we planned to get there by hook or by crook. Ye lay on the shore of the Andaman Sea. From it we thought we could sail from Ye in a sailing-vessel. However, if we chanced to be captured, the record so far showed that we should be executed. I determined our plan must succeed at all costs. It was a tragic thing to contemplate, but we judged our party of ten men were competent to see it though. It was of course rather a large party and having to disclose to them the plan beforehand increased the risk.

The members of our party were as follows: Bill Anker was a Captain, RASC, 18 Division. He and I came out on the same transport ship so we knew each other, and on the march from Banpong we became friendly. He was very fit, a powerful mover, with a good appetite. He survived unscathed and I am happy to say he is still fit and well. At Songkurai he was in charge of food supply and had been able to carry into my hut a reserve stock of food.

Bill's brother-officers, Jack Feathers and Robbie Robinson, both RASC, 18 Division, had come out with him. Jack married just before leaving for the front but he never knew his son had been born (he was an Oxford cross-country Blue). Robbie hailed from Liverpool (he was the child illustrated on boxes of Meccano).

Ian Moffat was like myself a Lieutenant in the Royal Engineers. His family lived in the Argentine whence he came to join up (after the war he joined a fellow ex-prisoner-of-war in America but in 1982 he was known to be alive back in Argentina).

Guy Machado was a schoolmaster when he was drafted into The Straights Settlements Volunteer Force as a Lieutenant. When we landed on Singapore Island he was appointed SSVF liaison officer to my company. His painful experiences in recalling escape and recapture preyed on his mind and he took refuge in the religious life, regrettably ending his life in 1950 at the age of 50.

Lieutenant T.P.D. Jones was another Malay Regiment Liaison officer. He had a simplified map of Burma printed on a silk handkerchief. It was inaccurate but no one knew the coast of Burma so we had no option but to rely on it. We guessed it was about 80 km to Ye and planned on the basis of a three weeks' walk. In actual fact, because of the density of the jungle we were unable to get through in three weeks and we ended up taking six weeks.

The seventh member of the party was Jones's friend, Corporal Brown (Futamatsu wrote *sōchō*, serjeant-major, but Brown was a Corporal).

The eighth man was an Indian fisherman called Nur Mohammed. Shortly after the Pacific War started he was transferred from Chittagong to India, was captured by the Japanese *en route* and became a prisoner-of-war. He knew Burma and understood some of the local dialect: his skin colour differed from ours and so if we encountered any local inhabitants he would have few worries about being challenged (after the war Captain Anker helped him to get a grant of land in Malaya and a permanent pension. When he joined the escape party Colonel Wilkinson promised to get him some recognition of his services if he survived. The Colonel did not survive but Anker approached Lord Louis Mountbatten, who agreed to honour this promise).

To these eight men Wilkie and I were added and made up our escape party of ten men. We exchanged pledges that *en route* if a situation arose when one of us became an encumbrance he would be abandoned. It was a binding, merciless pledge but the party as a whole must not be hindered: it helped no one to call a halt. Each individual was mutually resolute and before he started confirmed he would not alter his pledge.

Our prime objective was to get to the coast of the Andaman Sea near Ye. The escape plan was to make our way through the jungle to the bank of the Ye River, build a raft and float down the river to the coast. We assumed that on the coast we would acquire by some means a small sailing craft and sail West of the Irrawaddy delta and be able to struggle along through the Andaman archipelago. We estimated that we would make about four kilometres a day through the jungle and that it would take three weeks to float down river thereafter on the Ye River. It would take a week to get through to the river and we stocked up food for the four weeks for our trip down river, calculating four or five ounces of rice per man per day. The party decided to go at the end of June, and apart from checking the food and preparations we set out within ten days.

The escape point from Songkurai camp was fixed as being from the isolation hut I was living in, from which I had already cut a path to the Huai Song Kalia stream. Once the escape was discovered it was essential that we should have got as far away as possible from the camp. After leaving camp there would not have been enough time to cut a path through to the stream, but the guards took no notice of us and I had previously made logging noises in cutting firewood for cremations: the guards would mistake it for that. Our anxiety was that we did not know there was time enough to search out a path to the far bank of the stream. The senior officer in camp was Lt-Col.

A.T. Hingston, RAOC, and Colonel Wilkinson confided in him the escape plan when he decided to go. Colonel Hingston would cooperate by delaying his report of our escape as long as he could, which he willingly promised to do. Unfortunately, in the event, shortly after we had gone there was a snap roll-call and our absence quickly came to light. The guards at once searched the outskirts of the surrounding jungle. However, they were confident that escapers would have little chance of survival and appear to have abandoned the routine search.

At sunrise on the morning of 5 July 1943 Wilkie and his confederates were all ready. Each man had to break out of camp individually. In the event of his being discovered he had to make his own excuse for leaving camp. From the evening before until morning I could not sleep a wink from nervousness, but I had committed myself to the plan and deep down I was rather looking forward to the moment of departure. What lay in the future for us no one could know, one simply had to pray for success, but the chance of escaping was unlikely to recur. If a man fell ill or was injured he either starved or died. If captured by the Japanese he would either be shot or beheaded. In either case he was a dead man. Failure meant death and on that last night in camp my disturbing thoughts denied sleep. It was the turning-point in my life as a human being. Whatever happened I vowed in my heart that we had to succeed.

Our baggage consisted mainly of food. In addition to our staple food, rice, saved bit by bit, extra food like soy beans, salt and dried fish was packed in, each man carrying about 70 lbs on his back. In addition, each man had a groundsheet and a blanket. We shared out between us the additional load of quinine, mosquito cream, water purification tablets, hempen rope, string, candles, matches and lighters, mugs and mess-tins. We had an axe and three parangs for cutting our way through the jungle. Each man had a haversack or a gas-mask carrier, carried on the back, and into it went his personal effects. I had my traveller's cheques, material for celestial navigation and spare clothes. To keep it dry I wrapped the photograph of my wife Lindsay and our son Roger in a piece of oilskin, and put it at the bottom of my haversack. I devised a protective waistband out of blanket cloth and dealt with the ulcers on my leg by putting sulphonamide tablets in them. I wore boots. I took out the compass hidden in the bottom of my water-bottle and carried it with me as well as my collar-stud compass.

We said good-bye to no one. We thought it better not to let them know, to prevent us being a liability to them. Our start was a straightforward move along the path I had cleared as far as the Huai Song Kalia steam which was in flood after several days' rain. We waded upstream against the current and crossed to the far bank. The water left no footprints so we had no worries about that. Thereafter, whatever obstacles might be we took a compass bearing solidly West and went straight ahead, in fact a course *Towards the Setting Sun*. No one, however, had the slightest idea that, when we had crossed the steep hills West of Songkurai with our objective the Thai-Burma frontier, there ran a continuous mountain range through to the West of Moulmein.

After breakfast we set out again, with three of us clearing a track and one with the compass keeping our course steadily to the West. Right in front another couple of us took turns in cutting through the jungle with axe and parang. We took a rest about midday but, with no margin to spare of our rations, we ate nothing at lunchtime. We put a wide enough distance on our route for any search party to have little to go on.

Withered bamboos had collapsed above the bottom roots of scratchy big bamboo clumps and it was extraordinary hard work to fell them. In our circumstances we could not risk altering our bearing and this added still more to the difficulties. At five in the evening we stopped work and made the spot our resting-place. We made a platform a foot above ground and a substitute for a roof out of tree-branches. We built a blazing fire, had our meal and dried our wet rugs. As a precaution against tigers and other wild animals we kept the bonfire going all night. It rained nearly every day, a damp atmosphere. Around the thick bamboo clumps there was nothing but the deep green shrubs and trees of the jungle. The luxuriant undergrowth left no footprints and we had no fear of being tracked. There were snakes and leeches, hateful beasts.

On 9 July my son Roger would be five years old. My wife Lindsay (Futamatsu wrote 'Lindy', the name of Bradley's second wife) would be wondering, I thought, whether his father would ever be brought together again at his birthday parties.

On 18 July we had to climb a steep hill. Scratchy clumps of bamboo teemed with all kinds of creatures as we climbed and in this terrain of steep hills we barely progressed more than 50 metres a day. Whatever the cause, a bamboo scratch or a parang cut, Robinson had an injury to his hand which festered, got worse, and he could no longer do any hard work. We all found climbing hills very hard work and we got hideously tired. On meagre rations and with the extremely hard work our bodies became exhausted,. The plain truth was that it was taking us three weeks to emerge from the jungle and reach the bank of the Ye River, longer than we had anticipated, and we were disheartened.

From time to time, we heard monkeys howling in the jungle and saw them moving about. We were afraid of pythons (*kurohebi*). We ate wild bananas but they were full of black pips. On 25 July we finally ate the last bit of rice. I kept on trudging through the middle of this jungle forest with my prop being simply my wish to speak again in some way with my family at home.

On 29 July our first casualty occurred. When we woke up in the morning Corporal Brown had disappeared. For some days previously he had developed ulcers on his back and from time to time was unable to walk – it was beyond his strength. The previous night the temperature had dropped, the atmosphere became very damp, and so we did not let the bonfire go out. Someone would get up to put more firewood on it, so no one paid any attention to a man moving about and we had not realized that Brown had gone. We searched round his sleeping place but he could not be found. We could not waste our dwindling resources of physical strength and, heartless though it was, we had to abandon our search. There was no help for it, we had to abandon him in the light of our previous pledge. That night his absence weighed on us, we felt lonely, everyone was reticent and kept quiet. That day's incident could happen again, we thought, we could not know which of us was to die next and we could do nothing but despair.

On 2 August Feathers died during the night. He had got very thin and his swollen feet made walking extremely difficult. He was a splendid fellow, liked by everybody. His son was born soon after he left for the front but Jack's death prevented him from ever seeing his son, terrible bad luck, a pitiable case.

On 5 August, about a month after we had set out, we still had not reached the Ye River. We climbed a steep mountain track and in the evening Colonel Wilkinsion had spasms in a shack built as a temporary shelter. He was a big man, and due to lack of nourishment and the severe activity in walking the mountain sides he was on the verge of death and finally expired. He was my superior officer, we all relied on him so his death was a severe blow. I specially felt his loss and felt profound sorrow and discouragement. It was a bad omen for our future prospects. His death made the leadership for our further escape difficult because we felt we could not do without the Colonel's leadership. We overcame our grief but had to go on.

Every day the rain persisted. We went on and on to the west through the jungle. Our only bedding, blankets, took up water and got heavy. At night, although we wrung out the water from the rugs, sleeping in them was like sleeping in water. At times we could see no clear way through the trees and shrubs but none-the-less could not alter our bearing due West. There was nothing for it but to battle on.

On the night of 9 August Jones could not be found anywhere. We searched for a while on the back-track and found him lying unconscious. From the following day we pushed ahead, carrying him as he couldn't walk. That day, at last, we found a branch of the Ye River. We put him into an old hunter's hut on the river-bank, broke up part of it and made a blazing fire. While resting in the hut Robbie, who suffered from dysentery, showed symptoms of blood-poisoning and died. The wound on his hand, received shortly after the start, was painful and got worse. So another splendid colleague was lost and we were plunged into depths of grief. That night Jones lost his appetite and could not eat. He knew he could no longer move and begged us to start and leave him. No one could say no to his proposal. Despite our grief we left him in the hut, putting a full water-bottle beside him. No one thought he would survive but we told him we would send help if we met any local inhabitants within forty-eight hours.

We had set out on 5 July from Songkurai as ten men, by 10 August we had been reduced in the end to five. Our five colleagues who had lost their lives had used up daily all their energy on the escape, did it literally by sheer pluck, and collapsed. These men's deaths were examples to be respected. We thought it was a waste of human lives.

We had been walking through the jungle for six weeks. At the onset we had four weeks' food but after a fortnight it had looked unlikely to be enough. Still, we drank water every day, water from puddles and rainwater collected in our mugs. On the way we slept very little at night, all having painful buttocks and backs. In the depths of the forests bugs and mosquitoes afflicted us all the time and it seemed as if we were always hearing the hum of mosquitoes' wings in our ears.

On 14 August at last we groped our way to the bank of the main stream of the Ye River, a gently-flowing river, deep for its width. For some time we had been in the jungle hardly ever being able to see the sky. On the bank we made a temporary hut and spent several days building a raft, for our wasted physical strength quite a hard task. We were so weak we could walk only a few yards at a time and it took longer than we had expected to build the raft. The moment we put it into the water it could not be concealed and any local inhabitants would be certain to discover us. Our physical strength was near its limit, near exhaustion. If a local inhabitant did discover the raft, that was fate, and we could not avert it. On 17 August we floated our raft, it floated gently and began to move with the current downstream. As we had come clear of the jungle we no longer needed axe or parangs. All the same we would have to ride downstream for several days before reaching the river-mouth. We began to feel optimistic ... but optimism was misplaced.

We had expected the river to have bends and soon saw a gorge, narrow on both sides, and the current accelerated. We restrained the raft several times for colliding with the banks but it began to turn round and the fourth time it turned round completely, collided with a bank and disintegrated. We were tipped out in mid-stream and our baggage was lost. In some way we were not separated from our haversacks but everything else was lost. We exerted our last efforts to swim to the bank. Together with Moffat and Machado I was carried down river and a little downstream the five of us were able to join up.

Parangs and axe were gone and our blankets had disappeared so it was impossible to put the raft to rights as it was before the accident.

The five of us walked along the river-bank and some Burmese on the opposite bank saw us, the first human beings we had met since we started. They took us to their little shack and gave us some food, the first meal we had had for some time. Mohammed understood a little of the local language so we were able to give them some idea of what we were thinking. We slept the night in the shack.

The place was Kampong Karni (kampong means a small village). Never day we were taken to the village headman's house. He seemed cooperative and we were full of hope that we might have reached our goal. Kampong Karni was on a plain near the sea, several miles from the town of Ye. We had been walking in the wrong direction so had not reached our real objective. The headman had at one time been in the Army in Burma and could speak a little English. He gave us a couple of bananas each as substitute for a meal. His wife was with us in the room, the first individual of the opposite sex we had seen since leaving Changi. She was naked from the hips up, charmingly proportioned and to us a lovely, dazzling girl. We slept that night under his house, and we seriously thought that, compared with our colleagues who had died, we had deserted them and that it was a dreadful thing that they had had to die alone.

On 19 August the headman of Kampong Arkan came to see us and the next day we were transferred to Arkan. The villagers were curious, gathered to see us, brought us fruit. Our bodies were so debilitated it was difficult to eat their valuable presents but we thanked them for their kindness. Shortly afterwards we were taken to what seemed to be a police-hut, and were under surveillance of two young Burmese men. One of them allowed us to bathe, killed a chicken and made us a chicken curry.

When we met the headman of Kampong Karni, headmen had their eyes on a monetary award and would not hesitate to give information secretly to the Japanese Army that they had caught some British prisoners-of-war. This must be, we thought, the reason for our protective surveillance. Mohammed was worried and said it was dangerous to stay here, but we five had no physical strength left to back out, so in the end there was nothing for it but to submit to fate.

On 21 August a Japanese Army squad appeared. We had been re-captured, but there was some doubt as to who we were. We were resigned to being killed like those who escaped from Thā Makham and it didn't help to realize that our escape had failed. We were taken as suspects to Military Police HQ and there were interrogated by their commander. That we had walked from Songkurai was something he did not believe, nor how we did it, and suspected that a British Burma Army unit had made a landing on the coast near Ye. On 24 August we were transferred to the Moulmein barracks of the *kempeitai* (military secret police).

On 5 September, Lieutenant Bradley and his party were escorted back to Thailand. There were air raids on the way. In eight days they were escorted to the Thanbyusayat railway base camp and imprisoned for a fortnight. They recovered their strength slightly. Mohammed the Indian was taken away to some special place. Lt-Col. Banno, commander of prison camps in the Nikki area, came to verify that they were prisoners from Songkurai, and together with the *kempeitai* commander interrogated them again. They claimed that the reason for the escape was to tell the outside world about the miserable conditions of the prisoners-of-war on the railway. The *kempeitai* commander was suspicious about the possibility that during their escape they might perhaps have contacted a British Army unit. In the end they were not punished at Thanbyusayat and were sent back again to Moulmein. They arrived at Moulmein on 24 September, were seen by a medical officer and put into a hospital ward, and were finally back again on 7 October at No. 2 Songkurai camp from which they had started. Fortunately for them the Japanese in charge when they escaped had been relieved.

On 9 October, they were escorted to Nikki. It was intended to execute them there. It happened that Captain C.H.D. Wild, who had been the interpreter on the occasion of the British Army's surrender, frankly told Colonel Banno, 'To execute these splendid brave officers without trial would rebound as a slur on the reputation of the Imperial Japanese Army and leave a stain on their history' and they were sent to Singapore to be court-marshalled.

On 17 October at Konkuita the East and the West sides of the Thai-Burma Railway track joined up, and on 25 October at the joining-up point an opening-up ceremony was solemnized, as described in the following Chapter 33.

The following is also abstracted from Lieutenant Bradley's book:

When we were at Nikki, of the various methods of execution we preferred shooting rather than decapitation by a Japanese sword. But there was no indication of an immediate execution and some ten days elapsed, but on 25 October we were sent from Nikki to Singapore. Some six months earlier we had begun our march from Banpong to Songkurai, whence we made our escape into Burma. So from Moulmein via Tauk by railway we came back to Banpong. In sum, we had a round trip over the whole track of the Thai-Burma Railway. On 30 October, by train from Banpong, we finally returned to Singapore.

As well as being investigated in Outram Road police station, we were interrogated at Southern Army's GHQ in Raffles College. They would not believe we had contacted no one on our escape route, and we kept our pledge to state simply what was incontrovertible and what had been our difficulties. We were kept imprisoned as war criminals in Outram Gaol which had an evil reputation.

From November until the following June Lieutenant Bradley and his colleagues were taken from Outram Gaol to recover their health and were hospitalized in Changi. In June a court-martial was convened under the presidency of Major Ōmomo Yoshiraru and on 26 June they were tried and sentenced. In explanation of the sentence it was claimed that 'they were unable to endure conditions of confinement, abandoned their subordinates and infringed prisoner-of-war camp regulations', and that 'the point that the Japanese Army's treatment of prisoners-of-war was unreasonable did not apply'. Captain Anker was sentenced to nine years' imprisonment, the other three to eight years. At the President's discretion in that year for reasons of health their sentence was put in abeyance until 19 August 1945.

On 15 August, the war ending in Japan's surrender, the sentences of Lieutenant Bradley and his colleagues became void. Thus they were simultaneously liberated from sentence and from captivity and could be repatriated.[111]

Lieutenant Bradley makes the following summary in his book:

Of my formation, 18 Division, thirty per cent of the men lost their lives as prisoners-of-war on the building of the Thai-Burma Railway. This is a deplorable thing and we recall our worries when four years earlier we departed for the front from the waters of the Clyde, worries as to how many would return alive. For Japan, just before the war ended, 170,000 people lost their lives in the atomic explosions at Hiroshima and Nagasaki. Men of the Allied Forces as prisoners-of-war and natives of the southern countries totalled about 100,000 men who lost their lives as victims on the railway. Had the war gone on, to be sure many more would have been deprived of their lives. As for the hardships we suffered on the railway, in the well-known saying of the Bishop of Singapore, 'We must forgive but not forget.'

In circumstances like these, when the Japanese way of life relapsed from the civilized, the Japanese people quickly adjust to circumstances, and from primitive lapses seem not to have any difficulty in recovering their civilization. The English are not so clever at this and I don't know whether they can pretend in this context to act like civilized people, but they can hardly claim perfect humanity.

Chapter 33

OPENING TO TRAFFIC

On 17 October the Thai-Burma Rail Link track made its connecting-up point from Burma-side and from Thai-side at a point just West of Konkuita station about 40 km south-east of the Thai-Burma frontier, a joining-up point in mid-jungle, 262.53 km from the starting point at Nong Pladuk.

Respectively from east to west the track-laying squads of 5 and 9 railway regiments calculated their distances of track and aimed at meeting in the early morning at Konkuita on the day. Major-General Ishida Hideguma came to Konkuita expressly to take command of the act of making the connection. In the east on Thai-side it was 9 Railway Regiment's 2 Battalion, on the west on Burma-side it was 5 Railway Regiment's 1 Battalion, who each must recall how they had had the responsible honour of joining up the railtrack. They expected to complete it at noon on the day, and at 11 a.m. the contest started under the GOC's direction. The two squads had a gap of 200 metres between them.

Railway Official Katamura of 4 Special Bridging Unit was at the site and he described the scene as follows:

> I was at the time near the point at which the sets of rails joined
> up. The sky above the jungle at Konkuita was quite clear. There
> were massive growths of green leaves on the trees and although the
> tropical sunlight gave no shade they kept cascading down to the
> ground under the trees. The hour of noon drew near. Shrilling of
> cicadas assailed our ears. Work had stopped on the roadbed a day or

174

so previously. The railtrack stretched out making a straight line through the jungle. The embankment was low at this point. At 11 a.m. GOC Ishida gave the command to start the contest. Soon from both sides East and West in the jungle could be heard the shouts of command in unison of the two track-laying squads who braced themselves to the task in their race to get there first. Rails loaded on flatcars were propelled by rail-tractors, moved ahead and the work-squads lined up the sleepers. Then several soldiers with loud shouts in unison dropped each rail down on the sleepers. Gaps between rails were aligned and dog-spikes driven in with mells to fix the rails to the sleepers. The immediate section of track was adjusted and at once the leading flatcars were pulled by rail-tractors and moved forward. Both squads on the task, by their prompt work, shortened the gap between them in no time at all.

On Thai-side 9 Railway Regiment's squad had dressed suitably to make them agile at work, even the soldiers being naked from the waist up. A dozen prisoners-of-war, too, were on the task. The troops of 5 Railway Regiment on Burma-side were fully-armed in formal dress, carrying aslant on their backs cavalry carbines: they were gallant figures. With them worked Burmese coolies. The two sets of rails arrived at the joining-up point at virtually the same moment. It was at the 262.53 km point, equipped on both sides of the rails with a sheet-metal joint to make the connection fast. It was 17 October 1943. Colonel Imai, commander of Thai-side construction and Colonel Sasaki, commander of Burma-side construction, stepped forward in front of GOC Ishida and in a dignified manner reported completion. In an instant the troops at the site burst out spontaneously with a shout of *banzai* (ten thousand years). The prisoners and coolies looked pleased at the completion of their labour. Everyone's breast was filled with deep emotion and tears overflowed. So, for the hardship so long endured and for their comrades-in-arms who had died on the job they kept these things reverently in their hearts.

It was a solemn moment. The Thai-Burma Rail Link Line is finished at last! Ah, this railway is really finished. Barren lands have been crossed and rivers crossed by soldiers hollow-cheeked, bridges built over ravines, valleys filled in, the entire 415 km of railway line really completed!

A year and a half after construction started, nature in the form of jungle had been challenged in day-after-day sweltering heat, in cloudbursts of rain, battling with epidemic diseases, in the end we won the battle of linking the line from Nong Pladuk through to Thanbyusayat. Through unexplored jungle steam-engines' whistles reverberated and the day had drawn near when one would hear the deafening roar of trains rushing through. To the engineers numerous hardships had kept recurring day-after-day but today's joy brought tears to their eyes as their hearts filled with deep emotion. They thought of the many precious victims, their comrades and prayed that their souls might rest in peace.

On 25 October a pylon was set up in the enclosure at the ceremonial site to commemorate the joining-up point and the opening-to-traffic ceremony was solemnized. In the jungle nearby an AA-gun post was set up. Miraculously, Southern Army's military band was in attendance. From Southern Army Chief-of-Staff Shimizu was in attendance to represent his GOC. Under Ishida, GOC of Thai-Burma Construction, men of both the Thai and the Burma construction units were assembled. As a member of 9 Railway Regiment's staff I was permitted to attend the ceremony.

It began with the formal contest of closing the gap. At the joining-up point several sleepers and dog-spikes were put out ready. The two construction unit commanders, colonels Imai and Sasaki, had their equipment ready and with heavy mells drove special gun-metal dog-spikes into an ebony sleeper. Simultaneously an engine, which had stood by in waiting, did its test run to the joining-up point. This No. C5631 tank-engine, the first up from the East side, had been decorated with the crossed flags of Japan and Thailand, and moved quietly up to the joining-up point. After the ceremony when it went back into Thailand it was distinguishable by being decorated with the national flags as the engine which had been favoured to make its passage from the East to the joining-up point. The troops at the ceremony watched closely to be sure it made a successful test run. This after all was the day on which unexplored regions of Thailand and Burma could hear the sounds of trains thundering through.

GOC Ishida apologized for the hardships his men had undergone and declaimed his written speech of comfort for the souls of the victims. As commander he bowed to the assembled company and dedicated his report of a railway opened to traffic far away from their homeland. The band played the National Anthem which resounded impressively in the deep jungle forest. In the hearts of the troops a flood of emotional recollections gushed in. Above Konkuita there was not a cloud in the clear sky. From somewhere there floated in an impression of autumn in a jungle vibrating with the tropical heat and with the shrilling of cicadas. For myself, to be present at that ceremony filled me with deep emotion not only for the opening itself but also for the thought of the bones of the many victims buried in the soil of those unexplored regions and I dedicated my prayers as a memorial address for their meritorious deeds.

On the day of the ceremony Lieutenant Adams was in the prisoner-of-war camp at Konkuita and gives his recollections in his book:

> This day, for the Japanese Army, was the day of remembrance of the completion of the Thai-Burma Railway. For the prisoners-of-war, it was the day on which we had a holiday from work. The camp was alongside the newly-completed railtrack along which a special train was run for the Japanese general officers attending the ceremony, comprising two Toyoda diesel-engined boarded flatcars coupled together, on which *atap*-thatched roofs had been erected. We called it 'The Bamboo Express'. (The editor recalls prisoners calling it 'the Flying Kampong'.)

This railways construction created a heavy build-up of hardship for many taking part and a number lost their lives. None-the-less the opening of the Panama Canal with the crossing of the American continent by building a railway, and the construction of the Suez Canal, rank in line with the one we helped to build, known world-wide as grand civil engineering enterprises. Adams recalls:

> 'But we prisoners-of-war, far from thinking we might boast about helping to complete 'a grand piece of civil engineering enterprise', are left only with regret at the thought that people at home could have little sympathy with those who had helped to build a strategic railway inside enemy territory. We were, of course, utterly without any freedom of choice in the matter and may only console ourselves

with the thought that it was enforced labour in which we showed no cooperation.

Day and night it grew cooler as the dry season approached in the interior of Thailand. Morning mists swirled into our jungle billets, smoke from blazing fires at twilight floated out over the water, and we thought of autumns in our native land. Transport had started on the railway but it was difficult to maintain the expected tonnage finally hoped for, 1,000 tons. Rush-construction begun in the spring had admittedly reduced construction time but after the line opened to traffic deficiencies appeared here and there and complete equipment was still needed. This held up movement of transport.

Having been opened the line went beyond the Three Pagodas Pass carrying troops and supplies into Burma, infantrymen, field guns and ammunition. The Burmese Army supported us in transportation ... but we heard of no quick war results. About three years after hostilities had opened intelligence reports indicated that the war situation in Burma was not improving. There were many sick and wounded soldiers on trains coming back from the Burma front, where the British-Indian Allied Forces' counter-offensive was in action with hard fighting in a changing war situation.

Many victims had fallen by the wayside but the railway had been completed after a year and a half of hard toil with the objective of creating a viable transport system, but now that objective was far from being achieved.

Even today, some forty years after the railway opened to traffic, the sounds of trains bound for Burma echoed in my imagination, through jungle beyond the frontier. Still the sky is clear over unexplored jungle. Still tropical sunlight sparkles in the tree-tops and the black smoke from engines will never be put out as it floats through the air in my mind's eye ...

Chapter 34

THE BOMBING

In the Spring of the year in which the Thai-Burma Railway opened to traffic, from about the time when the order for rush-construction was received, the strain of the war situation was becoming intense. The year before, the America Navy, who began their counter-offensive after the start of the war, in June 1942 in the action off Midway Island sank most of the Japanese Navy's aircraft-carriers, inflicting a heavy loss on us. This naval battle complicated things for us and the Japanese Army, with the now enlarged Pacific battle-line, ran risks in their lines of communication. Our Army assaulted the Australian perimeter but their attacks collapsed after hard fighting at various points. In the SE Asia war theatre our Army's dispositioning of fighter aircraft proved to be inadequate.

For the Burma Expeditionary Force in their assault on India, after capturing Burma, the supply-line was to be the construction of the Thai-Burma Railway, of which the opening-to-traffic coincided with enemy air raids which damaged their carrying-power of this supply route.

In the circumstances with a number of Allied Forces' prisoners-of-war employed on it, from the time when construction started it looked as if detailed intelligence information was being reported from the prisoners. From early 1943 recce aircraft frequently flew over. In June 1944 there was damage to tools and materials accumulated at the base at Thanbyusayat, and concurrently the prisoners' quarters were bombed. The base on Thai-side at Nong Pladuk was also raided and prisoners-of-war injured. To avoid injury to their own men as prisoners, the enemy appear to have made surveys of the locations of camps.* From the Japanese angle, enemy attacks were to be expected but, having no fighter-planes, our AA arrangements were inefficient, yet despite it all we had opened the railway to traffic. In May 1943 the Mae Khlaung steel bridge was completed. AA-gun posts were set up and they gave partial protection to the bridge itself.

The enemy's attacks had effectively started with the opening to traffic of the railway. Obviously, to hinder rail transport, to collapse railway bridges was the most effective stratagem. They began with the steel railway bridge over the Mae Khlaung and went on to the very large number remaining of small wooden bridges. On Thai-side, apart from the Mae Khlaung bridge, all the others were wooden. The Mae Khlaung railway bridge 300 metres West of Kamburi was the enemy's primary target for air attack. In Burmese territory his primary targets were the three steel bridges over the Zami, Apalon and Mezali rivers which between them amounted to over 100 metres in extent.

With autumn in 1944 enemy air raids began in earnest. At the end of September there was a raid on Kommā near the base depot at Nong Pladuk and engines and good wagons received some damage. (See the editor's footnote earlier. This was the raid which caused so many deaths and injuries in Nong Pladuk prison camp.)

Mr Carl Fritsche, who lives in Ohio State, USA, and was a bomber pilot in the USAAF bomber force, gave an account of the bombing of the Thai-Burma Railway in his article in 1983 entitled 'Liberators on the Kwai' on pp. 78–91 of Aerospace Historian, vol. 30, No. 2. Here are extracts:

In 1943 a USAAF squadron was based in India and my No. 10 Squadron liaised with the British RAF. Our B24 Liberators set out for attacks from this Indian base. They took a bearing south-east and from Akyab came down to sea-level across the Andaman Sea, to

* For this raid see the editors account on p. 36 of Lt-Col. P.J.D. Toosey's Report on Malay and Thailand PW Camps. Futamatsu's account is meiosis carried to extremes. Ninety-four prisoners were killed, 290 injured. Document in Imperial War Museum, London.

avoid detection by enemy radar, passed the Andaman Archipelago at
50 feet a.s.l. and made landfall on the Malay Peninsular near Tavoy,
over which they flew in formation at high level. A lone pathfinder
guided us to our objective on the Thai-Burma Railway. The main
target was the bridges, and of these the bridge west of Kamburi in
Thailand was our most important objective. From the Spring of
1943 bridges had frequently been reconnoitred by air and progress of construction noted. The Allied prisoners-of-war were being
employed on this heavy work and recce planes not only looked for
places where heavy work was being done but also looked for prisoners' barracks, and special precautions were laid down in order to
prevent casualties among them.

The GHQ of the Thai-Burma Railway Construction was bombed on
8 and 11 November 1944. Adjoining it the HQ of 4 Special Railway
Bridging Unit was also bombed and a number of engineers were killed
in the action. GHQ was evacuated and moved back to the Thāmoan
neighbourhood.
The article goes on:

On 13 December the railway bridge and a Japanese Army AA-gun
post was attacked but the weather being bad the attack was unsuc-
cessful. The third attack was on 23 January 1945 but again the
weather was bad and the attack was not successful.
In the fourth attack on 4 February an AA-gun post was wiped
out. (Futamatsu interpolates that it was the Masuda AA-gun Unit.)
Parts of the bridge-piers and several spans of the wooden bridge were
also damaged. Further damage was done to the railtrack leading on
to the bridges.
The fifth attack was on 13 February. All AA-gun posts being
wiped out we went with low-level attacks at about 200 metres.
On the railway bridge, counting from the East, the third, fourth
and fifth steel trusses of these spans were brought down and we
had succeeded in damaging the bridge. At the same time the temporary wooden bridge was damaged and we had succeeded in
our objective of reducing the carrying-power of the Thai-Burma
Railway.

181

Sjt Sharp, a former prisoner-of-war who was in the Thā Makham camp (an American. He also gave an account of how tool-containers began to be carried in small boats while bridges were out of action: Editor) wrote in his diary that on 19 December the Kwae Yai came into flood: part of the wooden bridge was washed out, and he gave an account of the work involved in repairing it:

> On 3 April in the sixth attack it was clear to us that the steel bridge had been patched up and work was in progress gradually to clear obstructions caused by the collapse of the wooden bridge after the attack on it on 13 February. The repaired wooden bridge was bombed again, and again damaged.
>
> In the seventh attack on 22 April several formations kept up a night raid, one after another, lasting about seven hours, with the result that both bridges were reduced a second time to an unworkable condition. The eighth attack was on 24 June. This time RAF bombers kept up a continuous raid and both bridges suffered further damage. (In fact, RAF and USAAF B24s made alternate runs one after another: Editor.)

Enemy air raids were not confined to attacks on the Mae Khlaung bridges. They had begun on Burma-side on various bridges as well as on railtrack, but on account of the successful way on which wooden bridges were repaired the effect on transportation was not as great as the enemy had hoped:

> In the ninth attack on 14 July leaflets recommending ending the war in line with terms suggested at the Yalta Conference in July 1945 were dropped in the compound of Kamburi station, and an engine and a goods-wagon were set on fire and damaged (and four Dutch prisoners were killed inside the officers' camp near the station, killed by machine-gun fire: Editor) and in the tenth attack on 28 July a single plane flew over Banpong and Nong Pladuk scattering leaflets advising surrender, based on the Potsdam Declaration.

Air raids, of course, also took place in the outback and one might look at a passage in the account of Mr Sato Minoru, a war correspondent attached to my home unit, 3 Company of the Bridging Unit:

Enemy air raids became more and more ferocious, and repairing damage to bridges and to railtrack on Thai-side kept bridging units busy. In the Konkuita area repair work was done on damaged bridges. When work was in progress in building up triple-pillar support to bridge-piers one had to watch out for the slightest sign of aircraft flying at low level over the trees in the jungle to the West. They were bound to be enemy planes making daring attacks on Kamburi: suddenly, out of the shadow of the mountain bombers came into view attended by fighter-planes. At once they gained height and attacked our repair-work. There was no room to hide on top of the pillar-supports. One ducked one's body out of the way of machine-gun bullets, then down came a bomb. One hid behind the shelter of a pillar-support, waiting for the bomber to pass by, and went hurriedly underneath any available shelf as they made a second run. At Konkuita, we could see below us what looked like bombs on the railway station but visibility was obscured by earth and sand dancing aloft. Fragments from the bullets of machine-guns ricocheted around: it was extremely dangerous with little time to dodge behind the pillars. Within the station perimeter were several big cavities seven or eight metres deep. We were virtually weaponless and it was mortifying to be unable to counter-attack on the enemy's raids.

As we got used to air raids we learned that to take refuge in what the American marines called a fox-hole was safest, each to his own hole (Futamatsu uses the term *takotsubo*, octopus-trap). From a fox-hole one would see high altitudes very well and could judge the bearing of an aircraft about to drop a bomb. When on occasion they flew in at water level and delivered several bombs we were able to judge the range and the location at which they were aiming. When you took cover you had to be quick and then have the nerve not to move. All in all, bombing was nerve-racking. These attacks on the bridges were critical and we could not for a moment let up in the repair work. In seemed never to cease, but our task was to ensure that transportation continued on the railway. In our repair work we were just like schoolboys playing at cowboys and indians in mutual rivalry.

The spans on the bridges were all five metres apart and the construction was based on clamps. When damaged the clamps were lost but scattered pieces of timber were collected and used to repair gaps, and repairs were made in the short space of two or three days. There was, of course, a limit to what could be done to damaged bridge-piers and bridge-abutments because one could not have materials ready from previously damaged bridges in the area. This repair work to damage caused by bombing was something of an endurance test. But one must admit that partial denial of railtrack resulted in reduced carrying-power. When opened to traffic in 1943 it was planned to move 1,000 tons a day. By 1945 that had declined to 500 tons. (In the original plan for the railway in 1942 the transport planned was 3,000 a day: Editor.)

The main defence against engines being hit was their ability to run on one-way systems. Sidings off the main line were built into the jungle with cover against high-level bombing. On an air-raid alarm engines took refuge in these sidings. If there was no concealed line near at hand steam was suppressed and engines hidden under camouflage-nets. Enemy bombers even detected single cars moving in a railtrack area. In the end, even a solitary soldier by himself became a target for machine-gun fire. We lacked the armaments to ambush the bombers and they came down in low-altitude attacks, virtually skimming the tree tops in the jungle undergrowth. All the same, a defenceless railway was taking on these enemy attacks.

In April 1945 the Japanese Army's campaign to take Imphal ended in failure. The INA's advance attack collapsed, our Burma Expeditionary Force acknowledged recapture of Imphal by the Anglo-Indian Army, and so we withdrew. In the withdrawal our soldiers were able to move along the railtrack. There being no trains left, they had to trudge on foot over the Three Pagodas Pass into Thailand. At the time, responsibility for the railway east of the pass rested with 4 Special Railway Unit, and West of the pass 9 Railway Regiment had charge of l.o.c. and track repair. In May, when the retreat from Burma started, 5 Railway Regiment and 5 Special Railway Unit combined in supervising the maintenance work and in preparing a defence position in the Three Pagodas area and in holding their own on it. Both the regular military and the *gunzoku* were resolved to die honourable deaths, and in Bangkok, too, our expatriates and our *gunzoku* performed the solemn act of Roll Call as in days before the war.

The wretched condition of the Thai-Burma Railway became apparent for the first time in the war. In 1945 on the India front the GOC, General S.R.W. Slim, wrote in his book (Wm Slim, *Defeat into Victory*, Cassell, third edition May 1972, pp. 170 et seq.: Editor), in a very interesting passage, that lines of communication to the front line in Burma were the critical factor on which he depended. From Calcutta the Ledo Road and from the rear of Imphal to the base at Dimapur depended on railways and canals for supply. From Calcutta to Dimapur it was 750 km by rail, at Parbatipur the rail-gauge changed and to effect a transfer to the new gauge all cargo had to be man-handled across. Further, there was no bridge over the River Bramaputra so to cross it goods had to be ferried. At the outbreak of war, Slim points out, in 1941 the transportation capacity of this section was about 600 tons a day, but after war broke out it was boosted to about 2,800 tons. Early in 1944 a daily total of 4,400 tons was carried.

About that time on the Thai-Burma Railway the volume transported was 300 to 500 tons a day, supply quantities notably difference by comparison.

Further, in General Slim's book he makes the point that Lt-General Kawabe, GOC, Burma Expeditionary Force, burnt his boats in the campaign to capture Imphal when he crossed the River Chindwin. Kimura, too, who took over from him as GOC was faced with the same situation. The Anglo-Indian Army dropped about 30,000 paratroops over the East bank of the Chindwin and succeeded in cutting off Kimura's supply-route. Thus the Japanese Army was unable to maintain its position on the left bank and the Anglo-Indian Army extended its lines of communication, and one can see that these factors were pivotal for victory or defeat in the campaign to retake Burma.

Chapter 35

END OF THE WAR

In early August 1945 I was sent officially to Saigon from Southern Army Field Operations Railway HQ. My task was to have some engines, which had been sent urgently from Japan, transported to Bangkok. The war situation was deteriorating daily, and even in Bangkok enemy planes came over and bombed our HQ and godowns in the wharves. There was no answering gunfire from AA-gun emplacements in Bangkok and rumours were generated among the worried citizens that we had run out of ammunition. The Army of Occupation in Thailand were making preparations for the final decisive battle (see the editor's Introduction) and the local Japanese residents thought they ought to join up.

It was four years since the war started that I had visited Saigon. It had seemed quiet and peaceful. It was a beautiful town, tidy, and both the greens of the avenues and the Western-style buildings in the ordinary streets seemed not to have changed in those four years, but the citizens in their life-style were feeling something of a strain in financial difficulties.

Immediately on arrival I contacted Inoue Unit, the Saigon materials workshop of Southern Army Field Operations Railways. I went to the wharf in the harbour where the engines were being landed. Several of them had been dismantled (presumably c.k.d.) and the parts piled up. To arrange to get these engines transported I called on the HQ of the French Indo-China Japanese Expeditionary Force. Thereafter by daily visits I kept contact with the HQ asking for transportation either by lorry or by ship whichever proved convenient.

Southern Army GHQ had moved from Singapore to Saigon. At the Japanese French Indo-China Army HQ, too, there were two *gunzoku* sent by Railway Bureau. They were Kawakami Juichi who had been my contemporary at the Ministry of Railways and Kikkawa Kichizō who had been my contemporary at university. We went into quarters, found within the city limits with HQ's help, and inevitably in these quarters talk of the departed spirits of our friends came uppermost in our conversations. One evening at midnight we heard the sound of footsteps in sandals on the lower floor, but when we got up and looked there was no sign of anybody. The next night at the same time we heard the same footsteps. Someone seemed to say, 'Have you come, too?', someone apparently near at hand. From what a neighbour told us a woman who had lived in this room had been strangled, and it was rumoured that her departed spirit revealed itself. For several days the transportation plan for the engines remained unclear until 10 August. On that day I went to HQ we heard the news that atomic bombs had been dropped, one on Hiroshima on 6 August, one on Nagasaki on 8 August, and that the damage and casualties had been enormous. It was explained what an atomic bomb was but we didn't really understand it. On the way back, an officer from the internment camp for French civilians told us that they had learned from an intercepted short-wave radio news item that 'Japan has accepted the Potsdam Declaration.' It seemed to be the end of the war at last. No longer in danger, we thought we could stop worrying. This particularly unexpected outcome had not been envisaged by us but from what we knew four years earlier at Saigon at the start of hostilities it came as no surprise. The peoples of the countries in the theatre of war in the south would feel some peace of mind. No longer were we at a loss, wondering how we would fare. The atomic bombs which fell in these two or three days employed the use of atomic chemical reaction and were said to have the equivalent power of several hundred 50 kilogram bombs. We did not understand the size of the destruction caused by them. The immediate cause of His Imperial Majesty the Emperor's determination to surrender forthwith sprang from the fact that no one could possibly understand this new thing which caused such uncountable casualties.

On the morning of 15 August 1945 we heard from Inoue Unit of an important radio broadcast from our home country at noon, Japan time, and we came over to join them to hear it. Because of the time difference we assembled in front of Inoue's Unit's radio set at 11 a.m. There was some static but we were able to hear the serious tone of the broadcast. It was His Imperial Majesty who personally broadcast aloud in the Imperial Voice his declaration of the termination of the war. We could not grasp the detail but were able to hear what followed, the cabinet's respectful announcement in accordance with what the Emperor had proclaimed, that the war was ended. I knew that accepting the terms of the Potsdam Declaration meant that we had surrendered unconditionally that day to the Allied Forces. When we realized what kind of outcome had eventualized, that the war had ended in the form of a Japanese surrender, we all wondered how we could have felt relieved. The Army having surrendered we became prisoners-of war. We, who until this day looked on our enemy as prisoners-of-war, ourselves just the same became in turn prisoners-of-war. If the Allied Forces had any idea of revenge we would be interned somewhere and have to yield to hard labour, and we had no idea how many years would pass before repatriation; for this there was no tangible evidence. Some Japanese officers lost their nerve and became depressed, but Frenchmen living in Saigon who were released came and talked to them and said, 'My friends, you must not be so discouraged! Japan started the war and was defeated in it but France has been defeated many times!' So they said with a smile in consolation. When we heard this sort of talk we realized there is more than one way of looking at things ...

On 22 August I went in a tricycle-cab to invite my friend Kawakami to lunch in the Sholon district of town. Just as we were finishing our meal at a Chinese cookshop, there was a noise of firecrackers and of cheering. We looked out of the window and saw that Chinese national flags had appeared under every eave in town. We began more and more to doubt the feasibility of repatriation and we were not allowed to call up a tricycle-cab to see what was going on. There was nothing for it but for the two of us to take to the streets in Saigon. Just at the moment on the side-walk across the road we saw a procession of townspeople who carried in the van the national flags of England, America, Russia and China, and you could see they paraded exultantly. We were in a miserable mood because Japan had surrendered and it was as if the full force of realization had come on us in a sort of delayed reaction. The townspeople's procession had the air of a victory parade.

We had acknowledged the end of the war on 15 August and with its end our duties ceased but as far as we could see there was no indication of what immediately lay ahead. Anxiety about our future prospects weighed heavily on us. I longed to return to my unit. I called back into mind my distant native land and my family there. Faced with the sad reality of a Japanese surrender I was concerned also about my comrades-in-arms. On 30 August, at the instance of Japanese French Indo-China Army HQ, I returned to my post in Field Operation Railway Bureau HQ in Bangkok. It was a strange coincidence that four years before hostilities had opened in Saigon and that I was now welcoming their end in the same city. Then, I passed through Pnom Penh in war-like mood, travelling to Bangkok on a Cambodian Railways train. When war broke out I had carried on my course with the Japanese Army of Occupation in high spirits. Now, my mood could only be one of deep depression.

On my return to my HQ in Bangkok I found the unit personnel strengths had been notified to the Allied Forces in my absence, and it was not clear that I really was a *gunzoku* attached to HQ. By the same token when I had been stationed in Bangkok there was uncertainty about which particular unit I had been attached to, so by good luck I had escaped the Allied Forces' inspection by my absence.

In the streets of Bangkok Allied Forces' troops released from captivity held dignified marches, singing cheerfully, marching to music. They had put on their proper uniforms which they must have kept somehow in the personal effects. Against my own repatriation I had put on full *gunzoku* dress uniform and bore myself proudly as a Japanese, secretly wishing I was landing in my own country.

At the end of August my unit was put into concentration internment in Nonhoi. a Bangkok suburb. When we were waiting for a train in Bangkok Central Station a young British Army Officer abused us roughly, 'Be quiet! You're as noisy as pack of monkeys!' I understood his English and, without thinking, my heart full of mortification at having surrendered, I flung back at him, 'You brute!'

Chapter 36

INTERNMENT

It was in Thailand that we were stationed and with the end of the war were dispossessed there of our arms and interned. Japanese troops in French Indo-China (Vietnam), Malaya, Sumatra, Java, The Philippines and Burma comprising the southern regions' war theatre and the zone occupied by the Japanese Army, were all at war-end dispossessed of their arms mostly in Thailand, as we were, and interned together with Japanese overseas residents in various centres like Bangkok, Singapore, Soerabaya and so on. Men attached to Army units, soldiers, *gunzoku*, all without distinction were treated alike as prisoners-of-war and of course were employed on work for them. It was notable that in the cases of Allied Forces ex-prisoners-of-war, who now had direct control, that they received retaliatory treatment. Apart from Army units in positions on battlefields, there were also Japanese overseas civilians. For them the Allied Forces' policy was that they were to be repatriated but first their assets had to be administered by the Allied Forces and they were under regulations laid down about how they behaved during internment, the freedom of the individual being greatly restricted.

In the Thai-Burma area, many of the prisoners had been shipped to Japan after the railway opened to traffic, but there were still a number left in the area. For them, in each prisoner-of-war camp, there was the sudden reversal from Japanese management to their own. In this unexpected reversal of affairs, there were disorders at every camp and one cannot deny there was a revengeful spirit among them. The Japanese units themselves carried out the instructions of the Allied Forces and were coerced into various procedures. Those who understood English were used as interpreters.

Japanese troops on the whole complied with the Edict of His Imperial Majesty by 'enduring the unendurable and suffering what is insufferable' and obeyed the instructions of the Allied Forces, kept alive their hope of repatriation, and were interned. Some, however, unable to bear the disgrace of defeat, committed suicide and some, unwilling to live under British conditions, escaped. (As did Colonel Tsūji Masanobu, the fanatical architect of the *doro nawa* training camp in Taiwan in which he laid down the principles of action in General Yamashita Tomoyuki's campaign to capture Singapore, to whom he was chief-of-staff. After wandering for three years undetected in East Asia, he was eventually returned to Japan, becoming a Member of the Diet, in which he became a member of the House of Councillors: Editor.) Irrespective of the unease and perplexity inherent in our nature as Japanese, we had to comply with the Allied Forces' treatment of us at war end. It was ironic that command in our work now came from Allied Forces NCOs and not from Japanese commissioned officers.

Besides the Japanese battle-line troops, there were also civilians on board ships who in their several ways experienced the turn-round of affairs caused by the Japanese surrender, but after the initial shock and discouragement they calmed down. Somehow they managed to survive in the insecurity and hardships of life in internment which supervened; their heart's desire lay in their wish to return one day soon to their fatherland. No one could forecast when the opportunity for repatriation would come and they passed their time uneasily: they could not sleep at night for nostalgic thoughts of love for one's own home.

In the Spring of 1942 the Allied Forces' troops had surrendered when there seemed no point in going on fighting and their attitude was one of hope that when the war was over they could wait for the opportunity of repatriation: similarly now, prisoners after three-and-a-half years enduring hardships, the attitude of Japanese troops was to hope for the joy of release and the chance of repatriation.

On the termination of hostilities all Japanese troops were disarmed and interned. Obviously their standpoint differed from that of the Allied Forces' troops who had surrendered in the middle of the war. The policy of the Allied Forces still in post and in command of the Japanese

191

military and civilians was to repatriate them as soon as possible, but it was no easy task to transport Japanese from overseas when Japan had lost several million tonnes of shipping in the war.

Mr Adams has the following account of his own experiences as a prisoner-of-war:

> In Japan the true aim of spiritual education is to render loyalty to the Emperor and the nation, the national constitution, and especially in the Army they are educated to prefer death to the disgrace of being captured: they feel compelled to show courage of the do-or-die sort. This is why Japan did not ratify the Geneva Convention's Pact relating to prisoners-of-war taken in battle. In their way of thinking Japanese troops tended to be contemptuous of men who were not ashamed of being prisoners. Not understanding at all the stipulation of the Geneva Convention their violations of it were not therefore barbarous acts. We in turn were harassed by treatment which was cruel to us as prisoners-of-war.
>
> In August 1945 we were unexpectedly released from prisoner-of-war camps and became free men. In the camps the Japanese guards were replaced by our own men. The Japanese guards were escorted from the camps to other places (in the case of Japanese troops from camps along the Thai-side of the railway they were put in the first place into Changi gaol). It was hard for them not to know where they were going but I fancy it would be less hard than it had been for us, and there was little sympathy for them.

In action on the battlefield the mutual antagonism between enemies created some feeling of hatred for opponents, and there was some retaliatory action on Japanese troops, although one cannot deny there was retaliation by Japanese troops on Allied prisoners-of-war. However that may be, in the Allied Forces' courts-martial Japanese were judged as war criminals. It was a pity there was no customary usage on which one could decide how to judge the treatment of Japanese which could be thought of as based on retaliatory intent.

For about a month after the war ended we were left in peace at our internment place at Nonhoi in Thailand. So far officers were allowed to wear their swords, but now an order came to hand over all arms.

My own sword had gold and ivory inlaid studs (*menuki*, studs on both sides of the hilt) which I kept as a memento of this family heirloom. The Gurkhas who were now our guards looked through our belongings from time to time and took watches, fountain pens, etc. Our meals had a rice ration but side-dishes were scanty. We softened bananas in brine from unripe trees, there were also wild plants to cook but they had little taste, were tough, and were difficult to eat. Once we tried sucking opium and other wild plants but they were poisonous to the taste. Bamboo shoots, noodles, goats' milk and vegetables were good, but they were tough and hard to eat.

In November those interned in Bangkok were moved to Nakhon Nayok. Our internment was expected to last a long time so our quarters were built with timber posts and floors instead of bamboo, a site we called *Mizuho mura* – being rather like an old-time Japanese hamlet. In it, in addition to a unit stationed here, were the quarters of a unit back in retreat from the Burma front, and with them were field-hospital nurses: in the closing stages of the war Army prostitutes became temporary nurses, and in Rangoon and elsewhere restaurant waitresses served in Army quarters.

We still could not forecast repatriation day and the daily worry in camps was whether a ship would be sent for us. Fortunately, by order of the Allied Forces, we had little manual labour. Each individual used his common sense to get on top of life in internment, using various devices to that end. There was unease about whether a man would be able to go back to his old occupation after repatriation and so short occupational training courses were started. Among us there were not a few specially talented for this. By early 1946 men put on displays of plaited bamboo containers, etc. made by novices who learned by practice. How the materials and parts came to hand I don't know: there was no rope, yet remarkable displays of apparatus for plaiting matting appeared. In the 'hamlet', in no time at all bean-curd and malt were made. Someone fired glass in unglazed pots and made porcelain-like pots for medicines. In the jungle we had found plants which could be used for making paper, and men surprisingly made a matt squeezed-out thinly to make white paper.

Believing Japan would have to be a democracy we held talks to improve culture and civilized behaviour. Troops who were understood to be specialists in professional fields, including *gunzoku*, became the lecturers.

At Nakhon Nayok I entered my fifth year since coming into the war zone and reached the age of thirty-five (by Japanese reckoning). Happily I kept in good health ... but when we might be repatriated remained unclear. Members of units connected with the Thai-Burma Railway were said to be under suspicion as war criminals, so there was the risk that I might be summonsed. At the time I was privately studying English. It was a pleasure to be able to do it in internment life. Men of like tastes made plays and one really could not tell they were a troupe of amateurs. They created a make-shift theatre by setting up bamboo posts with a portable tent-roof. Every week they put on performances for two days running, each unit's troupe, with its own individual style, performing in verbal contest. Enthusiasm for these plays gradually increased, and at the public performances the voting of the judges on the excellence of performance became a fine act of judgment. In the performances, too, new scripts of productions appeared regularly. The men who acted each day were exempted from manual labour and did their rehearsals out in the jungle. I often recall those plays even to this day. Many Ōsaka alumni of the Kōike Unit, in act twelve of the 'Spring Dance' revue, regard the stage-setting and the performances as an exceptional masterpiece, and the female-impersonators who played the New Year Pine & Bamboo daughters in the stage opera gave pleasure to large audiences. The singing and dancing skills of 'The Tale of Shuzenji' (taken from the film) with 'songs of taste and refinement' sung to the *samisen*, and so on, with the costumes of the female impersonators made of paper, and their acting, became popular. The youngest soldiers were only eighteen years old so they did not need to make up as female impersonators but played the part naturally. In medieval dramas they looked the part in death-in-battle scenes. The Miyama Railway Materials Workshop Unit's *gunzoku*'s new productions of old drama in modern style was thought to be intriguing. 7 Railway Regiment's steel band used frying pans and steel drums as musical instruments and gave splendid recitals of light music: they were admired as geniuses. In the course of all this the men of each troupe would join together and form novel groups. One from a neighbouring internment camp, who came from Takachiho village, gave a public performance.

Stage-lighting apparatus and costumes had to be prepared. Wigs were made out of unravelled hempen rope, and paper costumes indistinguishable from the real thing were got ready. There was no electric light in internment camps, so performances were always matinées, and a unit was halved with one half one day on two-day performances. We enjoyed our theatre going. When Spring came, a mass meeting was to be held for the Emperor's Birthday on 29 April: work had been started on rebuilding an old-style stage, even with a revolving stage.

Suddenly, on 28 April there came an order from the Allied Forces for a move from our 'traditional' village site to Banpong. At dead of night at 2 a.m. we eventually went by train from Prachinburi which is 40 km south-east of Nakhon Nayok, but the move involved a march on foot for nearly 3,000 men. From our departure at two in the morning we had to make a forced march at about 4 km an hour and if you straggled behind you were set upon by thieves. We burned down the quarters in which we had lived for over six months and when we set out it looked as if we had been driven away by the blaze and the smoke. Our personal effects hung heavy on our shoulders, it rained and as we walked through the night we got wet and our shoulder burdens became twice as heavy. We wondered how often it would be like this until the day of repatriation, and we trudged on resignedly without uttering a word.

On the eve of the Emperor's Birthday we went into quarters in a military encampment halfway between Banpong and Nong Pladuk. This was one of the districts where men had been disarmed and the arms had been stored in a godown and a guard put on them. At night thieves got in and stole some rifles, among them Japanese soldiers who got away. The guard professed to know nothing about it and let it pass that the burglars were Allied Forces men.

On a day in mid-June came the orders for repatriation we had been waiting for. The Allied Forces detailed an initial 1,000 men and they were to embark at Bangkok. Immediately we called a conference of those responsible for the Banpong internment camp and the first party for repatriation was chosen. As senior *gunzoku* I was at the conference and claimed that non-combatants should have priority, a claim happily approved, and apart from myself a minimum of 100 JNR *gunzoku* were put on the first embarkation list. Next day there was an inspection at Nong Pladuk. The previous evening I had been talking to the former Bridging Unit commander Major Kōya, who was certain I'd be left behind as a participant in the Thai-Burma Railway construction, and I had accepted the situation and disposed of some personal effects. Against the time of repatriation I had hoped to wear full *gunzoku* uniform which I now jettisoned. In fact, I was passed through the checkpoint at Nong Pladuk without any difficulty and was handed my permit to embark. I had had so much disappointment so far that it was truly good to dispel tension and get some peace of mind. I reflected that on the business trip to Saigon as the war drew to a close there existed the same situation of being omitted from an official list of personnel and here again I had been omitted from an official list by Allied Forces. That final trip at the end of the war began to look like a piece of good luck. From the bottom of my heart I was relieved to have my equanimity restored. At this time we had no news of the men with whom we had departed for the front in 1942, but I must admit we spared little thought for the safety of others not immediately connected with us. One cannot deny this was self-centred, it being mankind's tendency to be preoccupied with his own crises ... but do so, and you feel ashamed.

Chapter 37

REPATRIATION

On 16 June 1946 we boarded a Liberty-type transport moored at the quay in Bangkok. We stayed overnight at the Bangkok leisure centre but until we actually went on board there was still the fear of being left behind and we were under some strain. Guards playing cards at the companionway checked each man's licence to embark as we went on board. The previous day at the checkpoint at Nong Pladuk small white permit cards had been issued, our passports to repatriation. When at last I stood on deck an immense feeling of security swept over me, for this ship was to carry me home to my motherland. I would have liked to cast off right away but familiarity with Thailand over so many years came back into my consciousness and I had mixed feelings about leaving it. But soon came a sound which dispelled all uncertainty, the deep, continuous sound of the ship's siren reverberating over and over, and she calmly cast off from the wharf. We left the harbour.

The River Menam flowed quietly and gently. The sky over the city was clearing up well. In the distance against the dark blue sky the pagoda of the Temple of Dawn glittered in the afternoon sun, sparkling, dazzling. Soon the rows of houses and banana plantations at the water's edge on the far shore began to look small as they receded. Farewell, Bangkok! Farewell, Thailand! As I stood on deck there welled up in my mind intimate memories of my war travels, memories coming and going one after another in an ever-changing panoramic picture. I wondered whether I should ever revisit this country, revisit its capital city ...

My thoughts made a complete switch and flew to my own country. If this ship arrived safely at a port in Japan and I really met my family, all that lay in the inmost recesses of my heart would be fulfilled. Thus ran my meditations, savouring anew the joy of repatriation.

The ship bore south of the capital into the Gulf of Siam and passed in the offing of Cape Sanjak in French Indo-China. Up to this point precise information had been lacking and it was only hearsay that we were heading for Japan, but we had a strong feeling that we were going home. On the fourth day after leaving Bangkok we entered the South China Sea. At nightfall the Southern Cross made a brief appearance.

On 27 June on the horizon on the port side we saw the summit of Mount Fuji. The entire ships' company rushed on deck; we remembered how many years had elapsed without being able to view our beloved Fuji. Closer and closer we drew near Japanese soil. This really was our fatherland.

Before long, in the evening, our ship entered the Uraga Channel and made the town port, but she had come from areas infested with contagious disease and we were not allowed to disembark and lay for two days at temporary anchorage in the port. Seen from the ship Uraga town looked quiet in the light of early summer with its fragrant scent of new leaves on the trees. We saw young women strolling by themselves with parasols over their shoulders: it was a tranquil way of life beyond what we had imagined, and in a defeated Japan we even thought it was incompatible. As we were about to disembark a map was put up on the bulletin board showing clearly the war-damaged zones in towns and cities. The men in front of the map were each, for weal or woe, learning the present state of their own homes. We went home by train from Uraga station. When the time came at last for our permits to return to our respective homes and to our wives and children, comrades-in-arms parted reluctantly on the train, hoping for reunions, but the wheels of the train went on vibrating ... it was a not-to-be forgotten journey from the war front, our expectation after return to renew our several ways of life, all this was blended and confused in our minds ... the wheels went on vibrating. Worn out by those over-lengthy four years of our war journey, feeling the relief at having come home, all this called for a short sleep for our weary bodies. The train, its loaded men who had willingly entrusted themselves to the vibrations of its wheels, ran alongside fields and mountains of our homeland. It took us on to our home towns ...

FOOTNOTE

In the evening of 16 April 1981, I waited on Kyōto station for the No. 26 *Hikari* limited express coming up from Hiroshima on the home side of the Bullet Train platform. The train stopped and two Englishmen got out. They saw the 'welcome' placard I was carrying and came up to me. They had come all the way from England to visit me, Mr Adams and his close friend Mr Janis. It was the first time we had met and we shook hands warmly. It was a wonderful occasion. Forty years ago we had worked on the Thai-Burma Railway and it seemed like an old relationship, and we were overcome by a feeling of familiarity.

Mr Geoffrey Adams lived in Poole in England and was a former Lieutenant in the British Army. In the Second World War he became a prisoner-of-war when Singapore fell. From November 1942 he was employed on construction labour on the Thai-Burma Railway but after it opened to traffic he was moved to Japan itself, on heavy labour in a zinc-smelting plant at Ōmuta. In 1945 he was sent to Mukden and was released by the Russians when the war ended. Now in Kyōto Mr Adams and his friend Mr Morris Janis travelled together, the latter a former captain in the British Army. At the time of the fall of Singapore in February 1942 Mr Adams was in the same unit with Mr Janis, and after the railway was opened to traffic they were both sent to Japan, travelling in the same ship, but later Mr Janis worked in a carbide plant at Kanose in Niigata Prefecture.

They had left England in late March, visited Singapore, Hong Kong, Bangkok and Kanchanaburi and the cemeteries where their comrades-in-arms are buried, and on 11 April flew to Japan, landing at Fukuoka aerodrome. Thence to Yamaguchi and Hiroshima through the good offices of old friends from 5 Engineer Regiment whom they knew in Singapore, a nostalgic visit to the flowering cherry trees round their homes in the Hiroshima district, and thence on to their visit to me in Kyōto. They had a trial run on the Ōigawa Line in the cab of the C56-type engine which had been repatriated from its use on the Thai-Burma Railway, and paid a visit to the Yasukuni Shrine to see the C5631 commemorative engine which was present at the opening-to-traffic ceremony on the Thai-Burma Railway.

Mr Adams had been introduced to me in the first place through Professor Peter Davies of Liverpool University. Mr Ewart Escritt of Oxford University had also been introduced to me by him, and I also met in Japan a former USAAF officer called Mr Carl Fritsche who lived in Ohio State, whose account of the bombing of the Mae Khlaung bridges is given in Chapter 34. Mr Adams kindly gave me a copy of his book, *No Time for Geishas*, about his experiences as a prisoner-of-war over four and a half years, an unbiased, dispassionately-written, objective account, a narrative largely about the Thai-Burma Railway. Also, in 1983, his friend Mr James Bradley kindly sent me (at Ewart Escritt's suggestion: Editor) his book called *Towards the Setting Sun* from which extracts are given in Chapter 32 about his escape from the railway at Songkurai.

These two volumes of remarkably instructive memories helped me to round off my war chronicle, and both these gentlemen kindly consented when I asked their permission to quote from their books. Here once more I formally give my cordial thanks for their great kindness.

POSTSCRIPT

When I completed my draft of *Across the Three Pagodas Pass* I felt there was something missing from it. My account was mainly restricted to my own experiences on Thai-side and there was not enough about what lay beyond the Three Pagodas Pass in Burma. Again, my knowledge of the Allied Forces' administration of the railway was limited to hearsay only. I regret this, and feel there is no excuse for it.

Records about the railway are scarce and I used much unofficial data, using articles in foreign magazines to aid my efforts. If you find errors and inaccuracies please be so kind as not to hesitate to point them out, do not hesitate to correct or to amend.

The quotations from the two ex-prisoners' memoranda are abridged versions and are translated into Japanese as best I could from the English texts. I shall be glad if my little record enables people who had experience in the railway in those days to recall it, glad, too, if those who knew nothing about a railway we left in a corner of south-east Asia take an interest in such historical facts.

So I close, and first express my thanks for the kindness of several people from whom I received data and photographs and have been allowed to quote from their works. Especially I have the honour to salute the former prisoners-of-war, Geoffrey Adams and Jim Bradley.

Futamatsu Yoshihiko

July 1986

END NOTES

1   P.N. Davies, *The Trade Makers: Elder Dempster in West Africa, 1852–1972* (George Allen and Unwin, London, 1973, re-issued 1980), 526 pp.

2   A comprehensive guide to the background to the film is provided in Julie Summers, *The Colonel of Tamarkan: Philip Toosey and the Bridge on the River Kwai*, (Simon and Schuster, London, 2005), 410 pp.

3   A copy of these tapes have been deposited with the Imperial War Museum in London.

4   P.N. Davies (with Tomohei Chida), *The Growth of the Modern Japanese Shipping and Shipbuilding industries* (The Athlone Press, London, 1990), 252 pp.

5   Teruo Saitoh was called up in 1930 at the age of twenty. He served in the 10th Division of Horse in Manchuria and China for most of the decade before being moved with the rank of Sergeant-Major to the Bridge Camp at Tamarkan in 1942. See author's interview with Saitoh, 11 January 1984.

6   Carl H. Fritsche, 'B.24 Liberator', in R. Highan and C. Williams (eds), *Flying Combat Aircraft of the USAAF and USAF* (Iowa State University Press, Ames, 1978) Vol. II and 'Liberators on the Kwai', in *Aerospace Historian*, Vol. 30, No 2, June 1983.

7   Kazuo Tamayama, *Building the Burma-Thailand Railway. An Epic of World War II: Tales by Japanese Army Engineers.* (The World War II Remembrance Group: Senson Taikenn wo Kiku Kai, Japan, 2004). Takashi Nagase, *Crosses and Tigers* (Allied Printers, Commercial Printing Division of the Post Publishing Co. Ltd., Bangkok, Thailand, 1990), 75 pp. An additional point of view is provided in a book by Air Commodore Ramesh S. Bengal, *Burma to Japan with Azad Hind. A War Memoir, 1941–1945* (Lancer, New Delhi, Frankfurt in association with Terra Firma, Chennai, 2009).

8   *Sunday Times*, 23rd July 1978. (See details of Louis Allen's publications in the Bibliography).
9   Author's interview with C.E. Escritt in Oxford, 21 September 1978.
10 P.N. Davies, *The Man Behind the Bridge. Colonel Toosey and the River Kwai*. (The Athlone Press, London, 1991 – reprinted 1997 and 2000), 233 pp.
11 P.N. Davies, *The Diary of John Holt* (Ed). (International Maritime Economic History Association, St John's Newfoundland, 1993), 205 pp. P.N. Davies, *The Trade Makers: Elder Dempster in West Africa*, (Second Edition). Reprint of original publication which covered the period 1852–1972 with an additional section which includes the final years from 1972 to the company's demise in 1989. (International Maritime Economic History Association, St John's Newfoundland, 2000), 555 pp.
12 P.N. Davies (with D.M. Mason), *From Orchard to Market*, (Lockwood Press, London 2005), 308 pp. P.N. Davies, *The Business, Life and Letters of Frederick Cornes: Aspects of the Evolution of Commerce in Modern Japan*, (Global Oriental, Folkestone, 2008), 514 pp. P.N. Davies, *Japanese Shipping and Shipbuilding in the Twentieth Century: The Writings of Peter N Davies*, (Global Oriental, Folkestone, 2010), 194 pp.
13 Kunio Katayama is Professor of Economics in the Faculty of International Studies at Osaka Gakuin University.
14 P.N. Davies, *The Man Behind the Bridge*, op. cit., see p. 34.
15 P.N. Davies, Ibid., p. 35.
16 P.N. Davies, Ibid., p. 59.
17 P.N. Davies, Ibid., p. 68.
18 P.N. Davies, *Japanese Merchant Shipping and the Bridge over the River Kwai*, (Clark G. Reynolds, Ed., Global Crossroads and The American Seas Pictorial Histories Publishing Co, Missoula, Montana, 1988), p, 202.
19 P.N. Davies, *The Man Behind the Bridge*, op. cit., p. 90.
20 Full details of Japanese merchant ships constructed during the Pacific War and of their losses shows a steadily declining level of tonnage. See S Woodburn Kirby, *The War Against Japan*, H M S O, London, 1969, Vol. V, p. 475.
21 P.N. Davies, *Japanese Merchant Shipping and the Bridge over the River Kwai*, op. cit., p. 203.
22 P.N. Davies, *The Man Behind the Bridge*, op. cit., p. 93.
23 P.N. Davies, *The Man Behind the Bridge*, op. cit., p. 196.
24 Interview with Yoshihiko Futamatsu in Tokyo, 14 January 1984.

25 P.N. Davies, *Japanese Merchant Shipping and the Bridge over the River Kwai,* op. cit., p. 210.
26 P.N. Davies, *The Man Behind the Bridge,* op. cit., p. 154.
27 Letter from Y. Futamatsu to P.N. Davies, 27 September 1979.
28 Sir William Slim, *Defeat into Victory,* (Cassell, London, 1958), p. 170.
29 Letter from Y. Futamatsu to P.N. Davies, 26 October 1979.
30 Interview with Y. Futamatsu and Renichi Sugano in Tokyo, 14 January 1984.
31 Y. Futamatsu, *Materials about the Thai-Burma Railway.* Note dated 15 January 1984 sent to P.N. Davies.
32 Y. Futamatsu, *Across the Three Pagodas Pass*: (Translated by Ewart Escritt and reproduced below). Hereinafter referred to as: Escritt Translation: p. 10.
33 Escritt Translation, p. 99. Note also p. 43 and p. 46 which helps to make clear his role in surveying and selecting the route of the *Railway.*
34 Escritt Translation, pp. 111–12.
35 Escritt Translation, p. 34.
36 Escritt Translation, p. 53.
37 Escritt Translation, p. 37 and p. 54.
38 Escritt Translation, p. 58 and p. 104.
39 Escritt Translation, p. 107.
40 Escritt Translation, p. 31.
41 Escritt Translation, p. 109.
42 Escritt Translation, p. 134.
43 Escritt Translation, p. 35 and pp. 122–3.
44 Escritt Translation, p. 136.
45 Escritt Translation, p. 97.
46 Escritt Translation, p. 184.
47 Escritt Translation, p. 185.
48 See below, footnotes 68 and 69.
49 Sir William Slim, *Defeat into Victory* (Cassell, London, 1958).
50 See also K. Tamayama, op. cit., pp. 93–7.
51 Escritt Translation, p. 53.
52 Escritt Translation, p. 29.
53 Escritt Translation, p. 128.
54 Escritt Translation, p. 186.
55 Escritt Translation, p. 187.
56 Escritt Translation, p. 189.

57 Escritt Translation, pp. 194–5.
58 P.N. Davies, *The Man Behind the Bridge,* op. cit., p. 205.
59 Escritt Translation, p. 195.
60 Interview with Y Futamatsu, 14 January 1984.
61 Interview with Renichi Sugano, in Tokyo, 8 October 1994.
62 Pictures of Locomotive C5631 appear between pages 48 and 49 in P.N. Davies, *The Man Behind the Bridge,* op. cit.
63 Keibunsha Publishers, (Engineering Specialists), Kita-Ku, Tokyo, 1986.
64 See Ewart Escritt's *Introduction* to his Translation, p. xl.
65 P.N. Davies, *The Man Behind the Bridge,* op. cit., p. 144.
66 See Ewart Escritt's *Introduction* to his Translation, pp. ii.
67 Julie Summers, *The Colonel of Tamarkan: Philip Toosey and the Bridge on the River Kwai.* (Simon and Schuster, London 2005) has many references to Boon Pong a Thai trader who smuggled many items into a number of POW camps.
68 See G.P. Adams, *No Time for Geishas.* (Lee Cooper, London, 1973).
69 See J. Bradley, *Towards the Setting Sun.* (Phillmore, London, 1982).
70 J. Bradley. op. cit., pp. 107–15 provides a full account of his trial and of Wild's testimony. A brief obituary of Wild (who was killed in an air crash in Hong Kong during 1946) by Lt-General A.E. Percival is included in this publication. Cyril Wild was in business in Japan prior to the war and not only spoke the language fluently but had a wide understanding of Japanese culture and mentality. He acted as interpreter for Percival during the surrender talks with the Japanese at Singapore in 1942. See also, S. Woodburn Kirby, *Singapore: The Chain of Disaster.* (Cassel and Co., London, 1971), pp. 248–50.
71 See Ewart Escritt's *Introduction* to his Translation, pp. vii.
72 Western readers may find revealing two articles in *Japan Quarterly*, first, in the issue for January-March 1989, Professor Takeda Kiyoko in her 'Conflicting concepts on the Emperor', second, in the issue for April-June 1989, journalist Kurita Wataru's 'Making peace with Hirohito and a militaristic past?' These could be read at the Japanese Embassy, 101–104 Piccadilly, London W1.
73 Letter from Futamatsu dated 7 February 1981 to G.P. Adams.
74 Letter from Futamatsu dated 24 February 1980 to Ewart Escritt.
75 Letter from Futamatsu dated 15 November 1979 to Ewart Escritt.
76 S.S. Pavillard : *Bamboo Doctor* (Macmillan, 1960), pp. 82–3.

77 Letter from C.F. Colchester dated 21 September 1977 to Ewart Escritt.
78 *Railway Gazette International* (IPC Transport Press, 3 April 1925), p. 488.
79 *Map of Burma Railways* (Waterlow & Sons, 1898).
80 *The Encyclopaedia Britannica* (14ᵗʰ ed., vol. 24, 1929), p. 66.
81 *The Numismatic Circular* (Spink & Son, January 1976). My unbuffed specimen is in the Imperial War Museum.
82 *World Construction* (issue for August 1982), pp. 14–15.
83 Sugano Renichi : *Taimen tetsudō no kiroku* (Tokyo, 1978).
84 See also : J. and C. Blair Jr., *Return from the River Kwai* (Simon & Schuster, New York, 1979).
85 *Blackwood's Magazine* (vol. 259 : issue for April 1946): article, pp. 225–35, by Charles Hugh recording that the Japanese in charge was the syphilitic but otherwise fine soldier Shimojō Harukichi *sōchō* who had with him 'The Undertaker', Kaneshiro Takashi *heiho*, with whom my earlier clash is described in Rohan Rivett's *Behind Bamboo* (Angus & Robertson, Melbourne, 1946), p. 358.
86 Obituary notice, *The Times*, issue of 17 February 1982.
87 Details of the death of General Shimoda Senriki are provided in the Papers of C.E. Escritt, (Item 24) held at the Imperial War Museum, London.
88 Captain Wild wrote the official 'Narrative of F Force in Thailand, April-December 1943' (IMTFE Narrative Summary, B. & C. Offences, vol. 2 of 11, pp. 768–856.
89 G.P. Adams, op. cit., pp. 112–13.
90 See also: Laurens van der Post: *The Night of the New Moon* (Hogarth Press, London, 1970), p. 59.
91 For this item the best copy on de-acidified paper is in The Nissan Centre for Japanese Studies, 1 Church Walk, Oxford. In the UK there are also copies in The Imperial War Museum, The British Museum, The School of Oriental & African Studies, and The Wiener Library, Institute of Contemporary History.
92 Julie Summers, op. cit., provides much background to the making of the film.
93 G.P. Adams, op. cit.
94 J. Bradley, op. cit.
95 Further details can be seen in I.C.B. Dear (Ed.) *The Oxford Companion to the Second World War*, (Oxford, U.P. 1995), p. 913.
96 Don Muang was developed by the Japanese into an airport for the city with a large but sparsely-furnished hanger for passengers.

[97] W.C. Ramsey (Ed.), *After the Battle* (Magazine) The Death Railway, No. 26, October 1979.

[98] The papers of Lieutenant General Sir Lewis Macclesfield Heath are held at the Imperial War Museum, London. A brief account of his career is given on the WIKIPEDIA website.

[99] *The Island* means Singapore Island. Adams' recce may have been a further check that Pulau Ubin, the island in the Johor Straits, south-east of Johor, was no longer occupied by Imperial Guards who had executed a feint to mislead the British that the landing would be made on the north-east shore. My own company landed a search party on Pulau Ubin and found the guards leaving the island on 11 February.

[100] These guns had all-round traverse but their shells were armour-piercing, not explosive, and did little damage to installations in Johor.

[101] W.C. Ramsey (Ed.), *After the Battle* (Magazine), Singapore, No. 31, November 1981.

[102] See also: J. and C. Blair, op. cit.

[103] For further details of Thailand's involvement see: N.J. Brailey, *Thailand and the Fall of Singapore: a frustrated Asian Revolution*, (Westview Press, Frederick A. Draeger, Boulder, Colorado, 1986).

[104] Julie Summers, op. cit.

[105] P.N. Davies, *The Man Behind the Bridge*, op. cit., pp 161–3.

[106] See the papers of Ewart Escritt (Item 24) at the Imperial War Museum, London.

[107] A reasonable assumption, but the error I was describing was in the context of a widespread 'legend' among POWs that the tracks west and east at the joining-up point at Konkuita were out of alignment and had to be adjusted, a typical 'legend' among POWs. On the other hand, the 'legend' undoubtedly arose from the garbled stories about the détour which Futamatsu and Mōri had to make.

[108] Rudimentary, and for Japanese soldiers, *gunzoku* and *heiho* only. A 'hospital' for POWs was merely one of the huts, or part of a hut, in a POW camp.

[109] The POW was saying that the burnt rice lining the *kwali* in which the rice was cooked, a perquisite of camp cooks, was less inedible than *meshi*, cooked white rice. To a Japanese this appalling heresy had to be 'ironic humour'.

[110] J. Bradley, op. cit., pp. 15–17.

[111] Ibid., pp. 108–10.

GLOSSARY

ankh Hindu word for stout steel-tipped rod with which a mahout guides his elephant: spelt 'ancus' in *The Second Jungle Book*.

anopheles malaria-carrying mosquito.

Archa-shell a box-shell.

Asahi 'morning sun' (i) fighter-plane with Rising Sun roundel.

         (ii) *Asahi shimbun* daily newspaper.

ASEAN Indonesia, Malaysia, Borneo, Philippines.

atap roofing-slats formed of nipa-palm leaves, set at an angle to allow rain to run down sloping roofs.

'Auld Lang Syne' tune adapted for sentimental Japanese song commending assiduous students who go on studying their texts after dark 'by firefly's light' and 'snow on the window-pane'.

baht Thai unit of currency, in 1942 equivalent to the Malay dollar.

baka yaro! coarse expletive meaning 'You stupid fellow!' or 'You idiot!'

banjofish PW nickname for dried codfish opened out like a filleted kipper.

banzai! 'May Japan and her Emperors endure for ten thousand years!'

Basshō Matsu Basshō, 1644–1694, poet who spent much of his time in travel. His 'Summer grasses' *haiku* was written at Hakodate, 'the castle on the height', where Minamoto general Yoshitsune and his faithful followers were killed by the armies of his jealous brother, Yoritomo.

> natsugasa ya
> tsuwamonodomo wa
> yume no ato

'Summer grasses: the warriors are but traces of a dream.'

bonze Buddhist priest.

bridge-abutments reinforced ends on each end of a bridge, usually concreted.

bridge-piers support the trusses which carry the road or rail-track across a bridge.

bushidō the way of the warrior, medieval concept revived by early nineteenth century nationalists, and promoted in heavy propaganda by the Army in 1931–1945, in effect militaristic propaganda.

canary seed batteries for secret radio sets.

centre-line line along which the track is to be run, often on an embankment.

Chennault US Brigadier-general who created AVO, American Volunteer Organization, the Flying Tigers. He married a Chinese.

chikushō! expletive meaning 'You dumb animal!' or 'You brute!'

C-in-C Commander-in-Chief.

chop logic disputacious argument, one who chops logic is a sophisticated arguer.

Colonel Bogey military march for brass bands composed by K.J. Alford, played by Ace Connolly, bandsman cornet player, at Nong Pladuk as work squads marched out of camp past the guardhouse.

compradore Chinese agent for British trading house.

corduroy-logging logs set as stepping stones to provide foothold on steep slopes.

CSM company serjeant-major.

daihonéi see IJA GHQ. It means 'Chief Main Camp' or 'Chief Main Operation'.

DAQMG Deputy Adjutant General & Quarter-Master General.

DDST Deputy Director of Supply & Transport.

dog-nails or dog-spikes, used to secure rails to sleepers. The Japanese word *inukugi* means 'dog-nail'.

doro nawa nickname for Taiwan Army Research Centre at Taihoku in 1941, commanded by Lt-Col. Tsūji Masanobu for training specialist personnel in tropical jungle warfare for the Malayan campaign of Lt-General Yamashita Tomoyuki to whom he became Chief of Staff. The word *doro* means 'robber', *nawa* means 'rope' and the nickname was given as the unit was formed at the eleventh hour (you catch the robber and make the rope afterwards).

embankment earthwork to carry track over low-lying ground.

Emperor Meiji in whose reign Japan was opened up to the outside world. His given name was Mutsuhito.

Emperor Shōwa in whose reign the Pacific War began. His given name was Hirohito.

fox-holes term used by American marines for shallow holes dug to avoid rifle-fire, excavated by the marine *in situ*. The Japanese equivalent is *takotsubo* meaning 'octopus-pot', a form of trap.

fusuma opaque sliding doors.

Gatmel type of dredger for excavating earth and sand down to a hard bottom in constructing well-crib bridge-piers.

GHQ General Headquarters.

GOC General Officer Commanding.

godown planters' version of Malay *gadang*, warehouse.

gunzoku civilian auxiliary of Japanese nationality.

haiku Japanese poem in seventeen syllables in the syllabary, arranged in five, seven, five syllables.

hakama loose, black, divided trousers worn by men.

heiho auxiliary not of Japanese nationality.

hikari 'lightning'. Also *Hikari kyūkōsha*, the name of a particular express train.

HQ headquarters.

human wave tactics in Japanese *jinkai senjutsu*, the ultimate in employing people to complete a job in minimum time.

IJA GHQ Imperial Japanese Army General Headquarters in Tokyo.

INA Indian National Army, the Army of Independence supported by the Japanese Army.

IWM The Imperial War Museum in London.

JNR Japanese National Railways.

kaigun 'sea army', i.e. Navy. In the Pacific War there was no separate Air Force. Navy and Army each had their own aircraft, and there was rivalry between them.

kampong Malay or Burmese small village.

kanji ideograph derived from Chinese. The word means 'Chinese letter'.

kempi military secret policeman with authority over PW camp staff, feared by ordinary Japanese soldiers. *Kempi* were expert in tortures designed to extract information deleterious to Japanese Army interests.

kempeitai the corps of military secret police.

kimono general word for Japanese clothing, particularly those which hang or drape from the shoulders.

Kinsaiyok *kin* is a Japanese ideograph meaning 'new'. Placename given by Japanese railway engineers to a PW camp eleven kilometres beyond Saiyok, New Saiyok.

kora! vulgar expletive meaning 'Here, you!'

kurai tanima 'the dark valley', name given by liberal Japanese to the decade after 1931.

kurohebi black snake, python.

kyūsoku kensetsu rush-construction, literally 'hurried construction'. The first ideograph in the compound has meaning of 'to expedite', 'haste', 'emergency'.

kyūsoku kensetsu shingeki fu 'Assault on Rush-construction' a march composed by a railway engineer, members of whose regiment began to chant it as they got to grips with the new methods.

-maru suffix to name of Japanese merchant-ship or liner.

meirei superior order.

Menam River The word in Thai means 'mother of the waters'.

menuki metal studs on both sides of a sword-hilt.

miscanthus giant grass, *miscanthus japonicas*, about four-feet high with narrow blue-green leaves with white midribs. The leaves are the same length as nipa-palm leaves and can be used for roofing purposes (see '*atap*').

'Miya' nickname for Imperial Guards Division or one of its units.

MO medical officer.

mochi more usually *omochi*. Savoury rice-balls.

MV 'motor vessel', prefix to name of British transport ship.

Nai prefix to Thai surname meaning 'Mr'.

noi means 'small' in Thai. Kwae Noi, the tributary river.

NCO non-commissioned officer.

octopus-pots or octopus-traps (see 'fox-holes').

padang Malay word for a level open space, often a parade-ground.

panung Malaysian word for the black underskirt worn by men.

parang Malay word for a heavy sheath-knife with a curved blade used either as a weapon or as a woodman's hatchet.

pier see 'bridge-pier'.

piling-frame turret on a pontoon, used in pile-driving out in a river.

plank viaduct railtrack built from a vertical cliff face supported by a framework of timber poles down to the river bank.

pompoms motorboat engines which made that sound. Sampans so fitted were called 'fish-tails' from their movement through the water on a river.

pony engines tank engines of sturdy construction, a work-horse popular with engine-drivers, can be made with sloping axle-frames for steep mountain railways. Those used on the Thai-Burma Railway were part of a batch exported from Japan to Thailand and elsewhere in 1941/2. Of the ninety exported to Thailand, converted to wood-burning and with axles altered to 1 metre gauge, forty-six were still in use by Thailand National Railways after the end of the war, and several remained in Burma and Sagalien. By 1977 all those in Thailand were finished except four. C5644 is preserved in working order on the Ōigawa Line and C5631 is displayed at the Yasukuni Shrine. They were repatriated on 5 October 1979. In Thailand one was displayed, C5623, at Thā Makham station at the River Kwae Yai bridge, and another at Thonburi station. C56-type engines were made for Ōigawa Railway Company by a Mitsubishi subsidiary, Kishaseizō, in Ōsaka. C5631 at the Yasukuni Shrine is the engine which was present, decorated with the Thai and Japanese national flags, at the joining-up ceremony at Konkuita on 25 October 1943. It is kept in apple-pie order by the C5631 Preservation Society, surviving members of 5 and 9 Railway Regiments on a rōta, who polish up the paint and brass and keep working parts greased.

pony-type Warren curved-chord half-through trusses a form of sturdy steel trusses or spans.

Pratet Thai constitutional monarchy in Thailand.

PW prisoner-of-war, plural PsW. POW is the civilian equivalent, plural POWs, an acronym used initially by journalists and by most prisoners-of-war not in the Regular Army, now the form in common use.

RAE Royal Australian Engineers.

RAF Royal Air Force.

railbed surface on which sleepers and rails are to be laid.

railtrack line complete with ballast, sleepers and rails.

railtrack head or railhead, point to which railtrack has arrived.

RAPWI Returned Allied Prisoners-of-War & Internees.

RASC Royal Army Service Corps (now Royal Corps of Transport, RTC).

RE Royal Engineers.

rikugun 'land army', i.e. Army.

Rising Sun Flag Japanese National flag, in two forms, (i) sun with rays radiating from it, (ii) red circle in the centre, called 'the poached egg' by PsW.

'River Kwae March' Japanese term for the theme tune in the film *Bridge Built in the Battlefield* (see 'Colonel Bogey').

RNF Royal Northumberland Fusiliers.

roadbed line of track levelled off with sloping sides, ready for ballast, sleepers and rails, often on an embankment in low-lying terrain.

Royal Palace walled enclosure in Bangkok within which are many wellknown temples and formerly the living quarters of the Royal Family.

Saiyok in Thai means 'waterfall', a place name.

samisen three-stringed guitar played with a plectrum.

samlor man-powered tricycle-cab plying for hire in Thai cities and towns.

sampans cargo-handling river-craft.

sen 100th of a *baht*.

serjeant a military serjeant, abbreviations Sjt., Staff-Sjt., Colour-Sjt., Sjt-major. A civilian police-sergeant is spelt differently to save time and prevent confusion in writing messages and telegrams. Civilians are abbreviated Sgt.

shichi-go-san 7-5-3 lucky number ornaments for New Year ceremonial decorations.

shōji translucent oiled-paper sliding-doors.

Shōnan Light of the South, Japanese name for Singapore.

Shōwa Shining Harmony, era-name chosen by Emperor Hirohito on his accession to the Throne in 1926.

sleeper the Japanese *makuragi* means 'pillow-wood'. A Japanese pillow is an upright, shaped piece of wood, *makura*, often with an opening in it to hold paper. *The Pillow-Book* (*makura no sōshi*) by the Lady Sei Shōnagon, born c. 965 AD, is a shining example of Heian culture.

speedo PW name for *kyūsoku kensetsu*, rush-construction.

Staff Captain 'Q' executive officer responsible for action about billets, food and movement.

sumi Japanese ink.

switchback standard railway-engineering technique to avoid lengthy high-gradient hauls on mountain railways.

tatami floor mats of standard size, one by two metres.

tennō heika formal way of referring to the Emperor. The phrase means 'Below the Steps to the Throne of the Divine Emperor'.

tical colloquial term for *baht*, q.v., normally used by PsW.

tokay gecko, a kind of wall-lizard found in Thailand, Burma, Malaya, Sumatra, Borneo and Java.

track line of railtrack.

trackbed surface on which ballast, sleepers and rails are to be placed.

track-surface width of railtrack, on the Thai-Burma Railway 4 to 5 metres.

unit formation normally below regimental rank, e.g. battalion, company, platoon, section, and usually referred to by the name of its commander, for example the Survey Unit was the Mōri Unit, its commander being 2/Lt. Mōri.

USAAF United States of America Air Force.

well-crib lower base support for a bridge-pier, excavated down to hard river-bottom, preferably rockbottom, and successively built up to waterlevel and cemented. The pier continues above the well-crib to the required height.

Yai means 'big' in Thai. See *noi*. River Mae Khlaung was also known as River Kwae Yai, its tributary being River Kwae Noi.

Yasukuni Shrine Shintō shrine in Tokyo dedicated to ease the souls of Japan's war dead, whose ashes are enshrined here. Yasukuni means 'peaceful country' but the ideograph for 'peace' also means 'ease'.

yasumi a rest from work. Often confused by PsW with the vulgar imperative, 'Yasume!' the word of command for 'Stand at ease!'

Zeros Japanese military aircraft with the red roundel of the Rising Sun, in naval aircraft sometimes referred to as 'Navy noughts'.

BIBLIOGRAPHY

Adams, G.P. *No Time for Geishas* (Leo Cooper, London, 1978).

Adams, G.P. *The Thailand to Burma Railway* (Ashley Press, Poole, 1978).

Adams, G.P. *Destination Japan* (Ashley Press, Poole, 1980).

Allbury, A.G. *Bamboo and Bushido* (Robert Hale Ltd., London, 1955).

Allen, L. *The End of the War in Asia* (Hart-Davis, London, 1976).

Allen, L. *Singapore 1941–1942* (Davis-Poynter, London, 1977).

Allen, L. *Burma: the Longest War, 1941–45* (J.M. Dent, 1984). .

Arneil, S. *One Man's War* (Alternative Publishing Cooperative, Sydney, 1980).

Bantock, G. *This Modern Japan* (Kinseido Ltd., Tokyo, 1973).

Barker, A.J. *Behind Barbed Wire* (B.T. Batsford Ltd, London, 1974).

Barker, R. *Hiroshima Maidens* (Viking Penguin Books, New York, 1985).

Baynes, L.L. *Kept - the Other Side of Tenko* (Book Guild, Lewes, 1984).

Bennett, G. *The Loss of the Prince of Wales and Repulse* (Ian Allen, London, 1972).

Bergamini, D. *Japan's Imperial Conspiracy* (Heinemann, London, 1971).

Blackater, C. *Gods Without Reason* (Eyre & Spottiswoode, Edinburgh, 1948).

Blair, J. & C. *Return from the River Kwai* (Simon & Schuster, New York, 1979).

Boulle, P. *Le Pont de la Rivière Kwai* (Juillard, Paris, 1952).

Bradden, R. *The Naked Island* (Werner Leurie, London, 1951).

Brett, C.C. *The Burma-Siam Railway* (SEAIC Bulletin, No. 246, 1946).

Bradley, J.B. *Towards the Setting Sun* (Phillimore, Chichester, 1982).

Bryant, A. *The Turn of the Tide, 1939–43* (Collins, London, 1957).

Burton, R.S.M. *The Road to Three Pagodas* (Macdonald, London, 1963).

Caffry, K. *Out of the Midday Sun, Singapore 1941–45* (Deutsche, London, 1957).

Clarke, H.V. *The Tub* (Cori Books, London, 1971).

Coast, J. *Railway of Death* (Commodor Press, London, 1946).

Collier, B. *The War in the East* (Heinman, London, 1969).

Connell, B. *Return of the Tiger* (Sundial Publications, London, 1960).

Coombes, J.H.H. *Banpong Express* (Wm. Dresser, Darlington, 1948).

Cornelius, M.D. *Changi* (Arthur H. Stockwell, Ilfracombe, n.d.).

Cornell, M.W. *I Fed the 5000* (Mitre Press, London, 1975).

Craven, W.A. & Cate (eds) *The Army Air Force in World War II* (University of Chicago Press, 1953).

Davies, P.N. *Japanese Merchant Shipping and the Bridge Over the River Kwai* (Clark G. Reynolds, (ed.), Global Crossroads and the American Seas. Pictorial Histories Publishing Co., Missoula, Montana, 1988).

Davies, P.N. *The Man Behind the Bridge: Colonel Toosey and the River Kwai* (Athlone Press, London, 1991, 1997 & 2000).

Dowex, J.W. *War Without Mercy* (Pantheon Books, New York, 1986).

Dunlop, E.E. 'Medical Experiences in Japanese Captivity', *British Medical Journal*, Vol. II, 5 October 1946–7.

Durnford, S.J.H. *Branch Line to Burma* (Macdonald, London, 1958).

Edwards, Jack. *Banzai You Bastards* (Corporate Communications, Hong Kong, n.d.).

Escritt, C.E. Numbered items in the C.E. Escritt Collection in the Imperial War Museum, London:

(3)   'The 17-hour stand at Nong Pladuk on 8/9 September 1942' (1982)

(4)   'Note on the 'V' Organisation', September 1942 – February 1945 (1982)

(5)   'Narrative on 'F' Force in Thailand, April-December 1943', by Capt. C.H.D. Wild

(7)   Provenance of souvenir medallion (medallion in Department of Art)

(8)   'A Japanese railway engineers' trace of the Thai-Burma Railway (1981)

(9)   'Detail of sidings etc.' on (8) (1981)

(11) 'A Japanese railway engineers' trace of the Thai-Burma Rail Link Line in the Imperial War Museum' (1981)

(12) Japanese text of Futamatsu's *taimen tetsudō wo shinobu* (1980)

(13) Translation of (12) (1983)
(15) Japanese text of Tsukamoto Kazuya's *mekuron no eikyūkyō jitsuroku senjo ni kakeru* (1981)
(16) Translation of (15) (1982)
(22) 'Note on dog-spikes used on the railway' (1983)
(23) Extracts from Futamatsu's *Account of the Construction of the Thai-Burma Railway* relating to treatment of prisoners-of-war and coolies (1983)
(24) 'Death of General Shimoda' (1985)
(25) Bound complete translation of Futamatsu Yoshihiko's *Across the Three Pagodas Pass: the Story of the Burma-Siam Railway* (CEE 1985–1987)
(26) 'The Thai-Burma Railway' (September 1987)
(27) 'Beyond the Three Pagodas Pass' (1988)
(28) *Across the Three Pagodas Pass by Futamatsu Yoshihiko translated and edited with an introduction for the general reader* (1990).

Fergusson, B. *Beyond the Chindwin* (Fontana Books, London, 1955).

Fisher, C.A. *The Thai-Burma Railway* in *Economic Geography* (April 1947, pp. 85–97).

Fisher, C.A. *Three Times a Guest* (Cassell, London, 1979).

Fritsche, C.H. 'B.24 Liberator' in R. Hichan and C. Williams (eds) *Flying Combat Aircraft of the USAAF and USAF* (Iowa State University press, 1978, Vol. III).

Fritsche, C.H. 'Liberator on the Kwae' in *Aerospace Historian*, June 1983.

Futamatsu, Y. Japanese text of *taimen tetsudō ki* (The Thai-Burma Construction Record Association, Tokyo, 1955).

Futamatsu, Y. Japanese text of *taimen tetsudō wo shinobu* (privately printed, Tokyo, 1980).

Futamatsu, Y. Japanese text of *Santōge wo koete: taimen tetsudō wo kataru* (Yamamoto, Tokyo, July 1985).

Ghostwriter: Japanese text of *Kaetta Kita C.56* (Ōigawa tetsudō k.k., 1979).

Gilchrist, A. *Bangkok Top Secret* (Hutchinson, London, 1979).

Gilchrist, A. 'Diplomacy and Disaster: Thailand and the British Empire in 1941', *Asian Affairs*, Vol. XIII, 3 October 1982.

Gordon, E. *Miracle on the River Kwai* (Collins, London, 1963).

Grenfell, R. *Main Fleet to Singapore* (Faber & Faber, London, 1951).

Hall, L.C. *The Blue Haze* (National Library of Australia, Sydney, 1985).

Hardie, R. *The Burma-Siam Railway* (Imperial War Museum, London, 1983).

Hastain, R. *White Coolie* (Hodder and Stoughton, London, 1947).

Hugh, C. 'The Last Journey' in *Blackwood's Magazine* (April 1946).

Ishimaru, Tota Translated by G.V. Rayment, *Japan Must Fight Britain* (The Paternoster Library, 1936, London).

Jeffrey, A.B. *White Coolies* (Angus & Robertson, Melbourne, 1954).

Keith, A.N. *Land Below the Wind* (Michael Joseph Ltd., London, 1939).

Keith, A.N. Three Came Home (Michael Joseph Ltd., London, 1948).

Kinvic, C. *Death Railway* (Pan-Ballentine Edition, London, 1973).

Kirby, S. Woodburn. *The War Against Japan* (London, 1969), Vol. V of *History of the Second World War* (U.K. Military Series, 1957–69).

Kirby, S. Woodburn. *Singapore: The Chain of Disaster* (Cassell & Co., London, 1971).

Lane, A. *One God, Too Many Devils* (Chrysanthemum Publishing House, Stockport, 1989).

Lewis, R. *The Other Ultra* (Hutchinson, London, 1982).

Lomax, E. *The Railway Man* (Vintage, London, 1996).

MacArthur, B. *Surviving the Sword, 1942–45* (Time Walker Books, London, 2005).

Morison, S.M. *History of the U.S. Naval Operations in World War II* (Oxford University Press, London: Vol. XIV, 1960 and Vol. XV, 1962).

Nelson, D. *The Story of Changi, Singapore* (Stamford College Press, Bureau of Records and Engraving, Singapore, 1973).

Owen, F. *The Fall of Singapore* (Michael Joseph Ltd., London, 1960).

Parkin, Ray. *Out of the Smoke* (Hogarth Press, London, 1961).

Parkin, Ray. *Into the Smother* (Hogarth Press, London, 1961).

Parkin, Ray. *The Sword and the Blossom* (Hogarth Press, London, 1961).

Pavillard, S.S. *Bamboo Doctor* (Macmillan, London, 1960).

Pavillard, S.S. *Enemy No. 19* (Pentland Press, Edinburgh, 1997).

Peer, I.D. *One Fourteenth of an Elephant* (Doubleday, London, 2004).

Pratt, P.R. 'The Thai-Burma Railway – 30 years after', *Railway World*, February, 1976.

Rawlings, L. *And the Dawn came Up Like Thunder* (Rawling's Chapman Publications, 1973).

Rivett, R. *Behind Bamboo* (Angus & Robertson, Melbourne, 1946).

Roberts, D.R. *Spotlight on Singapore* (Time Press, Douglas, Isle of Man, 1965).

Roskill, Capt. S.W. *The War at Sea* (HMSO, London, Vol. 1, 1954).

Russell, Lord. *Knights of Bushido* (Cassell, London, 1958).

Slim, Sir William. *Defeat into Victory* (Cassell, London, 1956).

Smyth, Sir John. *Percival and the Tragedy of Singapore* (Macdonald, London, 1971).

Spector, R.H., *Eagle Against the Sun* (Penguin Books, London, 1984).

Spence, A. *The Pure Land* (Canongate Books Ltd., Edinburgh, 2006).

Stewart, J. *To the River Kwai* (Bloomsbury, London, 1988).

Storry, R. *A History of Modern Japan* (Penguin Books, London, 1960).

Summers, Julie. *The Colonel of Tamarkan: Philip Toosey and the Bridge on the River Kwai* (Simon & Schuster, London, 2005).

Swinson, A. *Defeat in Malaya* (Macdonald, London, 1970).

Takashi, Nagase. *Crosses and Tigers* (Allied Prints, Commercial Printing Division of The Post Publishing Co. Ltd., Bangkok, Thailand, 1990).

Takeyama, M. Japanese text of *biruma no tategoto* (Tokyo, 1966).

Tamayama, Kazno. *Building the Burma-Thailand Railway: An Epic of World War II, 1942–43: Tales by Japanese Army Engineers* (The World War II Remembrance Group: Senson Taikenn wo kiku kai, Japan, 2004).

Tantri, K.Tut. *Revolt in Paradise* (Heinmann, London, 1960).

Toland, J. *The Rising Sun* (Bantam Books, New York, 1971).

Toosey, P.J.D. See list of items filed under *Toosey* in the Department of Documents, Imperial War Museum, London.

Tsuji, Mansanobu. *Singapore. The Japanese Version* (Constable, London, 1967).

Tsukamoto, K. Japanese text of *mekuron no eikyūkyō jitsuroku senjo ni kakeru hashi*, in *Railway Fan* No. 246, 247, Tokyo, December 1981.

Warwick, E. *Tamajao 241* (Paul-Ledger Publications, Ashingdon, 1987).

Watt, Ian 'The Myth of the Bridge on the River Kwai', *Observer Magazine*, 1 September 1968.

Young, P. (ed.). *The Battle of Midway: World War II* (Orbis, London, 1983).

INDEX

Railtrack-head, 154
Railtrack-laying technique, 62
Railtrack line-curvature, 36, 69, 119
Railtrack location, 61
Railtrack track surface, 36
Railway Bureau, 187, 189
Railway Command, 42, 43, 62, 63
Railway Control, 36, 88, 99, 102,
106
Railway cost, xxxii
Railway embankment, 120
Railway flatcars, 38, 56, 62, 121, 175
Railway Gazette International, xxxiii
Railway gradient, 69
Railway Materials Workshop, 36, 38,
59, 62, 80, 82, 111, 114, 115,
159
Railway official title, xxviii, 36
Railway previous plans, xxviii
Railway route, 43, 49, 111
Railway tractors, 79, 121, 126, 175
Rainbow, 71
Rainfall, xix, 114, 124, 176
Rainy season, 35, 41, 100, 122, 125,
135, 157
Rakuyo maru, xxxix
Rama I Bridge, 45
Rama VI Bridge, 90
Rangoon, xviii, xxxii, 35, 193
RAPWI, xxxvii
Recce party, 69, 70, 71, 72, 73, 113,
114
Rengam, 56
Repatriation, xxi, xxx, 99, 191, 193,
197
Republic of China, 30
Repulse, HMS., 7, 17

Resistance movements, liii
Rhio Archipelago, 19
Rice, xliii, 32, 125, 129, 136, 161,
164, 167
Rikugun, 7
Rising Sun Flag, 143
River bed, 77, 100
'River Kwae March', xlvii, lxiii
RNF (Royal Northumberland Fusil-
iers), xliv
Roadbed, 127, 142, 155
Roberts Hospital, xli
Robertson, Major Robbie, RAE, liv
Robinson, Capt. R., 163
Robinson, Sjt., 139
Ronshii, 128
Route-chart, 127–34
Route in antiquity, xxxii
Royal Army Service Corps, xl, 18,
19, 163
Royal Australian Engineers, liv
Royal Corps of Signals, xli
Royal Engineers, 35, 163
Royal Palace, 65, 91
Rue Catenar, 6
Rush-construction, see Speedo
Russo-Japanese War, xxviii, liii, 51
Ryōdanchō, 31

Saigon, xxx, 3, 5, 6, 15, 186, 187,
188, 189, 196
St Andrew's Cathedral, 93
Saitō, Colonel, lv
Saiyok, 74, 127
Sakamoto, Major, 46, 49, 50
Sakamoto Unit, 46, 63, 82, 83, 84,
87, 89, 93, 94, 95, 96